TEX_T_XE_T

Studies in Comparative Literature 46

Series Editors
C.C. Barfoot and Theo D'haen

Also by Margaret Buckley

A Woman's Man and Family Portrait
Novellas

The Commune
A Novel

A Novelist in the Making
Autobiographical Sketches

CHALLENGE AND CONTINUITY

ASPECTS OF THE THEMATIC NOVEL 1830-1950

MARGARET BUCKLEY
AND
BRIAN BUCKLEY

Amsterdam - New York, NY
2004

The paper on which this book is printed meets the requirements of
'ISO 9706: 1994, Information and documentation - Paper for
documents - Requirements for permanence'.

ISBN 90-420-1603-5
© Editions Rodopi B.V., Amsterdam - New York, NY 2004
Printed in The Netherlands

For Karl Miller

The finest English literary editor of his generation

and the first to recognize

Margaret Buckley the novelist

Acknowledgements

Any book written and rewritten over a number of years incurs debts too numerous to list. The bibliography indicates to a small extent the assistance received from published work, in particular from the editors of the Cambridge edition of the novels.

More personal thanks for recent advice and encouragement are due to Michael Bell, Robert Burden, Bernard Capp, Keith Carabine, Alison Hoddinott, Mara Kalnins, Mark Kinkead-Weekes, Laurence Lerner, Karl Miller, Rosemary Sumner, Tony Tanner, John Worthen and Louise Wright; and the final shaping of the book owed much to that most alert and meticulous of editors, Cedric Barfoot.

I must also thank those who have permitted quotation from copyright material: in particular Lawrence Pollinger (for the Frieda Lawrence Ravagli Estate) and the Calder Educational Trust (for the Samuel Beckett Estate).

Brian Buckley

A Note on References

Page references to Lawrence's novels appear after the longer quotations from them and are to the Cambridge editions. References to other texts appear in the footnotes, where the author and short title are given. Full details of all these texts are in the Bibliography.

Contents

INTRODUCTION

This book is an expedition into the imaginative worlds of a series of novelists linked together in a tradition, each one successively exploring and developing it. The tradition in question is that of the thematic novel. The partial mapping of that area is the chief aim of the enterprise. Lawrence's novels, we will argue, provide a distinctive focus on the principles and practice of thematic structure. For this reason they are chosen as the lynchpin of this investigation. They provide the kind of unifying critical criteria that such a wide-ranging survey needs.

The initial focus of the enquiry then, for the purpose of definition, is on *The Rainbow* and *Women in Love*. What kind of novel are they? They are not novels of ideas in the ordinary sense, since the ideas in them are not wrested from the context in which they arise and offered to the readers to be applied directly to their own lives. They are not psychological novels as such because, although the characters in them are convincingly individual, they lack the kind of foibles and contradictions that make people amusing or pathetic, and above all their development is not the ultimate deciding factor in the structure of these novels: how else explain what happens to the Brangwens as they fade out or are seen in a different light as the narrative focus changes?

In them Lawrence was interested not so much in individual minds, with all their idiosyncrasies, as in the more universal underlying processes that operate in people. He said when he was embarking on them:

> I don't so much care what the woman feels – in the ordinary sense of the word. That presumes an ego to feel with. I only care about what the woman *is* – what she *is* – inhumanly, physiologically, materially ... as a phenomenon (or representing some greater, inhuman will) instead of what she feels according to the human conception.[1]

---

1. Lawrence to Edward Garnett, 5 June 1914, *Letters*, II, 183. He followed this with his famous comment on diamond and carbon. As Jack Stewart pointed out, Lawrence's mature art, like expressionism in the visual arts, "distorts, disintegrates

This is not the only instance of a major novelist disclaiming interest or expertise in the psychology of characters. Nearly all the major thematic novelists investigated in this study signalled in a similar way their departure from the tradition of the biographical novel. For them, as for Lawrence, the psychology of the characters' personal impulses and conflicts was to be brought into a wider context which included the sociology of their historical setting and the religious and moral ideology they shared.

Lawrence's determination to diagnose and separate out the destructive tendencies in life from the factors that make for growth generated his major controlling subject-themes. The word "theme" in literary discussion can range in meaning from something as trivial as a single feature common to several figures in the text to something as wide and all-embracing as death. Here it signifies an intellectual and emotional complex or area of exploration to which the author was drawn, operating in him like a profound problem returning compulsively to consciousness to be explored. In this the various factors, psychological, social and philosophical combine.

Character and theme in Lawrence's two masterpieces are so thoroughly co-extensive that the dramatic interplay of personal motives enacts the dynamic counterpoint of the themes. But the unity is not uniform. The fluctuating and self-contradictory stances from the juxtaposed characters oppose and qualify each other. For example, the ironies of the cathedral scene in *The Rainbow*, resulting from the clash of Anna's and Will's opposing views almost equally endorsed, the interaction expressed as much in the narrative as in the dialogue, show the development of a technique that became more complex and multiple in *Women in Love,* with the five main characters constantly quoting each other, as it were, using the same ideas, words, images, either consciously challenging, mocking, subverting, or else unconsciously expressing "a oneness of struggle". It is not an irony that implies negation, but one that awakens fresh perceptions of relationships. The dramatic clash is accompanied by a paradoxical ambiguity or multiplicity in the imagery and terminology, a pervasive relativity, as everything closely co-exists, fraught with "shifting dialectical tensions".[2] The whole creative enterprise remains exploratory and unfinalised:

---

and disrupts the image of reality" in order to reach the bedrock of human response (see Jack Stewart, *The Vital Art of D. H. Lawrence,* 73).

2. Barbara Ann Schapiro, *D. H. Lawrence and the Paradoxes of Psychic Life*, 1.

The novel is the highest complex of subtle inter-relatedness that man has discovered. Everything is true in its own time, place, circumstance, and untrue outside of its own time, place, circumstance.[3]

This kind of relativism is a definitive feature of these two novels and many of those that most strongly influenced them. In examining them and other novels like them it will be helpful, as several critics have recently found, to bring into play some of the conclusions drawn by Mikhail Bakhtin from his study of Dostoevsky's novels.[4]

The first three chapters of this book examine Lawrence's master-themes, primarily in *The Rainbow* and *Women in Love*. Briefly defined, the first consists of the criticism of a kind of mentality that governs and values experience according to a prescription of principles; in the second disillusionment and self-confinement develop and deepen the breakdown of assurances depicted in the first, and the third explores ways in which life can recover, struggling free of adverse conditions to go on and renew itself. But they cannot be boiled down to general definitions, not even those offered by Lawrence himself in his essays and letters.[5] We explore the complex experiences of the novels themselves.

In Lawrence's other novels there is not the same degree of orchestration and tuning, but a wide variety of aims and levels of achievement. This study follows the progress of the themes rather than of the novels themselves, in order to secure a sharper focus on the way these factors operated and developed. It traces the forms they assumed in the first three novels, as they emerged from the context of Lawrence's style at this time, which involved a more pragmatic and intuitive creation of people and events. It examines their development in the novels after *Women in Love,* when Lawrence performed with virtuoso skill several variations on thematic structure, taking his options eventually towards a prescriptive narrative in which people and events exist chiefly to illustrate concepts. The discussion of all

---

3. Lawrence, "Morality and the Novel" (1925), in *A Study of Thomas Hardy*, 172.

4. Bakhtin's *Problems of Dostoevsky's Poetics* will be discussed in Chapter 5. For discussions of Bakhtin's ideas in relation to Lawrence, see for example David Lodge, *After Bakhtin;* Jack Stewart, "Linguistic Incantation and Parody in *Women in Love*", in *Style*, XXX; and Robert Burden, *Radicalizing Lawrence*.

5. Statements in Lawrence's discursive writings go off at a tangent of their own, deflecting attention from the text of the novels, and in any case simplifying (as any generalisation must do) the complex experience offered there. With two exceptions, for specific reasons, this study avoids them.

these other novels takes up no more than a third of the Lawrence coverage because of their slighter relevance to the analysis of the central themes.

The enquiry next considers the immediately preceding traditions that fed Lawrence's achievement as a thematic novelist. The focus on Lawrence here limits the scope of the investigation but provides an organic homogeneous unity: as everything in the main area is related to him, we can hope to uncover some of the creative processes of challenge and renewal in this tradition.

His reading is fairly well documented, from letters, essays and the reports of other people.[6] In three instances, in order to clinch the argument, a novel is included without exact documentary evidence (although Lawrence might well have read it). His own comments on other authors range all the way from enthusiasm to hostility. Often, we shall see, the hostility was directed at writers whose influence was important to him in some way – a common enough trait in other writers. As he explained, "We have to hate our immediate predecessors, to get free from their authority".[7] There is no attempt here to discuss the details of his comments in his critical essays on other novelists. These often reveal more about him than about them, an interesting subject, but not ours here.

This part of the book aims to demonstrate the existence of parallels, not exhaustively explore them. With each writer we search for evidence of Lawrence's challenging, rejecting, adopting or continuing the exploration in his own way. It is rarely possible (though it happens with Hardy, Bennett and Wells) to identify specific items or features he used or refashioned. More often affinities of theme are noted. The themes as defined in the first three chapters in Lawrencian terms appear to reflect his personal preoccupations and obsessions. However, generalized a little, they appear in some form or other in every thematic novel he read. One realizes that he inherited not only the basic assumptions but their organisation. They are the embodiment of cultural imperatives, as much social as personal. In studying Lawrence's reading therefore we are looking at a tradition of thought and experience, not merely one of literary form. The formalities of structure register methods of understanding life. For the purposes of this study therefore, form and content are inseparable. The

---

6. See Rose Burwell, "D. II. Lawrence's Reading" in *D. H. Lawrence Review*, III.
7. Lawrence to Edward Garnett, 1 February 1913, in *Letters*, I, 509.

themes are defined and related through an analysis of the handling of their content.

Our assumption is that Lawrence noted the affinities noted here and responded to them in complex ways that can resist academic definition. Often, in such cases, the most important effects are what are sometimes called creative influences: when the writer takes in an influence and draws on it intuitively as a resource in the creation of his own work. Guesswork in this area can be so treacherously misleading that it is sometimes preferable to let the relations between the novelists (and not just with Lawrence) speak for themselves.

To illustrate the care that must be taken, and the way sound observations may easily slide into dubious assumptions, consider what Raymond Williams in his *Modern Tragedy* made of Lawrence's response to Vronsky's accident at the races in *Anna Karenin,* when his mare's back is broken. Williams equated its general significance in Tolstoy's novel with the scene in *Women in Love* where Gerald subdues his mare at the railway crossing: "The future of Gerald and Gudrun is revealed in it, as surely as was the future of Vronsky and Anna in Tolstoy's scene." This is truer of Lawrence's scene than of Tolstoy's. Vronsky's implication in the tragedy of *Anna Karenin* is too complicated to be equated in this way, and Tolstoy's symbolism does not operate like Lawrence's. As Barbara Hardy had pointed out, Lawrence's shows "the accepted foreshortening of psychology in a symbolic novel" while Tolstoy's is many-facetted, and part of "the complex histories of truly complex characters".[8] It may well be that Lawrence thought of Tolstoy's scene at some point in the composition or revision of his own, "an image", as Williams said, "which Lawrence understood in Tolstoy and used in *Women in Love"* but chiefly to challenge it and assert a difference (the two characters themselves are as different as chalk from cheese). Williams took supposition a step further when he suggested a deeper impact, which "played an important part in Lawrence's creative life, making new images in, for example, Ursula's meeting with the horses near the end of *The Rainbow* and, very powerfully, in 'St Mawr'".[9] The only common factor in these other scenes is the presence of horses.

The order of our study is not according to categories but chronological, because that allows greater flexibility of approach and a more naturally consecutive relation between one novelist and the

8. Barbara Hardy, *The Appropriate Form*, 180.
9. Raymond Williams, *Modern Tragedy*, 132.

next. Its scope takes in Lawrence's interest in the English novelists
that led from the Brontës to Meredith and Wells, and in the French
realist tradition and its followers. It examines his profound response to
George Eliot and Tolstoy and defines the kind of narrative discipline
they exemplify, which, although it deals in moral categories to some
extent, is focused sympathetically on individual development, in a
structure comparatively large and fluid, and "shapes its moral
argument tentatively through character and action".[10] It is a form
Lawrence turned away from.

Central to this study is the distinction drawn here between
biographical (or developmental) novels with their psychological
realism, and thematic novels as defined here. Both kinds of narrative
are of course valid in revealing, illuminating and ordering the truth,
and the forms overlap, amending and enriching each other. There is no
doubt that novelists of the first type, especially George Eliot and
Tolstoy, shaped the way Lawrence thought about the subjects of his
major themes, and this study intends to indicate conceptual parallels of
that sort, but their influence on the way he handled them in his
thematic novels was comparatively limited.

The search in this part of the book then is primarily for novels that
resemble the structure of Lawrence's masterpieces. In several we find
psychological and more general interests in coalition, aligned
precisely (as by Stendhal and Flaubert) or more loosely (as by
Turgenev and Hardy). In Hawthorne and Melville there is something
more like the Lawrencian cohesion of character, ideology and
imagery. But the novels that really match Lawrence's in scope as well
as structure are the major novels of Dickens, Dostoevsky and Conrad.
These three novelists relate to each other as Lawrence relates to them,
although they made no consistent study of their predecessors, but
often took them in uncritically at a very early age. It would be possible
to compose for each of these writers a thematic analysis of their major
novels along lines parallel to that given of Lawrence's.

This is the great tradition to which Lawrence's masterpieces
belong. A generic title might be coined for it. The term "polyphonic",
invented for Dostoevsky's novels by Mikhail Bakhtin looks promising
but was too sharply defined in relation to the one novelist to be an
umbrella for others. E.M. Forster once gathered together Lawrence,
Dostoevsky, Emily Brontë and Melville under the term "prophetic",

---

10. Barbara Hardy, *The Appropriate Form*, 105.

but his definitions do not fit the conclusions of this study.[11] Rather than foisting more categories on the infinite variety of narrative forms, we prefer to use the common term, thematic, with its other connotations, making sure that the context determines the meaning.

In the last two chapters of the book the Lawrence filters are removed to indicate both the context and the influence of his achievement. We examine thematic options by other authors, chosen for comparability with Lawrence, first in his generation and then the next (confining the view for the sake of homogeneity to the British Isles). The study continues to be illustrative, not comprehensive: one or two novels chosen from each author and no attempt made to deal with the author's other work, except for brief indications of where the chosen items stand in the sequence. The novelists chosen represent important continuities and breakthroughs. There are examples of contemporaries following a path parallel to Lawrence's out of the kind of structure determined by an interest in psychological development into one governed by themes. There are revealing instances of influence – Lawrence on Huxley, Joyce on Beckett – absorbed, challenged and renewed. Some of the novelists of the generation that followed Lawrence were moving away from the nineteenth-century century influences that had largely determined their immediate predecessors, towards older models from the eighteenth century and beyond.

We hope by the end not only to have created an outline map of part of a tradition but to have demonstrated some of the ways in which original genius or talent challenges, develops and renews its inheritance. The book is intended for the kind of reader for whom a fine novel is an area of exploration and self-discovery, a small invention of a real world where there are too many factors interacting to prompt insensitive judgment, where our curiosity is fed without satisfaction, and where we are not wholly subject to events, ideas or feelings but made to experience all together – as we do in real life, but objectively, as we cannot do in real life.

---

11. See Forster, *Aspects of the Novel*, Chapter 7.

1

THE NEGATIVES OF IDEALISM

Principles are over-simple precepts for action. In order to be implemented, an attitude must be singled out like a thread of a certain colour from a bundle of entangled motives, needs and conflicting assessments of a situation. As abstracts they are essentially unworkable, for any living context in which they might be applied is necessarily too complex to be resolved adequately by simple rules. They must be challenged by the entire context of each situation, otherwise they may become weapons for a predatory egoism or shields for those whose sympathetic responsiveness has been maimed. This is what Lawrence explored. He defined the basic mechanism thus:

> The inclination to set up some fixed centre, in the mind, and make the whole soul turn upon this centre. This we call idealism. Instead of the will fixing upon some sensational activity, it fixes upon some aspirational activity, and pivots this activity upon an idea or ideal. The whole soul streams in the energy of aspiration and turns automatically, like a machine, upon the ideal.[1]

His critique involved a challenge to the contemporary social and ethical codes that shape the mentality, and also (more radically) an investigation into the personal motives that power this kind of idealism and make it potentially dangerous.

In his early novels Lawrence, influenced by the nineteenth century traditions of psychological realism, was mainly interested in constructing psychological studies. Idealism shows as a feature of characters like Emily Saxton in *The White Peacock*, the lovers in *The Trespasser* (which will be discussed later) and Mrs Morel and Miriam

---

1. Lawrence, "Democracy" (1919) in *Reflections on the Death of a Porcupine*, 79.

in *Sons and Lovers*. It is illuminating to begin the study with the latter, for there we see some of the personal origins of the general theme.

Gertrude Morel is "a puritan ... really high-minded and stern". Lawrence began the story, of course, with a series of anecdotes taken from his mother's view of her past and his own childish recollections. The raw material had an imaginative life of its own, which gave rise to the astonishing vividness and immediacy of the scenes between the Morels. From the initial aim of giving a faithful picture of a much-loved woman emerged what Lawrence himself, after he had finished, called a "theme":

> It follows this idea: a woman of character and refinement goes into the lower class, and has no satisfaction in her life. She has had a passion for her husband, so the children are born of passion, and have heaps of vitality, But as her sons grow up she selects them as lovers – first the eldest, then the second. These sons are *urged* into life by their reciprocal love of their mother – urged on and on. But when they come to manhood they can't love, because their mother is the strongest power in their lives, and holds them.[2]

Over four intensive revisions Lawrence searched out his theme, but the structure of the narrative remained the same, never completely remoulded by the interpretation (as, for instance, was the substance of Joyce's *Portrait of the Artist as Young Man*). Anomalies and problems remained. How does it come about that, attracted as she has been to Walter Morel's "sensuous flame of life", she later abhors it? How does "one of those naturally exquisite people who can walk through mud without dirtying their shoes" give way to the "fanatic" who "wielded the lash unmercifully"? Without the kind of analysis Lawrence was capable of later, we are left to guess at the mechanism of these developments. He increasingly underlined Mrs Morel's guilt but, as John Worthen concluded in his discussion of the revision:

> The final manuscript was now in danger of splitting Mrs Morel into two – the loving, caring, deeply sympathetic mother on the one hand, the ruthless moral martinet on the other; the two sides are only just perceived as aspects of each other. She is now seen as dangerous, and as partly responsible for the quarrels, but her point of view also regularly dominates the narrative of the marriage.[3]

At times the narrator is conscientious in apportioning the blame and even laying it heavily on her as the stronger partner:

---

2. Lawrence to Edward Garnett, 19 November 1912, in *Letters*, I, 476-77.
3. Worthen, *D. H. Lawrence: The Early Years*, 437.

> So in seeking to make him nobler than he could be, she destroyed him. She injured and scarred herself. (25)

Then he makes amends with: "but she lost none of her worth."[4]

The threat the mother poses to the free development of Paul's life is finally veiled by the sentiment of filial devotion. At her death she relies to the last on a stoical self-will supported by make-belief: "She was holding herself rigid, so that she might die without ever uttering the great cry that was tearing from her." Afterwards:

> She lay like a maiden asleep. With his candle in his hand, he bent over her. She lay like a girl asleep and dreaming of her love. The mouth was a little open, as if wondering from the suffering, but her face was young, her brow clear and white as if life had never touched it. (443)

The praise of the mother's beauty and the readiness to accept at face value her evasions of past and present has a harrowing authenticity as a reflection the son's terrified love.[5] But an older Lawrence, the author of *Women in Love,* would have more ruthlessly dissected that suffering, disillusion and self-denial, at the same time, perhaps, exploring more thoroughly what justifies the devotion.[6]

Of course, Lawrence's "theme" in this novel lacks the ramifications of the critique of idealism in the later ones. Only if we view Gertrude Morel in the most general terms, as a crippled, vengeful egoism arming itself with principles and turning the family into a battleground with the children as victims can we discern its embryo.

In the portrait of Miriam Leivers, Lawrence had a starting point as intensely personal as with Mrs Morel: his own relationship with Jessie Chambers. From a sensitive and realistic attempt to portray a complex character – which Jessie at first welcomed and admired – again

---

4. The same sentence occurs in the third draft of the novel (1911-12) ending with the word "nobility" instead of "worth". Later in the same draft comes the observation: "It is a question, whether she was more intoxicated with suffering than her husband with drink." See *Paul Morel*, ed. Helen Baron, 188-93.

5. The virginal look on Lawrence's mother's dead face is admired in some of the poems written at the time of her death, such as "Virgin Bride".

6. In the stories and plays written or revised after the completion of *Sons and Lovers* in 1912, Lawrence was already moving towards a more severe view of characters derived from his mother. In the play, *The Widowing of Mrs Holroyd*, as revised in 1913, the wife looking at her husband's dead body says "I never loved you enough" (Lawrence, *Plays*, 108). In "Odour of Chrysanthemums", revised in 1914, a wife in the same situation asks herself, "What wrong have I done?" and the narrator adds, "She had denied him what he was".

emerged something more impersonal, which previsions the later theme.

There is a keen analysis of Miriam's idealistic predisposition, which has the power to keep natural vitality at bay: "She was cut off from ordinary life by her religious intensity which made the world for her either a nunnery garden or a paradise where sin and knowledge were not, or else an ugly, cruel thing."[7] Constraint, vivid life suppressed or redirected, betrays itself in her appearance and manner:

> Her body was not flexible and living. She walked with a swing, rather heavily, her head bowed forward, pondering. She was not clumsy, and yet none of her movements seemed quite *the* movement. Often, when wiping the dishes, she would stand in bewilderment and chagrin because she had pulled in two halves a cup or a tumbler. It was as if, in her fear and self-mistrust, she put too much strength into the effort. There was no looseness or abandon about her. Everything was gripped stiff with intensity, and her effort, overcharged, closed in on itself. (184)

As in the portrait of Mrs Morel, there are anomalies, which may well have derived from the author's impressions of his model:

> He saw her peering forward at the page, her red lips parted piteously, the black hair springing in fine strands across her tawny ruddy cheek. She was coloured like a pomegranate for richness. His breaths came short as he watched her. Suddenly she looked up at him. Her dark eyes were naked with their love, afraid, and yearning. (247)

Paul accuses her of holding her essential self back: "She had fought to keep herself free of him in the last issue." At the same time he accuses her of offering herself as a sacrifice. After his "test" on her:

> She would obey him in his trifling commands. But once he was obeyed, then she had him in her power, she knew, to lead him where she would. She was sure of herself. (342)

Miriam is at this point "sure of herself", whereas earlier she is full of "fear and self-mistrust". It is not clearly seen, as this kind of thing will be with Hermione in *Women in Love*, as a superficial assurance and an underlying lack of it, but as assurance and diffidence veering; and the veering is dictated by the onus the author wishes to put upon

---

7. More categorical comments along the same lines appear in the second (1911) manuscript of the novel : "She seemed like one of those haunted, wistful angels that have taken refuge in heaven .... one of those spiritual women whose passion issues in prayer, becomes religious service, rather than a carnal thing. She was born to be a nun" (*Paul Morel*, ed. Helen Baron, 81-82).

her at any one stage of the story. The kind of contradictions that go together to make up a complex and coherent picture of Hermione work against each other in the portrait of Miriam. Towards the end of the revision process, in the autumn of 1912, Lawrence was, as John Worthen pointed out, moving towards the construction in Miriam of "a pattern of manipulative and frustrated desire" that resembles Hermione's.[8] But the reconstruction remained incomplete.

Three years of intensive rethinking and revision took Lawrence to the completion of *The Rainbow*, where the critique of idealism is enlarged from the psychology of an individual and begins to take in his whole civilization.

    Will Brangwen's ideals themselves are of course rooted in a longing for creative contact and self-renewal. It is his use of them that turns them into a means of escape or aggression. This is grounded psychologically, as it is in all the later studies of idealism, in a personal inadequacy in his relations with others, and a sense of insufficiency. The basic insecurity is illuminated clearly during the crisis that occurs towards the end of Anna Brangwen's first pregnancy. His neurotic dependence – "Why, if Anna left him even for a week, did he seem to be clinging like a madman to the edge of reality, and slipping surely, surely into the flood of unreality that would drown him?" – provokes in Anna this reaction:

> He wanted her in his power. He wanted to devour her at leisure, to have her …. Then she turned fiercely on him, and fought him. (172)

She struggles to break through the self-insulation in Will that relegates her to the role of satisfying a neurotic need. She wants to break the hold of the abstracts which are supporting the insulation and are instrumental to restraining her freedom of spirit. She fights all Will's abstracts and symbols, whether they are stained-glass lambs, or cathedrals, or his particular practice of his art, or his view of himself. In these lie the wider context of his malady.

    In religion he needs the sense of identity with God or with an absolute beyond the variables of self that will not only harmonize the known with the unknown but act as a recurring theme to his life and as a shared source of passional response with others. He tries to dissolve his own individuality in an abstraction or ecstasy where the self can be forgotten. Lawrence treated Will's late-Victorian Christian mysticism sympathetically, seeing it as a genuine if limited appreciation of the

---

8. Worthen, *D. H. Lawrence: The Early Years*, 449.

mysteries of death and renewal: "In church he wanted a dark, nameless emotion, the emotion of all the great mysteries of passion." His imagination is stocked with typological Biblical images, as Virginia Hyde demonstrated.[9] The thematic analysis explores the psychological needs and functions involved alongside the cultural sources Will draws on.

The scene in Lincoln Cathedral in Chapter 7 for instance correlates the individual and the traditional features of Will's experience, revealing strengths and weaknesses in both, including the paradox that what stands for the expansive and creative is at the same time a refuge and negation. It is based on a triple contrast between his personal vision of the wholeness of life, the vision offered by the Church in his time and the perspective created by the novel as a whole. This is brought about partly by the imagery of the seed and the arch (related to the rainbow) which are here given a Christian interpretation as well as linked both with the basic symbols of the novel and Will's personal experience of courtship and marriage. But primarily it is achieved through the juxtaposition of Will and Anna. From the beginning of the scene, wherever Will responds, Anna is there to challenge and to relate what is going on both to their private lives and to the changing world:

> When he saw the cathedral in the distance, dark blue lifted watchful in the sky, his heart leapt. It was the sign in Heaven, it was the Spirit hovering like a dove, like an eagle over the earth. He turned his glowing ecstatic face to her, his mouth opened with a strange, ecstatic grin.
> "There she is," he said.
> The "she" irritated her. Why "she"? It was "it." What was the cathedral, a big building, a thing of the past, obsolete, to excite him to such a pitch? She began to stir herself in readiness. (186)

The exploration of their separate linked responses forms an appraisal of the whole religious experience.

In parts of the cathedral scene the overwrought lushness of the style used to describe Will's responses conveys the confusion of sensual and spiritual ecstasy in him (it is the same kind of confusion to be found in the adolescent experience of his daughter Ursula). Although a great deal of space is repeatedly given to a sympathetic expression of his religious enthusiasms, these are critically placed at

---

9. See Virginia Hyde, *The Risen Adam: D. H. Lawrence's Revisionist Typology*, 77-92.

every turn. That Lawrence worked hard to objectify and evaluate Will's emotionalism in this scene and deepen its universal significance can be verified by a glance at the fragment of an earlier draft:

> Like a shadowy rainbow, the jewelled gloom spanned from silence to silence, darkness to darkness, fecundity to fecundity, as a seed spans from life to life and death to death, containing the secret of all folded between its parts. (590)

It became richer in concept, imagery and rhythm:

> Spanned round with the rainbow, the jewelled gloom folded music upon silence, light upon darkness, fecundity upon death, as a seed folds leaf upon leaf and silence upon the root and the flower, hushing up the secret of all between its parts, the death out of which it fell, the life into which it has dropped, the immortality it involves, and the death it will embrace again. (187)

Anna's and Will's opposing views are almost equally endorsed. The styles of their dialogue and thought are quite distinct, and we are forced to identify vividly with each in turn. Will is less reflective and rational than Anna. He does not think his way through his problems: "His mind he let sleep." The narrative plunges us into the flow of his feelings, fluctuating and developing in sudden leaps and conveyed in a language steeped in the rhythms and phraseology as well as the imagery of the King James Bible. It is a style of writing moulded to his mentality quite as much as any in Joyce's *Portrait of the Artist as a Young Man* and without any of the condescension of the parodist. Each development in him is distanced and critically placed by what comes next and what went before, and usually by Anna as well.

Her attacks are countered, half-truth with half-truth, but Will cannot hold out against her, partly because he so desperately needs her support and partly because his natural vitality acknowledges the truth of her objections:

> He listened to the thrushes in the garden, and heard a note which the cathedrals did not include: something free and careless and joyous. He crossed a field that was all yellow with dandelions, on his way to work, and the bath of yellow glowing was something at once so sumptuous and fresh, that he was glad he was away from his shadowy cathedral. (191)

His artistic aspirations go the same way. The early wood carvings are done in the excitement and wonder of his discovery of Anna: he gives her a butter stamper carved with a phoenix and begins a panel showing the creation of Eve. The latter reveals in prototype both his worship of the female and his fear of her. Obsessed with the idea of her, he is desperate to minimize it. Again Anna does not miss its significance:

> She jeered at the Eve, saying:
> "She is like a little marionette. Why is she so small? You've made Adam as big as God, and Eve like a doll.
> "It is impudence to say that Woman was born out of Man's body," she continued, "when every man is born out of woman. What impudence men have, what arrogance!" (162)

He burns the panel. His interest in art has already by this time grown more passive and escapist, as we see when on escaping to Nottingham after a row with Anna he picks up a book of illustrations of the carvings in Bamberg Cathedral:

> The book lay in his hands like a doorway. The world around was only an inclosure, a room. But he was going away. He lingered over the lovely statues of women. A marvellous, finely-wrought universe crystallised out around him as he looked again, at the crowns, the twining hair, the woman-faces. (153)

Here the sources of his quasi-religious aesthetic enthusiasms are indicated, as Stephen Dedalus's are in Joyce's *Portrait*.

The final, rather defeated phase of Will's idealism involves the dream of becoming "unanimous with the whole of purposive mankind" (the idealistic phraseology still typical of him) which boils down to an enthusiasm for education: "about all the rest he was oblivious and entirely indifferent." This channels his artistic interests into teaching evening classes in woodwork. Ten years later he takes up modelling, jewellery and metalwork, producing vivid imitative pieces but disappointed with his failure to achieve "utterances of himself". The characteristic cycles of feeling are set to continue, although we lose sight of him in the preoccupation with Ursula Brangwen.

The glimpses we get of him in *Women in Love* illustrate the primacy in the dual novel of thematic over individual developments. The scene in Chapter 19 where Birkin turns up at Will's house to propose to his daughter is a curious comedy of misunderstandings, with each of the two men is at his worst: Birkin an insufferable prig and Will, now in his forties, a scarcely recognisable moralistic blockhead, although we see the continuance of his anxiety-prone discontent. It is understandable that Birkin should superciliously dismiss him as "not a coherent human being, a roomful of old echoes" but it comes as a shock to find the narrative letting the judgment go unchallenged. In Chapter 27, when Ursula tells Will her decision to marry, he is more recognizable. His outrage at not being consulted (he smacks her face) and her downright defiance recall the worst side of their history of powerful demands and resentments in *The Rainbow*. But her repudiation as she packs her bag and leaves the house for good is the last word on Will. Anna Brangwen takes hardly any part in the exchange. In this novel Ursula's parents are seen strictly from the point of view of those who are freeing themselves from the mould they represent, and who are absorbed (as the author and readers are) in the business of escape or renewal.

The latter theme takes over *The Rainbow* from the time of Ursula's adolescence, but the analysis of idealism continues alongside it for a while, beginning with the gentle irony directed at her sixteen-year-old infatuation with her cousin Anton Skrebensky, and then becoming more serious as it focuses on him.

His is an idealizing love, something from which she discovers her mother's kind of need to fight free. Skrebensky believes in the importance of principles and holds on to them in a kind of desperation. They shore up the "ghastly sense of helplessness" and uncertainty he feels at moments of crisis. To feel purposive and important he must give himself up to social aspirations or to a machine like the army or to someone with more vitality than himself, like Ursula.

He is seen chiefly and effectively in terms of her needs and responses. What is enough for her at sixteen is insufficient at nineteen and a menace later. Almost from the start his love turns into a neurotic craving for self-obliteration: "Even, in his frenzy, he sought for her mouth with his mouth, though it was like putting his face into some awful death." Later, on his return from South Africa, the brief honeymoon illusion of contact and communion, when "he seemed like the living darkness upon her" is followed by her increasing sense of oppression and dissatisfaction:

> He seemed to be made up of a set of habitual actions and decisions. The vulnerable, variable quick of the man was inaccessible. She knew nothing of it. She could only feel the dark, heavy fixity of his animal desire. (410)

Their love quickly becomes a fight for mastery.

From Skrebensky's feeling unable to match the bargeman in living sexual response, to his fear of being nullified and driven insane by Ursula we see the outline of a case that refers back to Miriam and forward to Hermione. But whereas with Miriam the character stood out partly in contradiction to the thematic analysis of it, here the universalized theme runs away with the character. His arguments with Ursula lead summarily to her categorical repudiation of what he stands for. Occasionally the author too chips in, making more obvious the dismissive handling of the character: "He could not see, it was not born in him to see." There is not enough substance in the character to stop Lawrence gaining momentum on other themes in the course of presenting him. There are suggestions for instance of the diseased reaction to idealism later worked out fully and personally in Gerald.

In *Women in Love*, however, the portrait of Hermione Roddice shows theme and character combined and objectified. Her relationship with her lover, Birkin, was derived in Lawrence's mind from Miriam's with Paul in *Sons and Lovers,* as is clear from the rejected Prologue, which in this respect reads like a recall of the earlier relationship:

> She would do anything to give him what he wanted, that which he was raging for, this physical fulfilment he insisted on. She was wise, she thought for the best. She prepared herself like a perfect sacrifice to him. (507)

In the novel itself the love affair is compressed into the service of the theme, and portrayed only in its last stages: his denunciations of her and the struggle, leading to her murderous assault on him, which puts an end to it. About the past there are only the hints she throws to Ursula:

> "You would have to be prepared to suffer – dreadfully .... He lives an intensely spiritual life, at times – too, too wonderful. And then come the reactions." (295)

Hermione is therefore segregated from the action of the novel, more than Thomas Crich, whose spiritual sickness has its continuing effect on his family and resolves itself in Gerald. Unlike the suicidal Gerald who attaches himself to the destructive Gudrun, Hermione has enough power and interest in life to attach herself to the vigorous struggling life in Birkin, wanting to save her own through him. But her role is to be spurned. She stands at bay. As a result it is the complexities of the character itself that fall under close scrutiny: that character against which in violent battle Birkin learns to define what he most needs from life. Through this static concentration a deeper insight is given into some of the psychological conditions leading to a tenacious hold on half-believed ideas.

Essentially she has lost faith in the universals of the nineteenth-century traditions, which includes the rationalist discourse she encourages at her country house weekends, and even the ideology of love which she tries to foist on Birkin. What she holds on to is the beneficial control of the mind. It is this alone she really believes in. This, only lightly trammelled by the old ideals, is the source of strength for her and the measure of achievement:

> "If only we could learn how to use our will," said Hermione, "we could do anything. The will can cure anything, and put anything right. That I am convinced of – if only we use the will properly, intelligently .... And in so many things, I have made myself well. I was a very queer and nervous girl. And by learning to use my will, simply by using my will, I made myself right." (139-40)

With her the novel stresses the paralysis involved in attempting to conform to mental regulation. Hence the almost grotesque brilliance of her appearance, with its fixity and "sinister grace". In her there is competence superimposed on chaos. The awareness of this brings even to the most casual observer a sense of danger that prevents her being jeered at. She walks a tightrope:

> She seemed to catch her thoughts at length from off the surface of a maelstrom of chaotic black emotions and reactions, and Birkin was always filled with repulsion, she caught so infallibly, her will never failed her. Her voice was always dispassionate and tense, and perfectly confident. Yet she shuddered with a sense of nausea, a sort of sea-sickness that always threatened to overwhelm her mind. (140)

On her introduction in the first chapter we are told that "she always felt vulnerable ... any common maidservant of robust temper could fling her down this bottomless pit of insufficiency". We see her suffering as she has to pass the wedding crowd outside the church, hear of her chaos when Birkin is not there as expected: "a terrible storm came over her, as if she were drowning .... It was beyond death, so utterly null, desert." The surface self-assurance shown at Breadalby, where she queens it over her guests and dependents, staging scenes and pressing her attentions insolently upon them, is worm-eaten with the craving for intimacy that unnerves Ursula: "she seemed to hinder one's workings." Bewailing her loss of spontaneous "unknowable" life, as she does in the classroom, she nevertheless holds hard, out of fear and obstinate egotism, to what she has got. Birkin, rounding on her at that point and later making his final cruel and dangerous attack in her bedroom at Breadalby, when he tortures her with her inability to live and understand with the open, connective responsiveness he identifies in the geese he is sketching, drives her to the near madness in which she tries to kill him. He recognizes that, however dangerous the demand is to him, however ugly the attempt she is making, she is nonetheless in the position of asking for help:

> He looked at her in mingled hate and contempt, also in pain because she suffered, and in shame because he knew he tortured her. He had an impulse to kneel and plead for forgiveness. (42)

The violence of his verbal onslaught on her measures the power over him of her will-ridden intellectuality and idealism, the desire to "know" he has shared with her. In attempting to destroy the source of that power he threatens the very keystone of her sanity: "but he would never, never dare break her will and let loose the maelstrom of her subconsciousness, and see her in her ultimate madness." In the knowledge and shame of what he is doing to her he goes back to her boudoir and almost invites reprisal, turning his back on her to read. Her physical attack on him concludes the relationship, as does Gerald's on Gudrun at the end of the novel.

The portrait of Thomas Crich gives us the most comprehensive definition of Lawrence's theme. In him there is an agony of confusion between love that denies the self and love that asserts it. His over-riding stress on the former sponsors the disruption of balance between giving and taking in all his relationships. The mental directive protects him from a strenuous involvement, a flexible responsibility, and this limiting of response dries up the sources of renewal not only in himself but in those closest to him.

   The social ramifications of his idealism are fully developed, for he is a large employer of labour. His is a late-Victorian style of philanthropy. At first, reacting against his father's obsession with the mere accumulation of wealth, he almost deifies his miners: "he had felt inferior to them, as if they through poverty and labour were nearer to God than he." His benevolence becomes outdated, however, as the class war intensifies, when from fear of anarchy and to preserve the *status quo* he has to side with the owners against the men.

   The social perspective is firmly linked with the personal. We glimpse his feelings of inadequacy in his personal relations with his employees. And his relations with his wife are grounded also in feelings of insufficiency, together with the attempt to compensate for it by an insistence on power prerogatives. In both spheres there is the same grinding dissonance between conscious, idealized intentions and the basic bond of use and abuse. In this battle his wife, whose natural pride and emotional need are baulked and humiliated, sullenly rages "like one of the great demons of hell". She is unable to challenge him as effectively as Anna does Will, and he is the nominal victor, but the fight consumes his strength. The development of the marriage is traced from his initial violating worship of Christiana's purity – "she was a wonderful white snowflower, which he had desired infinitely" – to his eventual terror at her fierceness, as her suppressed vitality (and his own) grow more vengeful. The deadlock, the destructive hold each has on the other is given its most extreme expression when Thomas identifies his wife with the pain that tears him in his death-throes.

The war runs its course through the family, as we hear from Gerald's old nurse. The children, neglected, are destructive and untrainable:

> "But she wouldn't have them corrected – no-o, wouldn't hear of it. I can remember the rows she had with Mr Crich, my word! – When he'd got worked up, properly worked up till he could stand no more, he'd lock the study door and whip them. But she paced up and down all the while like a tiger outside, like a tiger, with very murder in her face. She had a face that could look death. And when the door was opened, she'd go in with her hands lifted – 'What have you been doing to my children, you coward.'" (213)

Here the mother, although working to make up to the children for her essential lack of interest (the nurse says, "She wasn't going to be bothered with them herself") is still absorbed in her own battle for freedom and her rightful position in her husband's love and respect. The father takes over the correction of the children out of a sense of duty and to relieve his feelings: "'he had to be driven mad before he'd lift a finger'." His domestic affections are dissipated by his "Christian" ideals and practices. He does not form a close, demanding attachment within the family until Winifred, the youngest, much later in his life, claims it, and by then his charitableness is being proved, even to himself, insufficient, unworkable and even destructive. His "universal" love has been an evasion of personal love and responsibility. Evasion is the keynote sounded by his wife at his deathbed:

> "Blame me, blame me if you like, that he lies there like a lad in his teens, with his first beard on his face. Blame me if you like. But none of you know." She was silent in intense silence.

His dead face is like Mrs Morel's – "as if life had never touched it" – but Christiana reacts with hatred:

> Then there came, in a low, tense voice: "If I thought that the children
> I bore would lie looking like that in death, I'd strangle them when
> they were infants, yes – " (335)

The analysis insists on what has controlled and sanctioned the violation:

> And now he was dying with all his ideas and interpretations intact ….
> Only death would show the perfect completeness of the lie. (218)

The portrait is brilliantly explicit, and most of it achieved in one chapter, but it is exploration, not exposition: we see the sufferings of a human being, not the dissection of a case.

In the novels completed in the following few years (from *The Lost Girl* to *Kangaroo*) Lawrence sniped at the ideals themselves – those he had already impounded – rather than considering the dangerous maladies that drive people to adopt and misuse them.

In *Kangaroo*, for example, there is a whole firing-range of ideals, from the Sermon on the Mount to Mrs Somers' romantic preferences. If we are looking for the kind of development we have found so far, the most promising area is in Ben Cooley ("Kangaroo" himself) who professes love as his motive and offers it as the sole "inspirational force". He offers Somers, the author figure, as Hermione does Birkin, a lopsided version of Somers' own doctrine, the revulsion from which enables him to define more clearly what he really needs to believe. Unlike Hermione, however, Cooley is not a character one can take seriously, and the general presentation of him degenerates at times into pantomime:

> And Kangaroo was hanging forward his face and smiling heavily and
> ambiguously to himself, knowing that Somers was with him.
> "'Tiger, tiger, burning bright
> In the forests of the night–'"
> he quoted in a queer, sonorous voice, like a priest. "The lion of your
> might would be a tiger, wouldn't it? – The tiger and the unicorn were
> fighting for the crown. How about me for a unicorn? – if I tied a
> bayonet on my nose?" He rubbed his nose with heavy playfulness.
> "Is the tiger your principle of evil?"
> "The tiger? Oh dear no. The jackal, the hyena, and dear, deadly
> humanity. No no. The tiger stands on one side of the shield, and the
> unicorn on the other, and they don't fight for the crown at all. They
> keep it up between them. The pillars of the world! The tiger and the
> kangaroo!" he boomed this out in a mock heroic voice, strutting with

heavy playfulness. Then he laughed, looking winsomely at Somers. Heaven, what a beauty he had! (114-15)

The last sentence reveals an infatuation on Somers' part which leaves Cooley virtually exempt from personal analysis of the kind we expect in Lawrence's treatment of an idealist. Only his doctrines are put to a test, in the riot in Chapter 16, where his political party reveals the brutality hidden behind its benevolence. The general situation is compelling, but the action in these scenes is separate from the two characters and remains corroborative merely of the direction Somers' thoughts are taking. There is no dynamic relationship between Cooley and Somers; no development, that is, evolving from the close relationship of two individuals, merely from the proximity of two streams of ideas that at points converge.

In the next phase of his writings Lawrence began to allow the desire to promote his own convictions take precedence over any sympathetic alertness to the predicament of those in the novel opposed to them. The critique of idealism was no longer a matter for exploration but for exposition. In *The Plumed Serpent* Carlota, the spokeswoman for Christian love, stands in Hermione's position in *Women in Love,* attacked and eventually repudiated by Ramón, who claims that their marriage has been based on passionate possessiveness – "either ravishing or being ravished" – and they have never recognized each other's individuality. He does admit a share of responsibility – "with Carlota he failed absolutely" – but there is no sharp retrospective analysis. Ramón's verdict is that her love has been forced, so that now its only genuine motive is the will to power. There is some staleness in the narrative that endorses this:

> Life had done its work on one more human being, quenched the spontaneous life and left only the will. Killed the god in the woman, or the goddess, and left only charity, with a will. (208)

Even their friend Kate Leslie, supposedly sympathetic to Carlota, adopts Ramón's line on her: "Kate knew at once that Dona Carlota loved him, but with a love that was now nearly all will."

One gets little convincing verification of Carlota's inward condition. She is depicted in tearful or frenzied opposition to her husband, victim of a situation she cannot understand and unable to challenge him in any effective way. Nowhere else in Lawrence's novels is a character who suffers so much dealt with in such a summary and unsympathetic way. While she breaks down in the frenzy that leads to her death, Ramón (quite unlike Birkin in a much less critical situation) shows a deadly acquiescence in it:

> Not a muscle of his face moved. And Kate could see that his heart had died in its connection with Carlota, his heart was quite quite dead in him; out of the deathly vacancy he watched his wife. Only his brows frowned a little, from his smooth, male forehead. His old connections were broken. She could hear him say: *There is no star between me and Carlota.* – And how terribly true it was! (343)

Carlota is given all the obtuse and dismissive treatment by her partner and by the author that was handed out to Walter Morel at the other end of Lawrence's ideological pilgrimage. Like Walter she can offer surprisingly telling comments on the partner's failings, in this case on the vanity of Ramón's self-apotheosis:

> "he wants to be worshipped. To be worshipped! To be worshipped! A God! He, whom I've held in my arms!" (165)

As we shall see more fully later, Lawrence was backing in Ramón something akin to the fanaticism whose dangers he had so tellingly analysed earlier. He was intent on the advantages of a new faith and laying up as many sacrifices for it as the old one did.

What his novels at their best condemn is not the half-truths of liberalism and contemporary Christianity – what doctrines are more than half-truths? – but how, when linked with a psychological disability, they may become dangerous substitutes for thought and responsiveness. This applies to all doctrines, including Lawrence's.

2

THE IMPRISONED SELF

Lawrence's second theme follows with a perverse logic of its own from the breakdown of assurances depicted in the first. Disillusion invents a mutation of the old ideals, transforming them into manias or fantasies which, like the ideals they replace, sanction an escape from the give-and-take of responsive and responsible relationships. In either case the passional and creative self is imprisoned, the "single" self coping with its isolation or sense of chaos – or else, enclosed within the self, inflicting it on others. The theme does not show itself effectively till *Women in Love*. There it is explored with an exhaustive finality that makes it the only possible starting point for this study.

Gerald Crich, who is both destroyer and victim, is at the centre, his tragic struggle given with a rare passionate intensity and its ramifications explored with great precision. The vivid and detailed psychology of the character fits at all points the universals of the theme. Trapped in the ruin of his parents' lives, his conscious attitude is a repudiation of all his father stands for, but the reaction itself enchains him. His rebellion drives him to transform the ideal of human equality into an equality in submission to a rational system, and romantic love, whereby one might lose the self in adoration of another, into an addictive craving for self-obliterative sensation. That is to say, he retains the slavish quest of fixed transcendent abstractions stationed beyond the variables of living response, the longing for an absolute. His development does not revalue or renew the tradition he has inherited but rather brings it to its death, sealing off individual thought and response more effectively than the older idealism.

While these and other general factors operate, we never lose sight of the personal and particular. The leaning towards destructiveness Gerald shares from the beginning with his brothers and sisters. Mrs Kirk the nurse says:

"If you wouldn't let them smash their pots on the table, if you wouldn't let them drag the kitten about with a string round its neck, if you wouldn't give them whatever they asked for, every mortal thing – then there was a shine on, and their mother coming in asking – 'What's the matter with him? What have you done to him? What is it, Darling?' And then she'd turn on you as if she'd trample you under her feet." (213)

The battle between the parents has been the reality of his life, his idea of "harmony" and security of purpose a later dream. His own act of violation in killing his brother follows from the parents' violation of themselves and him. The bewilderment and guilt produce a paralysis, an inertness that underlies the overt superficial evidence of initiative. It leaves the "fatal halfness" that Birkin comments on and the weakness and dependence that Gerald's women identify in him. His mother is scathing about it – "You're as weak as a cat, really – always were" – and Gudrun reflects:

Gerald! Could *he* fold her in his arms and sheath her in sleep? Ha! He needed putting to sleep himself – poor Gerald. (465)

He needs to put life into bondage, thereby reducing the danger and uncertainty associated with it. What he desires for himself in his reorganisation of the mines is the protection of a mechanically sure, monotonous activity – "a slumber of constant repetition" as Gudrun finally sums it up, "satisfied as a wheelbarrow that goes backwards and forwards along a plank all day" – a using up of himself in a way that leaves all basic conflicts unbroached.

To reinforce the semblance of "harmony" and keep himself in a position of control, it becomes inevitable that, like Dickens's Dombey, he violate others, in the name of mechanical efficiency, as his father had done before him in the name of humanitarianism. We see the kind of will required for this and the symbol of what is sacrificed in the scene where he subjugates the mare at the railway crossing. Gerald's will responds to the mechanical imperative of the engine and its trucks and co-operates with it in reducing the quivering vitality of the mare to subjection:

But he held on to her unrelaxed, with an almost mechanical relentlessness, keen as a sword pressing into her. Both man and horse were sweating with violence. Yet he seemed calm as a ray of cold sunshine. (111)

The more sadistic variant of this is in that keenly observed scene (amusing as well as sinister) where he masters the rabbit.

A sense of catastrophe shared with his family prompts Gerald's remark after his sister Diana's death at the waterparty:

> "There's one thing about our family, you know .... Once anything goes wrong, it can never be put right again – not with us. I've noticed all my life – you can't put a thing right, once it has gone wrong." (184)

The mother voices it in her outcry over the dead father:

> "Pray!" she said strongly. "Pray for yourselves to God, for there's no help for you from your parents."[1]

Nowhere is it more moving than in Gerald's response to his father's death. As he watches him die he feels he is "inheriting his own destruction" and "as if he himself were dealing the death even when he most recoiled from it". Afterwards:

> He was suspended on the edge of a void, writhing. Whatever he thought of, was the abyss – whether it were friends or strangers, or work or play, it all showed him only the same bottomless void, in which his heart swung perishing. (337)

Lawrence sustained the awareness of a family doom and its course throughout the history of the Criches, reinforcing it with the water imagery that is associated with all the ailing characters in the novel. In much of Lawrence's writings water stands, as it does in *Genesis*, for the submerging and dissolving of all bonds, the dissolving of the life we know. Lawrence once commented that he gave *The Rainbow* its title partly with reference to the biblical Flood.[2] In that novel it plays its traditional double role, both creative (as in the rainbow itself) and destructive (as in the flood which drowns Tom Brangwen). In its sequel, which Lawrence once thought of calling *Noah's Ark*, the destructive connotations prevail, although not completely: the complex ambiguity is carried, for instance, into Birkin's concern to come to terms with what he calls "the dark river of dissolution".

Thomas Crich's last words are about the leaking of water into one of the mines. Gudrun identifies Gerald's body, "stretching and surging like the marsh fire" with the succulent water plants that grow in its mud's "festering chill". At the waterparty, when Gerald has dived into the lake, "like a rat" and "like a seal" in an attempt to rescue the drowning couple, the ordeal is associated, as their love later is, with the magnetism of death:

---

1. *Women in Love*, 335. Not in the earlier (1916) version of the novel.
2. Lawrence to Waldo Frank, 27 July 1917, in *Letters*, III, 142.

Oh, and the beauty of the subjection of his loins, white and dimly luminous as he climbed over the side of the boat, made her want to die, to die .... She saw him press the water out of his face, and look at the bandage on his hand. (181)

He has caught it in a piece of machinery.

When the scene changes to the Alps in winter, the transformation of water into ice reflects the narrowing concern of the novel at this point in Gerald's story towards sterility, that idea of death without a promise of renewal which is expressed in the finality and abstraction of ice and snow. The imagery is fused with the action involving Gerald and Gudrun, between whom and for whom there is no growth, and it intensifies it.

Some readers attempting to come to terms with the tragedy have been drawn to some of Birkin's general pronouncements, such those in Chapter 19 where he tries to think out Gerald's destiny in terms of "the destructive frost mystery". But these sometimes pompous universals are bred of his own struggles, set within the context of his story and judged by it, and if we adopt them as authorial dicta we may miss the more delicate and subtle intuition embedded in the imagery, the alignment of the tragic action with the destructive phases of the natural life-cycle and of the elements – or, as Lawrence put it, in praise of Shakespeare and Sophocles, "setting behind the small action of his protagonists the terrific action of unfathomed nature".[3]

But the "mind-forged manacles" are not confined to the family. The social developments outlined in Chapter 17 stand separate but related behind the successive phases of Gerald's personal development, his wilfulness as a boy (mentioned by his nurse) moving from the idea of "savage freedom" through his interest in war and travel and into the "real adventure" of the mines. As this takes hold he becomes a natural victim of historical processes. His modernisation of the Crich mines is an enterprise typical of the era that includes the First World War, when direct personal contact between owners and workmen was diminishing and working relationships losing the sense of immediacy and human involvement that comes with smaller groups. When he makes the miners machine-minders, he fulfils the Victorian humanitarian ideal as he sees it. Equality becomes "equality in the Godhead of the great productive machine" and a worship of the machine is substituted for the old religious aspirations: "they were exalted by belonging to this great and superhuman system which was

---

3. *A Study of Thomas Hardy*, 29.

beyond feeling or reason, something really godlike." His feat of organisation represents the culmination of one phase of history and the beginning of another.

Graham Holderness complained that what happens to the Crich mines ignores the continuing "struggle between capital and labour".[4] But the given view is from Gerald's angle and is qualified by Gudrun's and Ursula's glimpses of the miners. The miners are seen in two lights. Their confusion or "rottenness of will" sponsors an escape like Gerald's from the challenge of immediate relationships, whose old assurances are changing, into the compulsions of a social machine. Against this   endorsement of what Gerald is doing is another dimension: their natural warmth and humanity, "a glamorous thickness of labour and maleness".

> In the backyards of several dwellings a miner could be seen washing himself in the open on this hot evening, naked down to the loins, his great trousers of moleskin slipping almost away. Miners already cleaned were sitting on their heels, with their backs near the walls, talking and silent in pure physical well-being, tired, and taking physical rest. (115)

These scenes show that Gerald's mentality has not been as completely imposed on them as he supposes.

After his reorganisation of the mines he is left vividly aware, like Ivan in *The Brothers Karamazov*, that a life based on recoil, however much it exalts the supremacy of his will, leaves a feeling of hysterical emptiness. He is horrified at his face in a mirror. He dares not touch it "for fear it should prove to be only a composition mask" and his mind feels "like a bubble floating in the darkness". This insecurity, his terror of the hollowness in him and the emptiness about him, drives all his subsequent actions. He has the kind of armed impotence one associates with Shakespeare's Coriolanus. It is a quality he shares with a whole gallery of Lawrence's characters: with the Prussian officer in the early tale, whose conscious will lords it over himself and others in brutal sadism; with Rico of "St Mawr" whose "anger was wound up tight at the bottom of him, like a steel spring that kept his works going" and with Cathcart of "The Man Who Loved Islands" whose sterility seeks its complement, like Gerald's, in the oblivion of snow. Gerald's case is treated more fully and with more penetrating sympathy than any of these. The main source of one's sympathy lies in the realisation that fundamentally he is vulnerable to fears and

---

4. Graham Holderness, *D. H. Lawrence: History, Ideology and Fiction*, 213.

longings springing from the spontaneous and unpredictable which he has spent all his life suppressing.

Two things stress his vulnerability and draw the reader into his plight: the way his development is weighted by his background, and the desperate attachment to Gudrun in which he is finally revealed a victim. Alongside these developments, the friendship with Birkin points to what is suppressed and lost.

Birkin feeds Gerald's urge to see beyond himself and his misfortunes, to make an effort, however abortive, at adjustment. He senses in Gerald's curiosity and the way he is "warmed" and stimulated by his talk a desire for vital contacts. On this intuition he bases his obstinate insistence on Gerald's freedom to choose a creative outcome for his life. Under his influence at Breadalby Gerald even appeals for help:

> "And part of me wants something else," said Gerald, in a queer quiet, real voice.
> "What?" said Birkin, rather surprised.
> "That's what I hoped you could tell me."[5]

Birkin however has to struggle for himself with his entire energy. When Gerald is most able to receive help (before his father's death and his involvement with Gudrun) Birkin is unable to give what he needs. The best he can offer is a *"Blutbrüderschaft"*, something that Gerald cannot agree to or understand because it requires the very faith and trust in another that his life has made it so difficult for him to feel.

We do see this potential in Gerald, however, this possibility of escape from defeat, at the water party, when he and Gudrun are sitting balancing each other in the canoe (the water imagery exerting its dual significance here):

> His mind was almost submerged, he was almost transfused, lapsed out for the first time in his life, into the things about him. For he always kept such a keen attentiveness, concentrated and unyielding in himself. Now he had let go, imperceptibly he was melting into oneness with the whole. It was like pure, perfect sleep, his first great sleep of life. (178)

Immediately afterwards the wrongness from within the family asserts itself in Diana's death.

Even after his father's death, when his downward course seems set, the novel insists on an alternative. One is aware of his impulse to be saved:

---

5. *Women in Love*, 97. Not in the earlier (1916) version of the novel.

> Another night was coming on, for another night he was to be
> suspended in chains of physical life, over the bottomless pit of
> nothingness. And he could not bear it. He could not bear it. He was
> frightened deeply, and coldly, frightened in his soul. He did not
> believe in his own strength any more. He could not fall into this
> infinite void, and rise again. If he fell, he would be gone forever. He
> must withdraw, he must seek reinforcements. He did not believe in
> his own single self, any further than this. (337)

From this point one sees how the impulse to be saved turns into a
craving to be destroyed. He is at first impelled towards Birkin for
"reinforcements" but "Birkin was away. Good – he was half glad".
The half gladness indicates that his choice is more than half made. He
goes then from his father's grave, revolted and stimulated by the
immediate contact with death, direct to Gudrun. In that episode the
surface realism – his getting lost, meeting the drunken collier,
burgling the Brangwen house – is governed by his bewilderment and
passion, so that the effect is like a dream, unpredictable yet seemingly
inevitable, the expression of an urgent unconscious need. The author's
grip on Gerald's feelings – and on Gudrun's when he falls asleep – is
subtle and unwavering, the sensitive objectivity even allowing a play
of comedy at the end when he is standing holding his boots ready to
leave.

There is in Gudrun's nature, in spite of her will, a servility that
invites him initially. It is seen at its clearest in the bedroom of the
Alpine hostel, where she almost succumbs in dread to his need for her
as an instrument of his gratification. Her nature, however, not only
offers satisfaction to Gerald's will to dominate, but through its own
acts of violence sharpens it. Her real challenge to him lies in her
resistance. This is clear even in the scene with the mare: in spite of her
preoccupation with the subject creature – "It made Gudrun faint with
poignant dizziness, which seemed to penetrate to her heart" – she
exults in the act. She screams out her challenge to Gerald as he passes
on: "I should think you're proud." Her self-assertion in fact matches
his, and the battle puts a keen edge on a sexuality that is desperately
determined on its own satisfaction.

The intensity of the lovers' excitement depends on their
separateness. It is an intensified self-consciousness. They define
themselves in assertion against each other, polarized in a way that
suggests ironic reservations about Birkin's ideal of love: they are "like
opposite poles of one fierce energy" that is destructive and self-

obliterative, not creative. Gerald wants to be his own god, with Gudrun administered unto him (it is what Ursula fears Birkin wants):

> "This is worth everything," he said, in a strange, penetrating voice.
> So she relaxed, and seemed to melt, to flow into him, as if she were some infinitely warm and precious suffusion filling his veins, like an intoxicant.

Gudrun, more timorous and secret, wants to satisfy her curiosity and test her power. The rhythms and imagery convey distinctly a different kind of predator:

> Her fingers went over the mould of his face, over his features. How perfect and foreign he was – ah how dangerous! Her soul thrilled with complete knowledge. This was the glistening, forbidden apple, this face of a man .... She wanted to touch him and touch him and touch him, till she had him all in her hands, till she had strained him into her knowledge. (331-32)

The two are imprisoned in themselves. There are now no conditions for growth, only collision – which takes place with great force in the winter expedition to the Alps at the end of the book, where sex becomes a war weapon, its "consummations" exclusive of the other person:

> His passion was awful to her, tense and ghastly and impersonal, like a destruction, ultimate. She felt it would kill her, she was being killed .... But always it was this eternal see-saw, one destroyed that the other might exist, one ratified because the other was nulled. (444-45)

Again the terms echo Birkin's concepts, in a gruesome mocking antithesis of the impersonality he postulates. The bifocal irony complicates and enriches our response to both pairs of lovers, sharpening our understanding of the essential thematic issues.

For Gerald, however, sex is not entirely warfare. Losing the fight for dominance discloses the vulnerability his mother knew about and a wistful longing for what was glimpsed in the canoe at the water-party:

> Though she treated him with contempt, repeated rebuffs and denials, still he would never be gone, since in being near her, even, he felt the quickening, the going forth in him, the release, the knowledge of his own limitation and the magic of the promise, as well as the mystery of his own destruction and annihilation.[6]

---

6. *Women in Love*, 446. The last clause was added in the final revision.

At the same time he vows to avenge his defeat with her murder. Giving up that attempt – described as if it were a sexual act – he walks away to his own death.

He makes his choice with all his personal experience and personal insufficiency, as well as his social environment dictating it. One is not allowed to feel that any one of the factors more than another tips the balance. The final balance is struck in the semi-delirium of his suicide:

> The snow was firm and simple. He went along. There was something standing out of the snow. He approached, with dimmest curiosity.
>
> It was a half-buried crucifix, a little Christ under a sloping hood, at the top of a pole. He sheered away. Somebody was going to murder him. He had a great dread of being murdered. But it was a dread which stood outside him, like his own ghost.
>
> Yet why be afraid. It was bound to happen. To be murdered! He looked round in terror at the snow, the rocking, pale-shadowy slopes of the upper world. He was bound to be murdered, he could see it. This was the moment when the death was uplifted, and there was no escape. (473)

The figure of Christ refers the tragedy back again to the general. Gerald, the transgressor, has from the outset denied life. He has killed his brother, enslaved the miners, nullified Gudrun. His dread of being killed is partly perhaps a fear of retribution. But the word murder suggests also the victim's sense of the agency of the factors that have helped to make him what he is. He "sheers away" from the figure of the crucifix, the reminder of his personal guilt; but the barrenness of snow lies around the figure of Christ as well as him. The traditions of the society he lives in, his family background, the battle with Gudrun, the failure with Birkin: all have a part in a tragedy whose main operative force lies in the damaged self, his inability to repair as Birkin does.

Gudrun takes the reader beyond the experience with Gerald into the final phase of the breakdown in *Women in Love,* which depicts those who, encased in themselves, and with not enough energy to power an obsession, see the will towards some artificial imposed coherence as futile.

Subtle parallels and distinctions are drawn between her mentality and Gerald's, which are delicately underlined by the rhythms and imagery of their thoughts. The way Gudrun in her art protects herself by means of mockery and spite – "finished off life so thoroughly ... made things so ugly and final" as Ursula says – is a denial and outrage of the object comparable with Gerald's, as we see clearly in the scene where she encourages Winifred to produce her malicious portraits of her pets and he sadistically subdues the rabbit. And her defiant, wilful "shuddering irregular runs" on the Highland cattle are her equivalent to his subjugation of the mare, given in terms of scornful dissociation instead of direct attack.

But the differences, drawing to him the preponderant sympathy, are more crucial in the end. Even as he is recognizing the futility and destructiveness of his relationship with her, he can tell himself that he has "broken forth, like a seed that has germinated, to issue forth in being, embracing the unrealized heavens". Gudrun never hopefully deceives herself in this way as to the import of her actions and responses. The passage that balances this in her development, as she gazes at "the final cluster" of Alpine peaks, is one that reveals her craving for the peace of total anaesthesia – her "consummation":

> If she could but come there, alone, and pass into the infolded navel of eternal snow and of uprising, immortal peaks of snow and rock, she would be a oneness with all, she would be herself the eternal, infinite silence, the sleeping, timeless, frozen centre of the All. (410)

Her longing echoes Birkin's (during his illness after Hermione's attack on him) for a "singling away into purity and clear being".[7]

However, although she is such a "closed thing" Lawrence created an unfailingly sensitive appreciation of her predicament. When, just after the description of the "open flower" of Gerald's suffering, one reads, "he tore at her privacy, at her very life, he would destroy her as an immature bud torn open is destroyed", her own personal suffering is clear, especially as it echoes her confession to her sister in the first chapter: "Everything withers in the bud." Uncertainty and self-mistrust have prompted her to hold on tightly to herself in fearful isolation. She too is the victim of insecurity and despair. She is stronger than Gerald only because she is the more resignedly despairing of the two. She has the strength of pliancy. She is not at war with the factors that destroy her, she is sodden with them. The pathos in the handling of the character ensures that the reader understands the sufferings as well as the dangers implicit in her

---

7. A comment from the narrator in *Mr Noon* (an authorial voice) curiously confirms how intimately Lawrence sympathized with some aspects of Gudrun's nature: "The beauty, the beauty of fate, which decrees that in our supremacy we are single and alone, like peaks that finish off their perfect isolation in the ether." An endorsement of "the ultimate perfection of being quite alone" was characteristic of this phase (1919-23) of Lawrence's development.

isolation: a severance from reality so extreme that the will, triggered off by fantasy, is the only remaining source of action.

There is an affinity with Hermione, but Hermione, in spite of what Birkin says of her, is more involved with others: she has grown dependent on Birkin and is sufficiently outgoing to attempt murder out of her baulked desire of fulfilment. The effort to communicate, to grow, to join a mainstream of life – however predatory the attempt – is there. She is able to do violence out of thwarted life, and in that respect is like Gerald. Gudrun never commits herself so far, she is never that outgoing. Her energies are taken up with the effort to minimize and insulate.

Her background and the psychological progression towards final dissociation are given in convincing detail. Filling her life with a succession of dreamy, shadowy pretences, like Emma Bovary, she has long lived in reliance upon Ursula's superior sense of realities. *The Rainbow* gives a brief sketch of her as a child:

> Gudrun was a shy, quiet, wild creature, a thin slip of a thing hanging back from notice or twisting past to disappear into her own world again. She seemed to avoid all contact, instinctively, and pursued her own intent way, pursuing half-formed fancies that had no relation to anyone else. (251)

When she is a girl this can be regarded as "a natural proud indifference". Only in the sequel is its negative potential revealed.

Fostering social factors are indicated. When *Women in Love* opens she has been the smart bohemian artist in London, relishing the "*réclame*" and suffering the boredom. At Beldover she plays for a while the local lass, sitting with her electrician boyfriend at the cinema, willing herself to be swamped with working-class feelings until she is overwhelmed by the converse of disgust. She graduates to Gerald:

> Under this bridge, the colliers pressed their lovers to their breast. And now, under the bridge, the master of them all pressed her to himself! (330)

There is the urge to be the same, the pride in the difference.

By conducting her activity in a dreamworld she reduces the terror of establishing a relationship sufficiently close and real for another person to take advantage of the confusion that lies underneath: "For always, except in her moments of excitement, she felt a want within herself, she was unsure." Her own will lacking direction, she is fearful she might give herself up to another's, as we see in front of the mirror

in the bedroom of the Alpine hostel. Gerald appeals to her, as he
stands for the power of the will and enacts a struggle to do something
with ruthlessness in the teeth of insecurity and disbelief. She is excited
and stimulated by it, as by an enactment of a drama akin to her own,
but in her insulation she is essentially dissociated from it and from
him: "She never really lived, only watched." She is the perfect
catalyst to his downfall, responding readily to his violence and helping
him faster towards destruction. But she is never able to identify her
own course of destruction with his.

She does not find her true partner in moral suicide until she meets
Loerke. She is aware of the blight: "Ah, this awful, inhuman distance
which would always be interposed between her and the other being."
Her going with Loerke, like Edith Dombey's with Carker in *Dombey
and Son*, is a measure of her despair, in as much as through it she
renounces interest in or attachment to all struggling life, embarking on
a career of charades. Gudrun travels from one world of shadows to the
next, the further removed from life.

In Loerke we see a native of chaos. His despair and rejection we are
made to understand as the outcome of his disrupted childhood:

> "My father was a man who did not like work, and we had no
> mother. We lived in Austria, Polish Austria. How did we live? Ha! –
> somehow! Mostly in a room with three other families – one set in
> each corner – and the W.C. in the middle of the room – a pan with a
> plank on it – ha! I had two brothers and a sister – and there might be a
> woman with my father." (425)

The definition of his physical presence is as vivid and memorable as
Hermione's, and with a rare comic touch. Gudrun notices:

> the look of a little wastrel ... and an old man's look, that interested
> her, and then besides this, an uncanny singleness, a quality of being
> by himself, not in contact with anyone else, that marked out the artist
> to her. He was a chatterer, a magpie, a maker of mischievous word-
> jokes, that were sometimes clever, but which often were not .... Out of
> doors he wore a Westphalian cap, a close brown-velvet head with big
> brown velvet flaps down over his ears, so that he looked like a lop-
> eared rabbit, or a troll. (422)

The novel has Loerke sketching in his own background and his views
on art and life, and attracting Gudrun to him, so leaving Gerald
isolated, within a few pages, achieving a personality so complete that
the logic of his responses is as readily if not as intimately understood
as Gudrun's. So that, when Birkin defines him as a sewer-rat and

Gudrun sees him as given up to "ultimate reduction, the mystic frictional activities of diabolic reducing down" he survives the bias of both pictures.[8]

Loerke takes everything further than Gudrun, in love as well as art. He hates what he calls

> "the *religion d'amour* .... I detest it in every language. Women and love, there is no greater tedium." (458)

For him every impulse is equally valid. Anti-convention, mere expediency, the indulgence of sensation, whatever distracts himself and keeps involvement at bay are the dictates of action. He is bisexual, expressing a preference for young girls together with a willingness for sex and "companionship in intelligence" with men or women. He is vehemently cynical about everything except his art. There he clings pathetically to delusions which he shares with Gudrun and which link them to ideals current in Lawrence's time and identified in the novel as sanctioning the disintegration of their lives. Both he and Gudrun believe in artistic Form, they trust in the act of representation itself to give the experience or observation within the work of art an immunity, a superiority and permanence. When Ursula attacks what she sees as crude in his statuette of a naked girl on a horse, Loerke replies, "with an insulting patience and condescension" in his voice:

> "Wissen Sie ... that horse is a certain *form*, part of a whole form .... It is part of a work of art, it has no relation to anything outside that work of art." (430)

The crudity of her assertions momentarily rouses the reader's sympathies for him. However, they finally vindicate themselves, especially as they are corroborated by what we know of his character and his life, when she asserts:

> "It isn't a word of it true, of all this harangue you have made me," she replied flatly. "The horse is a picture of your own stock, stupid brutality, and the girl was a girl you loved and tortured and then ignored." (431)

He and Gudrun use art as a form of dissociation rather than integration. It governs and seems to justify their other escapisms.

---

8. Gudrun's thought (*Women in Love,* 452) was added in the final revision. It is a lapse into Lawrencian jargon rare in the presentation of her responses.

Gudrun and Loerke are clues to a mentality that reappears many times throughout the novel, mainly in the minor characters, though Birkin is included too, with his response to the African statuette in Halliday's flat. There is Halliday himself, and his friends, and the young man Birkin notices in Beldover market, "somehow indomitable and separate, like a quick, vital rat" and some of the miners Gudrun observes in the ninth chapter. Without Gudrun and Loerke as touchstones this network would be flimsy. The beetle image for instance, used to describe Halliday's statuette, is properly elucidated in Loerke — "that little insect" Gerald calls him — and Loerke's own statuette is a product of just such a finality of experience as Birkin detects in the primitive carving. The scene in the Pompadour Cafe when Halliday reads out Birkin's letter climaxes in its impact on Gudrun.

It is to her that Lawrence keys the announcement in the first chapter of this aspect of the theme at its most general:

> The two girls were soon walking swiftly down the main road of Beldover, a wide street, part shops, part dwellinghouses, utterly formless and sordid, without poverty. Gudrun, new from her life in Chelsea and Sussex, shrank cruelly from this amorphous ugliness of a small colliery town in the midlands. Yet forward she went, through the whole sordid gamut of pettiness, the long, amorphous, gritty street. She was exposed to every stare, she passed on through a stretch of torment. It was strange that she should have chosen to come back and test the full effect of this shapeless, barren ugliness upon herself. Why had she wanted to submit herself to it, did she still want to submit herself to it, the insufferable torture of these ugly, meaningless people, this defaced countryside? She felt like a beetle toiling in the dust. She was filled with repulsion. (11)

Every detail of this paragraph is related to the design of the whole novel. The stress on "amorphous" and "shapeless" is the germ of the sociological thought which Lawrence develops in Chapters 9 and 17. The beetle image links Gudrun with a poetic complex that reaches through the book. But these elements are inseparable from the character through the medium of whose experience they are expressed. It is primarily her sensibilities we are exploring, which the style of the passage expresses, and which sensitize her to this aspect of the life around her. The moral complexity of the paragraph comes from the tension between narrator, character and situation. Gudrun's "torture" may reveal some truth about the town but more about herself. The reader, through the narrator, may partially corroborate

and partially condemn her response. Ursula's comment later –
"They're all right" – reinforces the relativity and limitations of
Gudrun's response, and the whole development of Ursula is set
against her.

This kind of balance and concentration was won in revision. In an
earlier version of the first chapter this quoted passage hardly exists,
and in its place is a snatch of conversation in which Ursula agrees with
Gudrun's revulsion.

Passages in a similar vein occur in the last few chapters of *The
Rainbow*. Ursula Brangwen looks at Wiggiston:

> The place had the strange desolation of a ruin. Colliers hanging
> about in gangs and groups, or passing along the asphalt pavements
> heavily to work, seemed not like living people, but like spectres. The
> rigidity of the blank streets, the homogeneous amorphous sterility of
> the whole suggested death rather than life. There was no
> meetingplace, no centre, no artery, no organic formation. There it lay,
> like the new foundations of a redbrick confusion rapidly spreading,
> like a skin-disease. (320)

The stress on the amorphous and inorganic reaches right through the
dual novel. Ursula's observations are the outcome of a phase of
indirection in her life and reflect what she notices in her uncle Tom
and his mistress Winifred Inger, who are in some respects prototypes
of Loerke and Gudrun. Tom believes "neither in good nor evil. Each
moment was like a separate little island, isolated from time, and blank,
unconditioned by time". Winifred, limited to the self and cynical
about men and the possibilities of love, has "at the bottom of her ... a
black pit of despair". In these last few chapters of *The Rainbow*
Lawrence's mind was on the move towards the structure and imagery
of its sequel. Tom resembles Gerald as well as Loerke, for he is a pit
manager with "something marshy about him" inflicting on his miners
an industrial system that reduces them to robots. There is both
dismissiveness and jargon in the presentation here, with the
generalities of the theme not firmly enough rooted in the psychology
of the characters, and over-riding them. However, Ursula's response
to Wiggiston is qualified and enriched by her later vision of the
creative potential among ordinary people.

There are three announcements of the theme in the earlier novels.

Annable in *The White Peacock* sticks out so much from the would-
be genteel sensitivities of the other characters that Lawrence was
forced to excuse his presence: "He *has* to be there .... Otherwise it's

too much one thing, too much *me.*"[9] He has been a curate, educated at
Cambridge, but his humiliating infatuation with Lady Christabel has
cured him of the delusions that go with his cultured existence, and in
cynical disgust he has chosen to live as nearly like an animal as he
can. He wearies and brutalizes himself. His expressions of opinion are
generally shrill or crude, especially on the subject of women, although
he does acknowledge at one point, about Christabel, that "It wasn't all
her fault". His declarations about being "a good animal" cannot be
taken as foreshadowing later developments of Lawrence's thought:
they express chiefly a cynical vindictiveness. A renegade against a
social system he regards as degenerate, he covers his total
irresponsibility with the affectation of a positive which exists outside
morality, declaring for instance, about his children, that they "can be
like birds, or weasels, or vipers, or squirrels, so long as they ain't
human rot". Those who have associated him with the other
gamekeeper, Mellors in *Lady Chatterley's Lover*, have been misled by
externals, for inwardly he is an obvious portent of Loerke in *Women
in Love*. Annable is shallowly and confusedly portrayed, yet he
announces at the start of his author's career that what he represents is
something to be reckoned with.

In *The Trespasser* the emergence of the theme is even more
striking, for it came to dominate a story that was not even Lawrence's
own. He was rewriting and developing Helen Corke's tale, which was
closely modelled on her own personal experience. Yet out of this
unpromising circumstance, at a time of personal uncertainty, and
written in a style he later deplored – thickly metaphorical, derived
partly from Corke's manuscript and partly from D'Annunzio's *The
Triumph of Death*[10] – came something we recognize immediately as a
forecast of Gerald and Gudrun.

---

9. Jessie Chambers, *D.H. Lawrence: A Personal Record*, 117.
10. Lawrence himself pointed to the affinity with D'Annunzio's *The Triumph of
Death* when he remarked to Catharine Carswell, "Take even D'Annunzio and my
Trespasser – how much cruder and stupider D'Annunzio is, really" (27 November
1916, in *Letters*, III, 41). In D'Annunzio's novel the hero's love affair begins as a
dream of ideal union and becomes a mortal antagonism. The action takes place
mainly on a seaside holiday, where Giorgio, like Siegmund, is on the beach in the
blazing sun, "fainting under the rapture" of the kisses of his beloved, who is younger,
stronger and more self-contained than he – a femme fatale "whose love, rapacious and
insatiable, sometimes became almost terrifying". An abject craving for sensual
ecstasy, a disenchantment with his dream, a sense of oppression, a longing for death –
"Oh, if I could but lie down and never rise again" – and a vengeful vindictiveness

Siegmund's Wagnerian name (chosen by Helen Corke) indicates the kind of heightened drama the authors had in mind. From the unloved isolation of an unsatisfactory marriage he escapes for a week with his girlfriend, Helena. His love seeks escape, intoxication and self-obliteration. From Helena he primarily wants comfort: he calls her "Hawwa – Eve – Mother!" But confined with her he finds instead a more intense isolation. The two lovers are always essentially apart, thinking their own thoughts, obsessed with their own emotions. The conflict between them is half-suppressed, while they struggle with their feelings in order to make believe that what they feel is rapture and ecstasy. Siegmund feels more and more estranged, oppressed by a "sense of humiliation ... a physical sense of defeat" which he cannot account for.

With a "sense of despair, a preference for death" Siegmund returns home, to be treated as an outcast there. He cannot face any future he can imagine. Sick with sunstroke, he sees death as the final release and comfort:

> Siegmund sat thinking of the after-death, which to him seemed so wonderfully comforting, full of rest, and reassurance, and renewal. He experienced no mystical ecstasies. He was sure of a wonderful kindness in death, a kindness which really reached right through life, though here he could not avail himself of it. (203)

He hangs himself.

Although this does suggest Gerald in *Women in Love*, the portrait is confused. The root causes of Siegmund's insecurity are never established – we are even offered inadequate simplifications like Hampson's about his being a *"concentré"*. The collapse of his marriage is excused rather than explained, on the most superficial grounds, and little attempt is made to understand the unsatisfactoriness of his experience with Helena except in terms of the inadequacies of her responses. Moreover, whatever its causes, Siegmund's malaise produces an inert self-pity which inhibits the reader's sympathies.

The portrait of Helena suffers from similar deficiencies. Her name, although derived from the original authoress's, suggests (in the mythic subtext of the story) the destructive potential envisaged in her conception: "She had a destructive force: anyone she embraced she injured." Like Gudrun in *Women in Love* she is dangerous because she

---

make up Giorgio's part in the affair, which ends in his suicide. (The quotations are from the translation by Georgina Harding published in 1898.)

is essentially unresponsive. She languishes self-consciously in her illusions and disillusions:

> Life, and hope were ash in her mouth. She shuddered with discord. Despair grated between her teeth. This dreariness was worse than any her dreary, lonely life had known. She felt she could bear it no longer. (125)

Her love for Siegmund is make-belief: "Her dream of Siegmund was more to her than Siegmund himself." Her strongest response is fear of his sensual demand: "The secret thud, thud of his heart, the very self of that animal in him she feared and hated, repulsed her." When she submits to it, it seems to her like death or a wish for death. But with her these factors fail to cohere as they do in Gudrun.

The tragedy misfires, and with it the obvious attempt to relate it, through the imagery, to universals: the fierce, consuming sun, which gives Siegmund sunstroke, and the sea which one day nearly drowns them. But the novel demonstrates how deep-laid in Lawrence's psyche the tragic aspect of this theme was.

How personal it was is revealed in the last part of *Sons and Lovers*, when after his mother's death the author-figure, Paul Morel, himself suffers "a lapse towards death". He feels "unsubstantial, shadowy" and "as if his life were being destroyed, piece by piece, within him ....The real agony was that he had nowhere to go, nothing to do, nothing to say, and was nothing himself." Like Gerald, Paul "dared not meet his own eyes in the mirror". He has a terror of "the void in which he found himself" and is on the verge of madness, before he finally resists and turns his face towards life again.

His erotic dependence on Clara during and after his mother's terminal illness, while it thrills her – "it healed her hurt pride" – places her in a consoling position: "she pressed him to her breast, rocked him and soothed him like a child." This leaves her dissatisfied: "He kept her because he never satisfied her." She eventually comes to dread his love:

> She was afraid of the man who was not there with her, whom she could feel behind this make-belief lover: somebody sinister, that filled her with horror. She began to have a kind of horror of him. It was almost as if he were a criminal. He wanted her – he had her – and it made her feel as if Death itself had her in its grip. (430-31)

Many of these details, together with the association between the destructiveness of his possession of her and the despair he feels at his parent's death, foreshadow the experience of "Death and Love" in *Women in Love*.

This development, together with the antithetical one of Paul's "belief in life" (to be discussed in the next chapter) marks the emergence of the major themes that were to be fully explored in the next two novels.

After *Women in Love* the non-tragic aspects of the theme prevailed, even in the tales, where its pursuit was keenest. Examples in the tales include the heroine of the "The Princess" with her yearning for "warmth, protection ... to be taken away from herself" which is opposed by her compulsion to keep herself intact; and Egbert of "England my England" (as revised in 1920) whose liberal principles, like Loerke's artistic ones, are part of his self-insurance policy (if other people ought to be free in their lives, he ought to be free of responsibility towards them). In the later tales any tragic features are balanced against the ironic, even in "The Man who Loved Islands" where Cathcart (who systematically eliminates human contact until he eliminates himself) dies like Gerald in the snow.

In the novels completed between 1920 and 1925 Lawrence was largely content to trace the theme in minor characters: the dilettantes and intellectuals at Florence in *Aaron's Rod,* for instance, and in *The Lost Girl* those specialists in self-display and retreat from life, Charlie May and James Houghton. *The Plumed Serpent* provides a more dynamic expression of it in the spectacle of the Mexican people, among whom is identified an "indifference to everything, even to one another" and a "helplessness, a profound unbelief that was fatal and demonish". This comes to life best in the first chapter in the "big concrete beetle-trap" of the stadium, where the bull-fight, with its sadistic overtones of sexual perversion, and the answering hysteria of both the Mexican spectators and the visiting American intellectuals are controlled and inter-related in a memorable way.

In *Lady Chatterley's Lover* Lawrence returned to the main issues. Now, however, his aims were expository rather than exploratory. Connie's lover is given us with an explicitness that lays everything on a plate: "at the very bottom of his soul he was an outsider and anti-social." In his affair with her, although "beneath his pale, immobile, disillusioned face, his child's soul was sobbing with gratitude to the woman, and burning to come to her again", yet:

> Mick *couldn't* keep anything up. It was part of his very being, that he
> must break off any connection, and be loose, isolated, absolutely lone
> dog again. (31)

He uses his literary success as a smack in the eye to "the smart
people" since he himself is a "Dublin mongrel". Like Loerke, he
maintains an illusion that enables him to snap his fingers at them and,
without touching his inward misery, distracts it. His physique too,
"curiously childlike and defenceless" is reminiscent of Loerke. Images
are used in the portrayal that are familiar from *Women in Love*: "the
silent enduring beauty of an ivory Negro mask" and "like rats in a
dark river."

Clifford Chatterley holds roughly Gerald Crich's social position
and some of his conventional opinions, and eventually commits
himself to the same effort of industrial reorganisation. But he shows
almost none of the dynamic conflict and suffering that makes Gerald a
tragic figure. His self-encasement makes him more akin to Loerke, his
physical paralysis only completing a psychic one. As Lawrence
expressed it in the first version of the novel: "He was always
paralysed, in some part of him." From the beginning of the novel as
finally composed one hears of his low sexual vitality. Even before his
injury, sexual intercourse is merely "one of the curious obsolete
organic processes" and after it "there was no touch, no actual contact".
What is stressed throughout his development is his "lack of sympathy
in any direction". The likeness to Loerke is confirmed by his taste for
the kind of art Duncan Forbes practises, as well as his own talent for
writing smart literature. Yet this major character in the novel rouses
less sympathetic recognition of his driving motives than did the minor
character Loerke. Sympathy for Clifford is inhibited by disgust, the
author "putting his thumb in the balance" to justify Connie's rejection
of her husband.

In the first version of the novel there is some pathos derived from
an appreciation of Clifford's predicament as an individual. He has a
more natural responsiveness here which engages one's sympathies:

> The instinct of self-preservation was so strong in him, he could only
> contemplate the thrill and pleasure of life, or else fall into apathy. He
> would have days of apathy, which swallowed up what would else
> have been bitterness and anguish. Then the thrill of life returned. That
> he could go in his motor-chair into the woods, and, if he remained
> silent, see the squirrels gathering nuts, or a hedgehog nosing among

dead leaves!! Each time, it seemed like something he had captured in the teeth of fate.[11]

Mixed with his self-pity is a genuine affection for Connie, which prompts a pathetic desire to allow her some fulfilment in spite of his impotence: "He loved her for her warm, still, physical womanhood." She in return admires him. These complications in the earlier version remain anomalous, not combined into a complex portrait, and they are over-ruled at times by explicit statements like, "in the vital sense, Clifford had no emotions". But at least they promise complexity.

In the final version of the novel they are almost entirely ironed out, and consistency gained by simplification. Lawrence himself, in his *Apropos of Lady Chatterley's Lover,* admitted the over-riding didactic considerations behind the portrait of Clifford: "the lameness of Clifford was symbolic of the paralysis, the deeper emotional or passional paralysis, of most men of his sort and class, today."[12] He is always limited, always emotionally paralysed. The only pathos is that evoked by the fact of his injury, and even that is somewhat neutralized in generalities:

> And dimly she realised one of the great laws of the human soul: that when the emotional soul receives a wounding shock, which does not kill the body, the soul seems to recover as the body recovers. But this is only appearance. It is, really, only the mechanism of the resumed habit. Slowly, slowly, the wound to the soul begins to make itself felt, like a bruise which only slowly deepens its terrible ache, till it fills all the psyche. (49)

Clifford develops of course, but the changes in him are like items in a repertoire of object-lessons in moral depravity, which suffer by recalling features of Lawrence's better work. First he is the aristocratic patron of a circle of intellectuals, their mental life flourishing with its "roots in spite". Then he is the literary entrepreneur preying "upon the ghastly sub-aqueous life of our fellow-men". He enters the power game proper, and the beetle imagery insists on the degenerate insulation: "one of the amazing crabs and lobsters of the modern industrial and financial world, invertebrates of the crustacean order, with shells of steel, like machines, and inner bodies of soft pulp." Eventually he is written off as Mrs Bolton's boy.

---

11. *The First and Second Lady Chatterley Novels*, 9.
12. *Lady Chatterley's Lover*, 333.

The negative emphasis in the portraits of Clifford and Michaelis is extended to their society, the intellectual milieu sketched in the conversations at Wragby and the industrial system that supports it. This is nowhere more obvious than in Connie's view of Tevershall in Chapter 11. Any dramatic or psychological context of the kind we have seen in Gudrun's view of Beldover is so flimsy that when F. R. Leavis quoted it in *The Great Tradition* for comparison with Dickens's picture of Coketown in *Hard Times* he felt able to write as if Connie were Lawrence's proxy directly commenting, like Dickens, on the contemporary scene:

> The car ploughed uphill through the long squalid straggle of Tevershall, the blackened brick dwellings, the black slate roofs glistening their sharp edges, the mud black with coal-dust, the pavements wet and black.

The repeated emphasis is not an expression of the character's neurotic aversion as it is in Gudrun's passage, but to hammer home the point:

> The utter negation of natural beauty, the utter negation of the gladness of life, the utter absence of the instinct for shapely beauty that every bird and beast has, the utter death of the human intuitive faculty was appalling. (152)

Connie does have her own reasons for the gloom that pervades the description, or at least for a hesitancy about her personal future that could plausibly promote gloom. But the strident emphasis – "ugly, ugly, ugly" – does not fit her character, and the harsh hysterical finality of the pessimism towards the end of the paragraph – "a people in whom the living intuitive faculty was dead as nails" – is out of keeping with her recent rapturous experience with Mellors and her quiet, persistently constructive approach to the future. It has neither the dramatic relativity that helps makes the portrayal of Gudrun's response to Beldover a complex one, nor the hope at the very end of *The Rainbow* that in retrospect does almost the same for Ursula's view of Wiggiston. In the earlier versions of the novel there is a kind of hopefulness in the general account of Tevershall, as there is in Ursula's responses to her environment in *The Rainbow*. The first version has Connie spotting in Tevershall "a certain feeling of blind virility, a certain blind, pathetic forcefulness of life". In the second there is an earlier draft of the passage we have quoted, which concludes, however, with promising complications later lost:

It was a sad country, with a grey, almost gruesome sadness. Yet it was not dead. It was alive, labouring under a queer, savage weight of dismalness and acquiescence. (363)

3

RECOVERY AND RENEWAL

The linking concept running through the breakdown Lawrence traces in his novels is the loss of a natural balance in which spontaneity and integrity, within the self and towards others, can operate together and as one. The breakdown is caused by the denial of spontaneity instead of the incorporation of it. In *Women in Love,* for instance, the elder Crich denies in the name of Christian idealism, Gerald under the name of efficiency, and Loerke and Gudrun out of mistrust, disbelief and despair. We have seen how ailing individuals are driven to know and to associate with the degenerative features of their society and its ideology and how this process is associated with the destructive phases of the natural life cycle. But Lawrence's portrayal of what leads to breakdown would not be so telling were it not defined against what leads to recovery and fulfilment. Those who achieve a balance do so not by some happily innate immunity to the influences that dog the characters we have studied so far, but rather through constant conscious struggle. The essential prerequisite is sensitive adaptability to the infinitely changeable conditions of life. The fullest definition of the theme occurs in the portrayal of Ursula and Birkin in *The Rainbow* and *Women in Love.*

In his first novel, *The White Peacock,* the presence of a constructive energy shows itself mainly in the incidental descriptive detail, when it is not over-written, of clouds, trees, flowers and birds. It provides a sense of power and resources even when as a whole this book is concerned to depict and in some ways accept failure.

The style of the novel was based primarily on an admiration of some of the English novelists, particularly Charlotte Bronte and George Meredith. Out of that context surface two motifs of the later theme, in the experiences of the narrator, Cyril Beardsall.

He resembles the author in as much as he combines physical frailty with a responsiveness to hope and promise. He refreshes himself after a depressing experience, in much the same way as Birkin does in *Women in Love*, by physical contact with the trees:

> I turned with swift sudden friendliness to the net of elm-boughs spread over my head, dotted with soft clusters winsomely. I jumped up and pulled the cool soft tufts against my face for company, and as I passed, still I reached upward for the touch of this budded gentleness of the trees. The wood breathed fragrantly, with a subtle sympathy. The firs softened their touch to me, and the larches woke from the barren winter-sleep, and put out velvet fingers to caress me as I passed. (152)

He also experiences homoerotic feelings (similar to Birkin's in the rejected prologue to *Women in Love*) for his friend George. They dry each other after a swim in a pond:

> I left myself quite limply in his hands, and, to get a better grip of me, he put his arm round me and pressed me against him, and the sweetness of the touch of our naked bodies one against the other was superb. It satisfied in some measure the vague, indecipherable yearning of my soul; and it was the same with him. When he had rubbed me all warm, he let me go, and we looked at each other with eyes of still laughter, and our love was perfect for a moment, more perfect than any love I have known since, either for man or woman. (222-23)

As in *Women in Love* the physical contact between the two men has no lasting consequences.

In *Sons and Lovers* Lawrence was initially concerned not so much to launch this major theme, which was still nascent in his imagination, as in the context of a psychological and social realism to build in Paul Morel a central character whose development would lead towards a creative outcome.

The various features of Paul's behaviour, with his mother, at the factory, with Miriam, with Clara and Baxter Dawes are loosely tied but vividly presented. The qualities his mother has fostered, ambition, reserve and idealism are at war with his keen hunger for life, the conflict promoting his instability and threatening to destroy him: "He had the poignant carelessness about himself, his own suffering, his own life, which is a form of slow suicide." Each phase of his development reveals further obstacles and personal deficiencies, yet if we look back over his career we can see, if not a pattern of self-liberation, at least the presence of a constructive energy and intelligent purpose.

While he is caught between his mother and Miriam it is the struggle to survive the confusion and resolve it that is uppermost. His resolution is neither despairing nor making do. He holds out for a real marriage, a permanent union of body and soul: "marriage was for life." In his arguments with Miriam (however unfairly prejudiced) he always drives towards an understanding. There is no real temptation to ignore the situation and become the victim of his own ignorance, as in the case of his brother William. One has to offset against his crippling despair at his mother's death the implications of how he hastens it. The mercy-killing of Mrs Morel and the burst of relief that follows it emphasize the upward motion of the whole of Paul's development. The chapter in which she dies is after all called "The Release".

This fine portrait demonstrates again an important distinction between *Sons and Lovers* and Lawrence's later style: it is wholly psychological, there are no wider thematic dimensions – not, that is, until towards the end. There, as we have seen, emerges the tragic theme of self-imprisonment to be developed in Gerald Crich. And when Paul takes a holiday from his problems with Miriam, by engaging in an affair with Clara Dawes, the experience promotes the statement of a "belief in life" which is a primitive germ of an aspect of the theme that would dominate the rest of the author's career:

> If so great a magnificent power could overwhelm them, identify them altogether with itself, so that they knew they were only grains in the tremendous heave that lifted every grass-blade its little height, and every tree, and living thing, then why fret about themselves: they could let themselves be carried by life. (398)

The opening paragraphs of the next novel, *The Rainbow*, launch the universals of the renewal theme, or rather the traditions, sensual, religious and social, that make up its cultural context, and emphasize in it the links between the human and non-human patterns of regeneration. This comes partly through the repetitive rhythms of the prose, which will be a characteristic of the whole theme, for renewal is the creative aspect of repetition itself, the progressive feature of mere recurrence.

In each generation of the Brangwens the recovery of life and hope comes about not through ideas, religion, duty or simple physical fulfilment but through the struggle of each individual towards the realisation of his or her own needs. Fulfilment can only come about in co-operation, not only with other individuals seeking the same fulfilment but also with the ideologies, conventions and institutions of society, which are in fact the stored and applied knowledge of other generations. They are to be challenged and accepted, fought and appropriated. They change historically, and the dual novel with its historical sweep from the middle of one century to the first decade of the next indicates them operating in the background as its people respond subjectively to them. The intense subjectivism of the novels, as well as the narrative style with its thematic and poetic organisation of material rules out the provision of conventional social history, but, as Mark Kinkead-Weekes showed, it can be traced in the background of the Brangwens' lives.[1] The picture has more substance even at this level than a mere "montage of myths".[2]

There is a sensuous richness and solidity in all the scenes with Tom Brangwen, a conviction and particularity in the portrait both of him and his setting, in spite of the shaping pressure of the theme as it propels him towards his self-renewal.

The hazards of getting there are not minimized. They are indicated in his brother, Alfred, the factory draughtsman who becomes "a silent inscrutable follower of forbidden pleasure" (he is Will's father). They are outlined in the references to Lydia Brangwen's first marriage to a man with humanitarian ideals, in which her nature has been thwarted and eclipsed, and from which she emerges, after a vividly sketched period of numb despair, with a defensiveness in which one might detect a reaction against self-conscious and idealistic love. Tom's development too has its hazards, with the threat of dissoluteness after his mother's death.

The scene where he proposes to Lydia is fraught with difficulties. But the fullness and directness of her responses, the outcome of a self-understanding derived (like Birkin's in *Women in Love*) from a painful past, make them almost like a wish-fulfilment for him because they present no extra obstacle to his effort of self-liberation. There is something miraculous about their first kiss:

> He turned and looked for a chair, and keeping her still in his arms, sat down with her close to him, to his breast. Then, for a few seconds he went utterly to sleep, asleep and sealed in the darkest sleep, utter, extreme oblivion.

1. See Kinkead-Weekes, "The Sense of History in *The Rainbow*", in *D.H. Lawrence in the Modern World*, eds Peter Preston and Peter Hoare, 121-39.

2. See Holderness, *D.H. Lawrence: History, Ideology and Fiction*, 180-89.

> From which he came to gradually, always holding her warm and close upon him, and she as utterly silent as he, involved in the same oblivion, the fecund darkness.
>
> He returned gradually, but newly created, as after a gestation, a new birth, in the womb of darkness. (45)

There is a powerful sense of the unexpected yet desired, revelatory and seemingly inevitable in the scene, in which his natural sensitivity is maximized.

Their love is sealed with the kind of sexuality that will reappear as an essential component of their offsprings' marriages:

> They looked at each other, a deep laugh at the bottom of their eyes, and he went to take of her again, wholesale, mad to revel in the inexhaustible wealth of her, to bury himself in the depths of her in an inexhaustible exploration, she all the while revelling in that he revelled in her, tossed all her secrets aside and plunged to that which was secret to her as well, whilst she quivered with fear and the last anguish of delight. (60)

The decision to be unspecific about sexual practices, whatever its other reasons, serves the important artistic purpose, here and throughout Lawrence's novels (including *Lady Chatterley's Lover*) of focusing attention on the emotional reactions.

There remains (Tom feels) a "shadowiness" in Lydia derived from her past, together with a maturity and patience upon which he relies. Her relegation to the background made it easier for Lawrence to focus on Tom's feelings to reveal the pattern of an achieved balance, although she is the more powerful determinant of its success:

> She waited for him to meet her, not to bow before her and serve her. She wanted his active participation, not his submission.
>
> She put her fingers on him. And it was torture to him, that he must give himself to her actively, participate in her, that he must meet her and know her, who was other than himself. (90)

The core of the renewal is sexual, but it is based on wider pre-requisites, including the balanced responsiveness that is characteristic of Tom: his "plentiful stream of life and humour, a sense of sufficiency and exuberance". This is consolidated through his marriage – "a new, calm relationship showed to him in the things he saw, in the cattle he used, the young wheat as it eddied in the wind" – but it is not complacent:

> He felt himself tiny, a little, upright figure on a plain circled round with the immense, roaring sky: he and his wife, two little, upright figures walking across this plain, whilst the heavens shimmered and

roared about them .... There was no end, no finish, only this roaring
vast space. Did one never get old, never die? That was the clue. He
exulted strangely, with torture. (126)

Tom and Lydia provide a touchstone of balance and a sensitive
alertness to life. This is the essential factor in Lawrence's theme. With
this achievement as a reference, the rest of the novel and the whole of
the next explore in greater detail the conditions and hazards of getting
to that point.

The main threat to the renewal of this achievement in the next
generation comes, as we have seen, from Will Brangwen's personal
insecurity and the idealism he uses to prop it up. Another comes from
Anna's own kind of insecurity, for besides her centrality, with its
bright, robust, adventurous spirit, which attracts Will's love, there
remains a scar from "the anguished childish desolation" of the period
after her father died, so that whenever she feels a threat to her stability
or independence she retreats into a wilful and obstinate self-
containment and self-assertion: "She clung fiercely to her known
self." The threat shows itself most violently in her dance to the
"nullification" of Will, in the chapter called "Anna Victrix".

The relationship is explosive, not inherently stable like Tom and
Lydia's. Moreover we see it at closer quarters, and from both their
viewpoints equally, drawn into intense identification with each in turn,
their opposing feelings almost equally endorsed. The scenes are
vividly particular and dramatic, and yet are governed by the requisites
of the theme. In them the major regenerative symbols of the novel
appear. The seed figures most memorably in the wheat-stooking
courtship scene and on the honeymoon: "Suddenly, like a chestnut
falling out of a burr, he was shed naked and glistening on to a soft,
fecund earth, leaving behind him the hard rind of worldly knowledge
and experience." The rainbow appears first (in the guise of the arch) in
the cathedral scene of Chapter 7 to create, as we have noted, a
complex poetic dialogue alongside the dramatic dialogue of the two
characters.

The couple fight their way through towards an equivalent of Tom
and Lydia's achievement, though fraught with more unresolved
conflicts and insecurities. Its sexual core is most fully revealed in
Chapter 8. There they are released from some of the earlier
constrictive personal demands of their love into a greater sexual
freedom. Now, as he worships "the separate, several beauties of her
body" (for him it is yet another prostration before the absolute) he is

no longer so tense with awe and resentment and she is freer to use him for her own pleasure: "He was the sensual male, seeking his pleasure, she was the female ready to take hers: but in her own way." In an earlier manuscript version of this scene their sexual experience is more thoroughly positive (and less characteristic of Will): "all the devious, the never-to-be-recorded ways of satisfaction" take them

> to the very end, till they had had everything, and knew no more. Whatever their imagination had wanted, they had. And they came through it all at last cleared, resolved, freed.[3]

In the final version negatives intrude which were absent between Tom and Lydia. There is violence: a "sensuality as violent and extreme as death" (like that between Gerald and Gudrun in *Women in Love*). And there are features of which Will at least is ashamed. His brand of shame – defined as "that part of delight of which a man is usually afraid" – is characteristic of his ineradicable fear of Anna's power over him, and this also contributes to his sense of the "sinister" and "death" in their lust. However, their neurotic insulation is so much less than Gerald's and Gudrun's, the violent lust appeases and does not separate them finally, so that they find "the secret, shameful things ... most terribly beautiful". As a result of their newfound pleasure in each other they become grateful and gain respect for each other's inviolability.

They are left with a feeling (stronger than Tom's) of discontent, sensing unrealized potential in themselves and unreached horizons around them. Anna Brangwen in particular, in looking forward to the next generation, is a standard bearer of the rainbow image that her daughter is to take up at the end of the novel:

> Dawn and the sunset were the feet of the rainbow that spanned the day, and she saw the hope, the promise .... She was a door and a threshold, she herself. Through her another soul was coming, to stand upon her as upon the threshold, looking out, shading its eyes for the direction to take. (181-82)

Ursula, that "soul" belongs as much as anyone to the context that stretches back to the beginning of the book. Throughout her development one is forced to awareness of a pattern repeating itself:

> Hesitating, they continued to walk on, quivering like shadows under the trees of the hill, where her grandfather had walked with his daffodils to make his proposal, and where her mother had gone with

---

3. Kinkead-Weekes, "The Marble and the Statue", in *Imagined Worlds*, eds Maynard Mack and Ian Gregor, 390.

her young husband, walking close upon him as Ursula was now
walking upon Skrebensky. (278)

It is important to realize that her achievement is as much because of as
in spite of her history, and is not the result merely of a felicitously
indomitable vitality. She grows in maturity partly because of the
personal, ideological and institutional influences, and these are not all
encouraging and beneficial. She has to take sides, for instance, in the
conflict between her parents, and her sensitivity to the difficulty of life
is increased by having emotional demands made on her by her father
which she cannot satisfy. Her parents become for her both an example
and a warning, the idea of their vigour and their potential contrasting
with the achievements of their lives. She sees them baulked and is
thereby driven to achieve a greater fulfilment in life and marriage.

The second half of *The Rainbow* exemplifies, to the exclusion of
almost everything else, the processes by which an individual comes to
understand her own needs as defined within and against the pressures
of society. This is the aspect of the renewal theme to be developed
here. It is so much given over to this that other features are
overshadowed by it. The portrayal of Skrebensky for instance (as we
have seen) is according to Ursula's criteria. He is a character not so
much explored as dismissed, and finally whittled down until he is
merely the instrument of the disappointment that pushes her onward.
The presentation of her other experiences, in school, college and
elsewhere, is framed in the same way and has provoked complaints
that Lawrence gives her responses too much authority. However, the
later episodes leave no doubt that it is the individual, and what she is
about, that we are to concentrate on, and not her indictments. It is her
spiritual pilgrimage that is being depicted here, and nothing else. She
is defining her needs: the indictment of her society is no more or less
than what is implicit in the dismissal of certain ideals and beliefs by
one individual passionate for a full life and single-minded in pursuit of
it. From the wreck of every experiment she gains a little more self-
understanding, a little more definition of an objective. Whether she is
exploring religion, education or love her basic criterion is constant:
she turns aside from those ideas and assumptions that she is able to
understand might cramp or distort her growth. The strength,
determination and widespread nature of her rejections take the
measure of the vitality needed at this stage.

Then she begins to understand what there is for her to be other than
the challenger. Looking at a cell under a microscope she sees it not as
an emblem of survival – "self-preservation and self-assertion" – but of

belonging to a creative continuum: "Self was a oneness with the infinite." Afterwards, the destructiveness and disillusion of the love affair with Skrebensky – protracted, exhausting sexual battles for dominance and self-survival – obscures the vision. Constrictive influences threaten to overwhelm her. Then her encounter with the horses makes the unpredictable and mentally unmanageable in life and in her own life-energy become real to her. In the illness that follows, what has been happening to her finally crystallizes, in an image that recalls her father's honeymoon and looks forward to her own:

> And again, to her feverish brain, came the vivid reality of acorns in February lying on the floor of a wood with their shells burst and discarded and the kernel issued naked, to put itself forth. She was the naked, clear kernel thrusting forth the clear, powerful shoot, and the world was a bygone winter, discarded, her mother and father and Anton, and the college and all her friends, all cast off like a year that has gone by, while the kernel was free and naked and striving to take root, to create a new knowledge of Eternity in the flux of Time. And the kernel was the only reality: the rest was cast off into oblivion. (456)

Here is the final coming to the core of her strength. The paragraph ends with her touch of grandiose idealism, but in the imagery of the seed lies a counter-suggestion that what she has been attempting to break free from has been a necessity to her. The shell has to exist in order that the kernel can grow undamaged, and to be cracked that it might strike root. The fight has been so that the protective might not become a death-trap.

At the very end of the novel her faith in life confidently superimposes itself on the world around her.[4] The optimism in the last paragraph of the book is characteristic of her as an expression of her own defiance and hope, of her desire and her power to develop, and is valid as such. There is every reason why she should read others, the colliers, by her own lights, for she has acquired a certain humility through her recent experience and implicitly understands, in

---

4. Over the past fifty years, academic critics have been about equally divided between applauding and deploring the optimism of Ursula's final vision of the rainbow. Against: Leavis, Daleski, Alldritt, Holderness and others. For: Kermode, Spilka, Balbert, etc. Peter Balbert most strongly insisted on the continuity of the two novels when he called the end of *The Rainbow* "not really an ending at all but an announcement of Ursula's realisation of the kind of marriage she needs" (Balbert, *D.H. Lawrence and the Phallic Imagination,* 78).

identifying her own potential with theirs, that she is not unique. She must wait for her fulfilment upon similar potential in others, even in her choice of a mate:

> The man should come from the Infinite and she should hail him ....
> She was glad that this lay within the scope of that vaster power in
> which she rested at last. (457)

She has found a greater tolerance, even of Skrebensky: "Who was she to have a man according to her desire?" It is the kind of "expectancy" noticed in her at the start of the next novel.

In *Women in Love* the theme enters a new phase, focused not so much on the pre-requisites of individual development as on those of union. As before, the needs of the theme govern the handling of the character. In this novel Ursula is no longer important on her own: her growth with Birkin is of the first importance and we see her almost entirely in relation to him. Even on the occasions when she is *tête-à-tête* with her sister the conversation almost always turns on marriage, love and her relations with him.

She has her fears and assertions and her setbacks of despairing self-pity but she is by far the more robust of the two, not as bowed by past experience. In her arguments with Birkin her greater assurance, her informed and penetrating criticism of him and her readiness to begin a new life are the outcome of a battle for fulfilment that is equivalent to his. Her intelligent, sensitive normality of response enlists the reader's sympathies more readily for her than for any other character in the novel. It makes her a match for him.

Recognizing in Birkin someone who like herself will not make do and is keen to live, she expects a passionate attachment. She herself feels a "normal" passion in the first stages of her love, though she expresses it in terms that betray a loneliness and the aggressiveness of a self that has never yet been admitted by her lovers:

> She believed that love was *everything*. Man must render himself up to
> her: he must be quaffed to the dregs by her. (265)

So at first she does not go along with, and partly misunderstands Birkin's fears of the self-assertive stages of love. She sees his fears as weakness – as they are – but sees them as a weakness towards her, a failure towards herself. In the course of her defensive campaign against his ideas, and her attempts to prevent him from avoiding the complexities of the relationship, she aligns herself to some degree with what he is attacking. He carries her with him much of the way because of the parity of their past experience, but her own fears for her chances of survival in the earlier stages make her round on him and bring him to face her, as at the end of the "Mino" chapter when she attacks his ideal of star equilibrium for its implication of female subordination (though it is if anything more vulnerable for its suggestion of insulation) and forces a confession of love.

After their marriage Ursula is sometimes suspected of sounding like her husband's mouthpiece. Cornelia Nixon, for instance, spotted that "by the end of the novel Ursula has submerged her life in his and accepted all his ideas with the sole exception of blood-brotherhood" and complained that "her acceptance of his way does not proceed from an intellectual recognition that he is right, but rather from the discovery, in the tearoom scene, that he is a superior being".[5] But that eager newly-wed acceptance of attitudes is mutual – he subscribing to her kind of warmth and receptivity – and it is qualified by rejections, as we shall see. The woman who throws herself so boisterously into the *Schuhplatteln* dance and afterwards finds her husband's sexy leerings slightly repulsive does not look destined to become a domestic cipher. *The Rainbow* has shown at great length how she is informed by her experience in a positive way, not driven away from contact but finally always more surely towards it. She remains in this novel the nearest to a norm of achieved balance.

The man she faces is the most complicated individual in the novel (or anywhere in Lawrence) whose every facet is directly related to the struggle for that sensitive adaptability which we've seen from the start is the essence of this theme. Although he is set in this direction, the negatives are not minimized. On the contrary, he is almost as maimed by his moral environment as those characters whose failure we have studied. Their maladies can all be found in him. Whatever balance he has is hard won, as his gaunt, ailing body testifies. He is sick or convalescent for most of the first two thirds of the novel and under no delusions as to the root cause:

> "One is ill because one doesn't live properly – can't. It's the failure
> to live that makes one ill, and humiliates one." (125)

He recognizes as "imminent in himself" a taste for the kind of sensuality typified in the primitive statuette at Halliday's flat and associated with Gudrun and Loerke. As Hermione's lover he has participated in the outrage of her kind of "ideal love". This kinship with the elder Crich is confirmed by the occasional effacement into a

---

5. Cornelia Nixon, *Lawrence's Leadership Politics*, 214-16.

"Salvator Mundi" that Ursula finds so distasteful. Birkin knows as well as Gerald or his father the dual urge to idolize and deny a woman, and his fear of self-obliteration within the relationship presupposes an inclination towards it. His passion for Ursula after the tragedy at the water-party – "extreme desire that seemed inevitable as death" – is analogous to Gerald's reactions in the later chapter called "Death and Love". He is acutely sensitive to the processes of dissolution, and as a result longs to be accepted in sensual terms "at the quick of death".

He is not, however, as crippled with dissensions as the Birkin originally envisaged in the rejected Prologue, in whom the two halves, spiritual and sensual "always reacted from each other" and who is split sexually: "feeling more at home with a woman than with a man, yet it was for men that he felt the hot, flushing, roused attraction."[6] The specifically sexual attraction to men was eliminated in the revision of the novel. The rejection was in line with the strategy that drew personal characteristics into a map of recovery.

The friendship with Gerald remains crucially important, but predominantly in impersonal rather than personal terms. Birkin sees Gerald's condition as a challenge: he realizes that he needs to be reclaimed from a similar degenerative process as is in himself. His impulsive suggestion of a blood-brotherhood – "we shall swear to stand by each other" – comes across as an attempt to force the issue of Gerald's salvation (as Birkin sees it) out of an anxiety that it might be too late. One is always as much aware of antipathy as of affection between them. They are both primarily engaged elsewhere. Their wrestling is initiated by Gerald's need for "something to hit" after his reorganisation of the mines, while Birkin, just snubbed by Ursula, has his own reasons for joining in. Nevertheless, instead of taking us into their personal needs it spells out more clearly their general inclusion and rejection of each other:

> They stopped, they discussed methods, they practised throws, they became accustomed to each other, to each other's rhythm, they got a kind of mutual physical understanding. And then again they had a real

---

6. The Prologue to *Women in Love* is not confessional, and it would be misleading to look there for a map of Lawrence's sexuality. Mark Kinkead-Weekes summarized the biographical issue quite judiciously: "He knew himself to be bisexual, but was convinced that a greater degree of 'otherness' made heterosexual relationship the more creative and transforming, if more difficult" (Kinkead-Weekes, *D.H. Lawrence: Triumph to Exile*, 303).

struggle. They seemed to drive their white flesh deeper and deeper
against each other, as if they would break into a oneness. Birkin had
great subtle energy, that would press upon the other man with an
uncanny force, weigh him like a spell put upon him. Then it would
pass, and Gerald would heave free, with white, heaving, dazzling
movements. (270)

Only circumstantially does the scene invite comparison with the one
between Cyril and George in *The White Peacock.* The essential
relationships involved are dissimilar. The discipline of Lawrence's
objectivity has made it one in which, out of an exceptional occasion in
an impermanent relationship, there is envisaged (in a dramatic
symbolism much like that in the episode between Gerald and the
mare) a "oneness of struggle" which reveals the closeness of the two
in kind. Afterwards they go their own ways. It is a struggle between
the hopeful and the despairing which in some ways dramatizes the
whole relationship between the novel's two major themes. Birkin is
refreshed and exhausted from the fight and from the intimacy and
understanding, the interflow with what he knows he himself is part of
and loves, and whose deathward career he rejects.

The other basic split in Birkin, envisaged in the Prologue, between
the spiritual and the sensual, does show up in the novel, but is pushed
to one side, along with his past with Hermione, who confides to
Ursula his "violent oscillation ... between animalism and spiritual
truth". It shows eventually in the style of his "licentiousness" in the
Alpine hostel when Ursula finds him "repellent":

> He was so attractive, and so repulsive at once .... The flickering fires
> in his eyes concentrated as he looked into her eyes. Then the lids
> drooped with a faint motion of satiric contempt. Then they rose again
> to the same remorseless suggestivity. (412)

It is the shamed and insolent sensuality of a man defiant of his
inhibitions. These features of a damaged individual are seen in
perspective in relation to his other more normally healthy attitudes.
Ursula is learning to accept them as aspects of the whole man.

Offset against all these negatives in the map of qualities is the
changeable spontaneity of his responses that gives him common
ground with Ursula. She calls it "his wonderful, desirable life-
rapidity". It shows up the bondage and paralysis of Hermione and is a
challenge to Gerald, who notices an "amazing, attractive goodliness"
in him. The effort to clear the ground for this to operate causes the
strain. He is a character in whom the effort must be made and the
strains endured. In rejecting not only Hermione's idealism but also the

sensuality he sees in the primitive statuette he is searching for an enlargement of experience, including thought and knowledge. It is his knowledge that saves him, for it involves a knowledge of what is fatal and crucial for life. Ideas must be for him the agents of change, not the dictators of conformity:

> Whichever way one moved, if one were to move forwards, one must break a way through. And to know, to give utterance, was to break a way through the walls of the prison, as the infant in labour strives through the walls of the womb. (186)

The more he finds out about life and its processes the more he can critically apply his knowledge to his own development. The violence with which he attacks the old is a measure of his capacity for new life.

His experience, dicta and aspirations work together to throw the struggle into prominence. All the ideas he evolves are bred of the difficulty he personally experiences and are designed to isolate a particle of truth against which he might define a need or course of action. In consequence the beliefs he holds, especially about love, vary considerably according to the situation he is operating in. His pronouncement to Ursula in Chapter 11 – "I don't believe in love at all" – flatly contradicts what he has said to Gerald six chapters before: "I want the finality of love."

With some ingenuity it is possible, as Michael Ragussis and Michael Levenson have shown, to treat Birkin's speeches throughout the novel as some kind of continuous though tortuous argument, which "affirms a belief, invokes a value, expresses a desire; then cancels the affirmation, the invocation, the expression; and then cancels the cancellation without restoring the original positive terms".[7] The sequence is not as self-contradictory and fruitless as this suggests. Each stance Birkin adopts is temporary, dictated by the exigencies of the situation and controlled over all by his desire for balance and a fuller understanding. Lawrence's aim was not to build the "continuous development" of an argument (or of a character in a George Eliot novel) but to outline a strategy. The shifts of response (more complex than the shifts of idea) always come under the overall dramatic relativity of one part to another. In the dramatic situations there is development though it is not smoothly continuous.

The ironic relativity is nearly all structural, drawn from the sequence of the attitudes in relation each other and to their dramatic

---

7. Levenson, *Modernism and the Fate of Individuality*, 154. See also Michael Ragussis, *The Subterfuge of Art*.

circumstances. One of the few instances of the more obvious kind of ironic underlining (where the author calls attention to his own critical dissociation) is when Lawrence was showing an idea crystallising, in the scene after Hermione's attempt to murder Birkin. He leaves her house, physically ill and sick with loathing, walks "barely conscious" across the park and takes off his clothes:

> To lie down and roll in the sticky, cool young hyacinths, to lie on one's belly and cover one's back with handfuls of fine wet grass, soft as a breath, soft and more delicate and more beautiful than the touch of any woman; and then to sting one's thigh against the living dark bristles of the fir-boughs; and then to feel the light whip of the hazel on one's shoulders, stinging, and then to clasp the silvery birch-trunk against one's breast, its smoothness, its hardness, its vital knots and ridges – this was good, this was all very good, very satisfying. (107)

The text conveys Birkin's sensations in such a way as to allow the validity of the experience – the way it answers his craving for "sensual reality" – to establish itself as separate from the escapism and eccentricity that belong to his feverish state. The delicate irony that ensures this distinction becomes more insistent towards the end of the episode:

> Really, what a mistake he had made, thinking he wanted people, thinking he wanted a woman. He did not want a woman – not in the least .... This was his place, his marriage place. The world was extraneous. (107-108)

Later on, the more usual dramatic relativity prevails. During his recovery from the subsequent illness, the experience that has served the immediate restorative purpose of putting him in touch with life uncomplicated by people has become rarefied, worked on, leant upon during the period of his withdrawal from activity. It becomes the sentimental notion he puts forward to Ursula when he next meets her: "You yourself, don't you find it a beautiful clean thought, a world empty of people, just uninterrupted grass, and a hare sitting up?"[8] It is a lapse into the childlike self-protective illusion that a world without human life could possibly be without problems. (Ursula resists it here, although it recalls some of her feelings near the end of *The Rainbow,* but she suffers her own lapse into life-weariness after the water-party.)

---

8. *Women in Love,* 127. The remark is a late insertion, probably made in September 1917 (see *Women in Love,* 546). Most of the sick-bed meditations at the start of Chapter 16 were added during the final revision, 1917-19.

Later still, when Birkin is ill at the start of Chapter 16, the idea becomes an evolutionary theory of love: "the singling away into purity and clear being of things that were mixed." This is an attempt to gather himself in the effort to define a central singleness upon which to rely and console his sense of being worsted by Ursula's possessive passion. But what is essentially valuable for Birkin in the experience returns and gets validated at the end of the novel in the "consoling" vision forced out of him by Gerald's death:

> If humanity ran into a cul de sac, and expended itself, the timeless creative mystery would bring forth some other being, finer, more wonderful, some new, more lovely race, to carry on the embodiment of creation. The game was never up. The mystery of creation was fathomless, infallible, inexhaustible for ever .... To have one's pulse beating direct from the mystery, this was perfection, unutterable satisfaction. (479)

He is affirming what Ursula saw in the cell under her microscope, but with a new (and characteristic) emphasis on the changeable adaptability of life.

The obvious self-portraiture, together with the way Lawrence generally let the development of Birkin's thoughts speak for itself without immediate dissociative pointers prompted many readers to search in his theories for keys to an understanding of the novel as a whole. The speculations in Chapter 19 for instance about the "African way" have been discussed on the assumption that here Birkin is a mouthpiece for the author's view. The passage is one of Lawrence's late interpolations and lacks the extreme finality of most of the seven-times-revised novel. But even here the thoughts are objectified as the products of a particular character in a particular situation. Birkin reflects on the African statuette after an attack of the illness that has dogged him since Hermione's assault on him. Under its influence he has wanted (as he tells Ursula the night they meet by the pond where he is stoning the moon) a cooler relationship – that they should accept the fact that they love each other and be "glad and sure and indifferent". The speculations follow the next day when he is alone. In them an offshoot of the anxiety shown in the moon-stoning (which refers a reader of *The Rainbow* back to Ursula's violence with Skrebensky) is given expression. He enlarges his fear of the possession and self-assertion involved in love by fearing what might co-operate in bringing about the kind of passion he wants to avoid since his experience with Hermione. The sense of what might be lost – "the goodness, the holiness, the desire for creation and productive

happiness" – runs alongside his desire for sensual fulfilment. He
frightens himself still further by thinking of the "Arctic" (Gerald's)
way of breaking off from "the happy creative being". Both before and
after the speculations he questions his attitudes and the stances he
takes. He has admitted his uncertainty as to the validity of his general
ideas:

> Perhaps he had been wrong to go to her with an idea of what he
> wanted. Was it really only an idea, or was it the interpretation of a
> profound yearning? (252)

Even earlier in this chapter he has commented to Ursula: "While ever
either of us insists to the other, we are all wrong."

Compared with the understanding of the novel as a whole, Birkin's
thoughts on the subject of what is happening to such characters as
Gerald and Loerke are not very illuminating. Moreover, they are
sufficiently trivial offshoots of Birkin's own preoccupations as to be
immediately set aside in his own case: "he could not attend to these
mysteries any more." When his anxiety has lapsed, the vital and
positive urge returns:

> There was another way, the way of freedom .... This was the other
> way, the remaining way. And he must run to follow it. (254)

The firm placing of the speculations within the context is reinforced
later by the retrospective parody of some of the notions by Halliday,
who in the cafe scene (Chapter 28) intones one of Birkin's letters so as
to bring out the latent pomposity and banality, the grandiloquent or
hysterical repetitiveness of Birkin's style of thought at its worst –
though its earnestness offers a telling contrast to Halliday's own moral
indifference. The whole dialectical process puts the reader through the
kind of discipline in flexibility needed to achieve recovery from
Birkin's scale of disability. It is what Mikhail Bakhtin might have
called "dialogic".[9]

Every character in a novel, in one form or another, gives
expression to the author's understanding. The articulate Birkin works
on his experience through words and in this way communicates
directly with the reader as well as from within the structure of the
novel. But what he says is only part of the means by which the reader

---

9. See Robert Burden's discussion of that scene (and others) in the light of Bakhtin's
theories, including "parodic, self-parodic and carnivalizing strategies" (Burden,
Radicalizing Lawrence, 174). David Lodge saw the classroom scene in Chapter 3 as
"dialogic" in Bakhtin's sense, because of its "fluid, flexible handling of 'point of
view'" (Lodge, *After Bakhtin*, 64).

is moved to an understanding of his recovery and has its validity only in relation to his experience. His theories never break through the critical complex of the book. They are all the product of an ailing character whose fear of life has almost equalled his love of it. Many of the key terms he uses, as we have seen, belong as much to Gerald and Gudrun. The fear of passion and its self-assertion and limitation; the fear of obsession expressed in the moon-stoning, the stoning of the Cybele; the fear of the very corrective he employs in himself – that is, the mind – these in turn give rise to the theories he evolves. In the course of the action what he believes is challenged, placed and changed. What has been valid in his aspiration remains after the change, what has been dictated by fear and desperation is attacked and altered.

Even the last part of the "Excurse" chapter, about which there have been complaints that it is rigged to fulfil Lawrence's own simplistic fantasies about love, is tied at all points to the dramatic situation and critically assessed by the novel at a later stage. The episode follows a fierce and exhausting quarrel between Ursula and Birkin which reduces them both to an uncluttered awareness of their need for each other and of the knowledge that their love survives the clashes. In Birkin immediately after the row is over there is "a darkness over his mind. The terrible knot of consciousness that had persisted there was broken, gone." They have reached a state in which they can (to apply his own dictum) "cease to be so that that which is perfectly ourselves can take place in us". Both, at any rate, feel released into a more complete trust. For Ursula by the time she reaches the inn:

> This was no actual world, it was the dream-world of one's childhood
> – a great circumscribed reminiscence. The world had become unreal.
> She herself was a strange, transcendent reality. (312)

Later they both feel "the world was under a strange ban, a new mystery had supervened". The episode is held suspended in this way as an experience produced by the elation the two lovers feel as a result of their exhaustion and relief. Romantic simplifications are engendered between them. Ursula has a grateful and worshipping vision of him: "his strange, whole body, that had its marvellous fountains, like the bodies of the sons of God who were in the beginning." And he of her: "a paradisal flower she was, beyond womanhood." These belong to their magical sense of removal and the discovery of creative potential.

The worst one can say about these passages, which were interpolated late in the revision, is that they stretch the reader's patience and are, for the most part, badly written.[10] The most disappointing passages – the two pages at the inn with Ursula on her knees in front of Birkin, together with the last three pages of the chapter, when they drive to Sherwood Forest and spend the night there – were added to the final version of the novel, 1917-19. Those last pages replace a conversation in the preceding draft where they affirm their love but admit to differences and problems of the kind seen in other parts of the novel. In the earlier (1916) version the characters are uncertain. Birkin admits that he is scared of the clinches of sexual "passion" and wants "peace" while Ursula, uncertain of his motives, ends in tears. In the final version the characters exude assurance while the scene itself lacks artistic conviction.[11]

The romantic or ideological simplifications do not finally break through the critical complex of the book. The essential meaning and value of their attachment and their commitment to it, securely enough established in dramatic terms before the generalities of the theme take over, are confirmed just before and after their wedding, in Ursula's "strange, open, dazzled face" when Gerald questions her about her happiness and by Birkin's "passion of gratitude": "This marriage with her was his resurrection and his life." They are later qualified by some of the Alpine scenes where the insufficiencies and adjustments in their relationship are emphasized. The problems of insecurity raised between them will not, of course, go away, no matter how many pledges are sworn, in whatever terms. The reiterative and sporadic rather than continuously progressive shape of their story is one of its convincing features, and that is one of the reasons why the belated attempt to inject something more emphatically final into the last seven pages of the "Excurse" chapter was misguided.

In their last scenes there is a nudge towards something more inclusive. Earlier, in Chapter 22, Ursula, faced with a lover's craving for physical acceptance – particularly intense from one with such high levels of insecurity and egoism – has felt reluctant: "He wanted a

---

10. David Lodge, unwilling to assume that Lawrence was unaware of the soap-opera effect of some of the phrases in these passages, suggested that they might be equivalent to the kind of "stylization" or parodic technique defined by Bakhtin, written that is with the purpose of putting the reader "on his guard against identifying too readily and deeply with the emotions of the character" (Lodge, *After Bakhtin*, 66).

11. Pierre Vitoux analysed the virtues and failings of both versions in "The text of *Women in Love*", in *Texas Studies in Language and Literature*, XVII (1976). John Worthen's "The First *Women in Love*", in *D.H. Lawrence Review*, XXVIII (1999) slightly favoured the earlier version.

woman to *take* something from him, to give herself up so much that she could take the last realities of him, the last facts, the last physical facts, physical and unbearable." He himself has, he thinks, "taken her at the roots of her darkness and shame – like a demon, laughing over the fountain of mystic corruption that was one of the sources of her being, laughing, shrugging, accepting finally".[12] Now, at the Alpine hostel, in spite of misgivings, she feels a readiness for a more "unrestrained" lovemaking, of a kind that recalls scenes of sensuality in both previous generations of the Brangwens – though she still registers some repugnance by calling it "bestial" and "shameful". For her now, even what she terms "repellent" is an opportunity for further self-liberation: "There would be no shameful thing she had not experienced." These feelings echo those of her mother and father.

Birkin's whole experience of life has led him to a ruthless assertion of what he believes to be the "growing" principles and in the assertion of them they have become over-defined and bound by the limitations of a conscious attitude. At this stage of her life Ursula's less conscious, more spontaneous and diffuse responses to the creative sources of life help bring Birkin's constantly in touch with living variability. While for him on their final departure to the continent the novel stresses (and these are the terms used) the remedial qualities of "darkness", "stillness" and "sleep" as the ones essential for him in their love, for her the stress is on "light", "openness" and "warmth" – the hope and happiness she characteristically feels now her own vigorous life has direction.

In them Lawrence presented more thoroughly, sensitively and critically than anywhere else his understanding of the pre-requisites of fulfilment, the factors that make for recovery, at the same time placing these in a strongly individual context which gives them undeniable life. The dual novel assesses their ability to attain a sense of pattern and of oneness with life – "to have one's pulse beating direct from the mystery" – and on the basis of this to achieve a balance within

---

12. *Women in Love,* 304. Not in the earlier (1916) version of that passage, which has this: "If she refused the union with him, he had failed in life, he had only known the terrible process of death, in which he was fulfilled" (*First Women in Love,* 279). The newly added sentence in this chapter (23) suggests the kind of struggle with inhibitions that Ursula later finds puzzling in Birkin's "licentiousness". Since the narrative records no close encounter between the lovers since the end of the water-party in Chapter 14 – and that was no "laughing" matter for Birkin – we have to imagine one in the intervening period.

everyday experience and contribute to constructive relationships with others. It ends with no pipedream fulfilment but with the promise of further challenge and battle, and now with a mate with whom they can essentially join forces. The ending is the portrayal of an achievement in the only realistic and honest interpretation of the word: they have formed one enduring and growing relationship and are expectant of others.

They resign their jobs (he has an annuity) because Birkin needs a removal from influences that might damage the new shoots of his union with Ursula:

> "One wants to wander away from the world's somewheres, into our own nowhere .... It isn't really a locality, though, it's a perfected relationship between you and me, and others." (315-16)

No mention is made of the most permanent and undeniable way a pair relate to others, through having a family. But there is another commitment, treated with the utmost seriousness in the final pages of the novel during Birkin's grief at Gerald's death when he insists that his repudiated friendship might have altered the outcome; and behind Gerald of course is the larger society to which he belongs. Birkin is not content to be an outsider. There is then finally no implied rejection of the whole of contemporary society, and no attempt to provide a recipe for its salvation. This is a mark of the novel's distinction compared with some that followed, and a confirmation of the processes so vividly explored in the earlier generations of the Brangwens.

Their histories in *The Rainbow* have both validated what Ursula and Birkin achieve and provided its context. Ursula's development has been fed by the traditions that her family has for generations creatively challenged and renewed. For all Birkin's end-of-the-world fears and obsessions, in the dual novel as a whole recurrence and continuity are essential features of renewal. *The Rainbow* is all about that. The continuity is stressed in the recurrent imagery: in the first novel the rainbow itself, symbol of opposites in unison, which stands as a pledge, a sign of the renewal of life and of hope through the achievement of the individual, and in both novels the imagery of the seed (or womb) and water. In Ursula's final recall of her past it is the gulf, "the great chasm of memory" that is stressed, but on the wedding journey across the sea to the continent with Birkin:

> They seemed to fall away into the profound darkness. There was no sky, no earth, only one unbroken darkness, into which, with a soft,

sleeping motion, they seemed to fall like one closed seed of life
falling through dark, fathomless space. (388)

The final emphasis is given to the continuity, the image of the seed
(added in the final revision) referring us back to its occurrence at
crucial moments in the lives of Ursula and her father, and reminding
us of all that is preserved in the new union. In a seed death and birth
meet, it transforms death into life. In their love are all the conditions
for growth together with the experience of death. It involves, like the
cycle of the generations in the double novel, the death of one form of
life and the birth of another.

In his exploration of this theme in the novels immediately after
Women in Love, Lawrence was relaxing from the strenuous ambitions
that had generated his masterpiece, into experiments with looser
thematic forms. The themes that had been defined with such sharp
complexity were now to be reworked in narrower terms, often with
more attention paid to ideology than psychology. They lie alongside
the people, sometimes superimposed on them. Some of the authorial
imposition is direct, some (hardly less so) through characters who
have physical and temperamental as well as mental attributes in
common with their author – continuing, with their partners, the kind
of exploration of his personal life that Lawrence had embarked on
with Birkin and Ursula, but now without the dramatic complexity. For
one thing, the female partners exist less as individuals, more as
complements of the men, sometimes challenging them but without
much explored independent status.

One important area of fresh exploration in these novels is
concerned with the problem of authority between the sexes. The kind
of complete and equal mutual acceptance that seems to be on the
brink of attainment between the newly-weds in *Women in Love* and
which has been Birkin's hope with Gerald now came under scrutiny
and was often seen as unlikely, impossible or even undesirable. In the
diminished doubles of Ursula and Birkin that appear in *Aaron's Rod*
and *Kangaroo* – Tanny and Lilley, Harriet and Somers – an uneasy
balance is struck and not closely investigated. In other pairs the hope
of stability lies chiefly in the achievement of control by one party or
the other, with the consolations of power or submission. That at any

rate is one of the options treated with serious if tentative endorsement.[13]

The Lost Girl began as a kind of ironic compliment to Arnold Bennett, whose best novel, *The Old Wives' Tale*, Lawrence had read some ten years before. He had felt challenged enough to draft a kind of rejoinder to it, which he called "The Insurrection of Miss Houghton". Of the two sisters in Bennett's novel, Lawrence was more interested in the livelier, Sophia, who, baulked in her ambition to become a schoolteacher, elopes with a travelling salesman and enters a life in Paris of romantic expectations and temptations. But instead of escaping the influence of her social inheritance she takes it with her into her rebellion and ends her life self-suppressed, obsessed with profits and respectability, and saddened: "the riddle of life was killing her, and she seemed to drown in a sea of inexpressible sorrow."

Rewriting his draft seven years later to make it into *The Lost Girl*, he produced a radical reworking both of Sophia's fate and of the structure of Bennett's novel, which had been born of an admiration for the French realist tradition. Lawrence's Alvina Houghton, like Bennett's Sophia, is a draper's daughter in a Midlands town and goes abroad with an unsuitable partner. But for Lawrence the story became an illustration of his regeneration theme, the action accompanied by a running commentary, just as the theme accompanies the character, without quite fusing with it. While Alvina is not as powerful as Ursula, she is presented as an exceptional individual – "We protest that Alvina is not ordinary" – who struggles against the limitations of her upbringing towards a fuller life. She spends her twenties in a middle-class moral bondage from which she is released by her marriage.

There is a lively sketch of her early life, though with some casualness in the handling, and some impatience with the conventional (Bennettian) style of biographical narrative:

---

13. This aspect of the theme dominates the tales written between 1917 and 1925. Sometimes the woman comes out on top, sometimes the man. Women are dominant in "Monkey Nuts" and "Tickets Please", men in "The Ladybird" (where Lady Daphne becomes Count Dionys' "bride of the darkness") and in "The Fox" where, in the "tail" tacked on in its revision, the wife acquiesces in her husband's desire for her to become "submerged in him". In others, such as "Fannie and Annie", "Samson and Delilah" and "The Captain's Doll" a balance is struck, the women showing an equal determination to have what they need in life, matching the male power or cockiness of their partners, who win their sometimes grudging admiration.

> Surely enough books have been written about heroines in similar
> circumstances. There is no need to go into the details of Alvina's six
> months in Islington. (32)

The author relies a lot on bald statement to remind the reader of the
basic issues: "She went right back on highmindedness .... Her own
inscrutable nature was her fate." The major events in her later
development are poorly prepared for. They are both predictable and
surprising: predictable because the narrator makes no secret of his
intention to turn her "topsy-turvy" and surprising in that they issue
from a "nature" which remains "inscrutable" – the reader isn't kept in
touch.

The process of Alvina's renewal is initiated by her response to
Ciccio, who is a composite of observations of an Italian type with
glamorous intimations of inner powers. He has what Lawrence later
observed in some of Giovanni Verga's characters, a "spontaneous
passion of life that spurts beyond all convention and even law".[14]
Alvina's responses to him supply the glamour:

> She seemed steeped in the passional influence of the man, as in some
> narcotic .... It was his physical presence which cast a spell over her.
> She lived within his aura. (290)

In love he is "inhumanly regardless". His enjoyment of her seems at
times like self-gratification and her submission to it like self-
immolation:

> White, and mute, and motionless, she was taken to her room. And at
> the back of her mind all the time she wondered at his deliberate
> recklessness of her. Recklessly, he had his will of her – but
> deliberately, and thoroughly, not rushing to the issue, but taking
> everything he wanted of her, progressively, and fully, leaving her
> stark, with nothing, nothing of herself – nothing. (233)

Through this willing rape her known self is stripped away, as the
Brangwens' was through mutual self-submission. She feels about the
subjection that "she could never endure it for a lifetime" and at the end
a shaky balance is achieved between the partners when Alvina, now
pregnant, insists on Ciccio's returning to her from the war, and he
appears to value her moral independence (from the social machinery
he fears) highly enough to make the promise. So for her, in a
development that is implied rather than explored, submission is a

---

14. Lawrence, Introduction to *Cavalleria Rusticana* (1927) in *Phoenix*, ed. Edward
McDonald, 244. What attracted Lawrence most to Verga was his "passion for the
most naive, the most unsophisticated manifestation of human nature".

phase in the growth of new capacities of feeling. The growth shows itself in several directions, as in the last Italian chapters of the book, where alongside her estrangement from the people there, she develops a sense of belonging to the natural world.

If *The Lost Girl* is a reworking of Bennett, *Mr Noon* is in some ways a reworking of Wells. Whereas in the former Lawrence fractured the structure of Bennett's realism, here he adopted something of Wells's thematic style, comic and message-bearing: it is the message itself and the whole mentality that constitute a critique of him. Other features of the style of this unfinished draft resemble Lawrence's letters. It initiates the movement in his novels at this time towards a narrative with a more immediate relation to his own personal life. The second part of the novel in particular shares with the letters a spontaneity and biographical authenticity. Some incidents provide clues (in addition to the letters and poems) to the biographical background of the story of Birkin and Ursula. Some actually recall scenes in *Women in Love:* such as the *Schuhplatteln* dance (249-50) or the quarrel and reunion of the lovers:

> He sat with his head dropped – brooding, oblivious in a kind of dark, intense inwardness. There was an unspeakable silence in the room. She glanced at him from time to time. But he was motionless and as if invisible to her.
>
> Rather nervously she slipped from her sofa and came and crouched at his side, and very timidly put her hand on his knee. He did not move. But awful fire of desire went through him at once, so that his limbs felt like molten iron. He could not move.
>
> "Are you cross with me?" she said wistfully. And her hand sank closer on his knee.
>
> He turned and looked down at her. A strange, almost unseeing expansion was in his eyes, as he looked on her. And he saw her face, luminous, clear, frail, like a sky after thunder-rain, shining with tender frail light. And in his breast and in his heart the great throbs of love-passion struck and struck again, till he felt he would die if he did not have her. And yet he did not move.
>
> "Say you're not cross! Say it!" she murmured. And she put her arms round his hips, as he sat in the chair and she crouched before him. And he took her in his arms – her soft, deep breasts, her soft sides – !
>
> Ah God, the terrible agony and bliss of sheer passion, sheer, surpassing desire. The agony and bliss of such an embrace, the very brink of death, and yet the sheer overwhelming wave of life itself. Ach, how awful and utterly unexpected it is, before it happens: like

drowning, or like birth. How fearful, how causeless, how forever
voiceless. (225-26)

The passage has a first-draft freshness, as well as biographical interest.
It belongs to a dramatic context not as complex (of course) as *Women
in Love,* but it casts a curious, even critical light back to some
passages in the "Excurse" chapter, as well as forward to some of the
later love scenes in Lawrence's novels, where the element of alarm
and danger felt in the self-surrender is lessened in various ways.

Gilbert Noon, while not resembling Birkin (he was modelled on
Lawrence's friend Neville) nevertheless gives utterance, along with
the narrator, to the Birkin philosophy. But it is brought to the level of
table talk. For instance:

> And the tree of life itself never dies, however many blossoms and
> leaves may fall and turn to dust .... You have got to release from
> mental control the deep springs of passion: and after that there has got
> to be the leap to polarised adjustment with the woman. (190)

Or (slightly misquoted from Tennyson's *Maud*):

> "And oh that a man would arise in me
> That the man I am might cease to be." (227)

The continual bantering tone, with its direct addresses to that
nineteenth- century construct, the "gentle reader" not only effect a
parody of a defunct style and its associated thought patterns, but also
suggest an undercurrent of conscious, comic self-parody.[15]

Aaron's Rod, written alongside *Mr Noon,* is less directly
autobiographical, but its episodic structure reflects, especially in the
geography of Aaron's wanderings, Lawrence's own life at this time.

Aaron's tentative regeneration is portrayed, like Birkin's, from the
time of the collapse of his "ideal love" – in his case for his wife. He
gradually comes to recognize that his hurt withdrawal from any
challenging relationship is a "malady". Recovering, he moves towards
"the responsibility of a new self in himself" and a sense of promise.[16]
The portrayal of this at one point echoes Ursula's in *The Rainbow,*
stripping her image of renewal to apply it to Aaron's mental and
emotional condition:

> Having in some curious manner tumbled from the tree of modern
> knowledge, and cracked and rolled out from the shell of the

---

15. David Lodge was one of the first to note this, in his *After Bakhtin*, 71-73.
16. Aaron's quest is underpinned with biblical analogies. See Virginia Hyde, *The
Risen Adam: D H. Lawrence's Revisionist Typology*, 199-41.

preconceived idea of himself like some dark, night-lustrous chestnut from the green ostensibility of the burr, he lay as it were exposed but invisible on the floor, knowing, but making no conceptions: knowing, but having no idea. (164)

As with Alvina, there is some vivid presentation of Aaron's experience, especially in the early domestic scenes. Its interpretation however is rarely left to the reader, who is not anyway given sufficiently complex data to form his own judgments and is often treated by the author with impatience. For instance, there are interestingly vivid details in Aaron's return home and his quarrel with his wife in Chapter 11, but little in the way of immediate, probing exploration of responses. Two chapters later (after he has gone to stay with casual acquaintances in Italy) we are offered a retrospective analysis of their marriage, followed by the image of renewal just quoted, and then this:

> If I, as a word-user, must translate his deep conscious vibrations into finite words, that is my own business. I do but make a translation of the man .... Don't grumble at me then, gentle reader and swear at me that this damned fellow wasn't half clever enough to think all these smart things, and realise all these fine-drawn-out subtleties. You are quite right, he wasn't, yet it all resolved itself in him as I say, and it is for you to prove that it didn't. (164)

Lawrence is admitting failure to convey Aaron's experiences with full conviction and cocking a snook at the reader: why should he bother? Was it partly the disappointment he experienced at the banning of *The Rainbow* and the blocking of *Women in Love* – the rejection of his major effort towards an honest and complex understanding – that prompted this stiffening reliance on conclusions evolved by himself and imposed on the raw material of the novels?

A turning point in Aaron's development is his submission to the physical ministrations of his new friend Rawdon Lilly (the Birkin figure). According to the doctor who attends Aaron in Chapter 9, he is "like an animal dying of the sulks" and Lilly sets about his cure:

> Quickly he uncovered the blond lower body of his patient, and began to rub the abdomen with oil, using a slow, rhythmic, circulating motion, a sort of massage. For a long time he rubbed finely and steadily, then went over the whole of the lower body, mindless, as if in a sort of incantation. (96)

The new feature in this scene compared with the wrestling match in *Women in Love* is the decisive domination of one man by the other. However, like Alvina's submission to Ciccio, it is not final. Lilly continues to preach the values of power and submission and Aaron, his "malady" half-cured, listens but remains largely unconvinced.

Lilly, as he takes over *Aaron's Rod,* making Aaron himself for a while almost a subsidiary, restates some of Birkin's fundamental convictions, but the contexts from which they spring are almost as generalized as they are: discussions of love, friendship, war and revolution. Any deeper relatedness fails to appear. Individual predicaments and even particular actions, such as the "punch in the wind" Lilly gets when he argues with Jim Bicknell, serve only as illustrations for the discussions. Without the illuminative reference to a varied and thereby more impartial dramatic context, Lilly's statements about individual integrity remain mere notions.

The same is true of Somers' much longer speculations in the next novel, *Kangaroo,* which was written in six weeks in Australia. Apart from the central episode recalling Lawrence's wartime experiences, it starts as a travelogue and develops into a discussion novel. It throws the ideological issues of the regeneration theme into the arena of Somers' mind or of his disputes with others. Birkin's idea of friendship as constituting a constructive relationship with society is recalled – "All his life he had cherished a beloved ideal of friendship – a David to his Jonathan" – and then:

> He couldn't go along with it. He didn't want a friend, he didn't want loving affection, he didn't want comradeship. No, his soul trembled when he tried to drive it along the way, trembled and stood still, like Balaam's Ass. (107)

He rejects the "bond of real brotherhood" offered by Willie Struthers and goes for the "the mystery of lordship ... the joy of obedience and the sacred responsibility of authority" which he tries to identify in Ben Cooley's political authoritarianism. But this cause fails him too and he moves on to a doubt-ridden search for a religious equivalent. Alongside the longing to believe in something unvarying – "The human heart must have an absolute" – is the knowledge that the dangerous unpredictable spontaneity of "the great life-urge" is at odds with the fixity of ideas and ideals. But underlying the irrepressible desire for absolutes is a permanent mistrust of the variables involved in personal commitment: "This individuality which each of us has got and which makes him a wayward, wilful, dangerous, untrustworthy quantity to every other individual, because every individuality is bound to react at some time against every other individual." Moreover, he admits, "human love is a truly relative thing". All this thinking round the issue is "human" enough, but we are not given a strong enough dramatic context for our sympathetic understanding to work on, only reformulations, often wordy and grandiose: "Alone in the darkness of the cavern of himself, listening to the soundlessness of inflowing fate .... Alone with God, with the dark God."

One of the more moving aspects of Somers' irresolution is the revelation that he is desperate. Towards the end of the book the moon appears over the ocean, a picture echoing major crises in the great dual novel. The threat ingredient is greater than it is with Birkin in the "Moony" chapter of *Women in Love*. The waves, with moonlight "like a menace on the nape of their neck" fall on the beach "like a rush of white serpents". There is hysteria and an uneasy melodrama in the scene. The whole night is "rocking with a cold, radium-burning passion, swinging and flinging itself with venomous desire". As with Birkin, the experience has sexual bearings. But without an effective dramatic correlation with his marriage (as there is with Birkin and Ursula) the experience is resolved into a generalised isolation and longing:

> Richard rocking with the radium-urgent passion of the night: the huge, desirous swing, the call, clamour, the low hiss of retreat. The call, call! And the answerer. Where was his answerer? There was no living answerer. (341)

In the next novel, *The Plumed Serpent*, tentativeness in all these matters gives way to dogmatism. The novel represents a serious struggle on Lawrence's part to relaunch the kind of enterprise seen in his masterpieces. It shows a re-wakening of passion and struggle after the stalemate or the impatient discursiveness of the previous four; but the passion and the struggle is now to sell the convictions, and not towards the alertness and fullness of response that was the objective before.

Of course, within the novel's schematic structure lies the same faith in life as ever in Lawrence's novels and the same awareness of the limits of personal achievement. As Ramón Carrasco, the protagonist explains:

> "Life makes, and moulds, and changes the problem. The problem will always be there, and will always be different. So nothing can be solved, even by life and living, for life dissolves and resolves, solving it leaves alone." (361)

There is the same belief in the value and necessity of the individual commitment to others (to a mate first and to the rest of society) and the same goal of harmony between the sensual and spiritual, each symbolized by a component of the Quetzalcoatl figure, the bird and the snake, with their attendant imagery of light and darkness. The morning or evening star, hung between earth and sky, between day and night, stands for the equilibrium that is possible between instinctual and conscious knowledge and between the self and others; it represents a "meeting-ground" for relationships in which no faculty and no party is worsted. The failure of the symbolic superstructure is partially due to its elaboration. It takes on too ponderously the appearance of a seriously preferred alternative religion, when in fact it is a passionately rejuvenated Mexican myth that Lawrence found would carry his interpretations and express the final, almost purely didactic or "prophetic" phase of his commitment to life and society.

It is not that the complexity and difficulty is no longer perceived. Ramón, who puts forward many of the forty-year-old Lawrence's newfound religious convictions, admits:

> "I am no longer a young man, who can afford to make mistakes. I am forty-two years old, and I am making my last – and perhaps in truth, my first great effort as a man .... It is very easy for me to make a mistake. Very easy, on the one hand, for me to become arrogant and a ravisher. And very easy, on the other hand, for me to deny myself, and make a sort of sacrifice of my life." (273)

But for him the struggle to live has become the struggle to live up to: "Quetzalcoatl is to me only the symbol of the best a man may be." He is not the reformed and self-critical idealist that Birkin is, but more like the kind Lawrence has made us suspect. A comparison between Birkin's experience in the woods at Breadalby and Ramón's self-created ritual of regeneration reveals an absence of the flexible ironic objectivity or variety of evaluation we saw there:

> He took off his clothes, and in the darkness thrust his clenched fists upwards above his head, in a terrible tension of stretched, upright prayer. In his eyes was only darkness, and the darkness slowly revolved in his brain too, till he was mindless. Only a powerful will stretched itself and quivered from his spine in an immense tension of prayer. Stretched the invisible bow of the body in the darkness with inhuman tension, erect, till the arrows of the soul, mindless, shot to the mark, and the prayer reached its goal. (169)

Kate Leslie, the foreign observer, spots the "heavy exertion of will" in him and on everybody around him:

If once the will of the master broke, everything would break, and ruin would overtake the place almost at once. No real relaxation, ever. Always the sombre, insistent will. (406)

She also notices "something cruel" in his "passive, masked poise" though generally his masculine self-will is idealized as much as Mrs Morel's feminine self-will in *Sons and Lovers*, and he is exonerated more than she from the moral consequences of his actions, even in his marriage (as we have seen in Chapter 1 above).

The will to power passes into his new church. The ritual of initiation for his second-in-command, Cipriano, is an act of physical bondage – the initiate tied, blind-folded and clasped by the master. At the end, like Birkin and Gerald after their wrestling, they are in a state of "perfect unconsciousness" but now the purpose and outcome is to reinforce Cipriano's already declared allegiance: "To me, Ramón is *more* than life." He in turn feels "the black mystery of power go out of him over all his soldiers". He exacts from them a militaristic discipline and treats his enemies with a brutally complacent mockery of justice:

"The Lords of Life are Masters of Death," he said in a loud, clear voice.

And swift as lightning he stabbed the blindfolded men to the heart, with three swift, heavy stabs. Then he lifted the red dagger and threw it down. (380)

There is no irony here. It is an idealism of power. Ramón and Cipriano become divinities – finally shedding, along with their vestiges of human reality, all their human responsibilities. "Why should I judge him?" Kate asks herself after the stabbing. "He is of the gods, and so am I."

Both men want the same kind of power over their sexual partners. Ramón chooses wisely in his second wife one who sees her own kind of "tigerish power" realized in serving him. Cipriano on the other hand gives himself a seemingly impossible task with Kate Leslie. Here the novel takes up the issue of male sexual dominance where Lawrence left it in *The Lost Girl* and pushes it to an untenable extreme.

Kate is an Irish woman of forty, veteran of two marriages and several children. Like Ursula Brangwen she has a well-defined personality and development. She is wearied to disgust with "mere personal contact" and aware that her conscious self is limited and needs renewal. Her experiences are presented with a sensuous reality that, at the start at least, is not entirely skimmed for its ideological significance. She supplies the only independent light on what she calls the "high-flown bunk" of the religious pantomime. But there is also a steady and increasing progress of endorsement from her. As she comes under the influence of the new religion she relinquishes rather than renews her individuality. At times her reactions are indistinguishable from the author's direct commentary, which in turn is indistinguishable from Ramón's thoughts. There are occasional apologies for this melting of identities – "she was surprised at herself, using this language" – but the ardour that causes it only increases until the point is reached where she assumes the title of the goddess Malintzi.

By this time she has succumbed to the attractions of Cipriano. Her decision emerges from her weariness of her past way of life, her need for peace in place of continual restlessness, and a fear of becoming "a horrible, elderly female". This is the realistically psychological element in the picture, equivalent to the dramatic context we have seen framing the romantic idealism of Ursula and Birkin. However, it fails to contain the idealism, which sporadically – "Only when Cipriano was present, and then only sometimes" – "overwhelms" her. The more realistic side of her mentality continues to operate – when she realizes she does not want "the little general, the strutting little soldier" whose nature is "just inert and heavy, unresponsive, limited as a snake or lizard is limited". But it fights a losing battle against the compulsion to be

> fused into a molten unconsciousness, her will, her very self gone, leaving her lying in molten life, like a lake of still fire, unconscious of everything save the eternality of the fire in which she was gone. Gone as the burning bush was gone. Gone in the fadeless fire, which has no death. Only the fire can leave us, and we die. (320)

Cipriano's "living male power" alters "the scale" in which she sees him, so that he becomes "My demon lover! .... The Master, the everlasting Pan". To this power – "this huge erection" no less – there seems to her only one response possible: "submission absolute, like the earth under the sky." It is more radical than Alvina's addiction.

When they become lovers, he insists on her sexual passiveness, deliberately withdrawing whenever she gets excited in the wrong way. She learns to set aside her former kind of "orgiastic 'satisfaction' ... the beak-like friction" in favour of a "soft, heavy, hot flow, when she was like a fountain gushing noiseless and with urgent softness from the volcanic deeps". She welcomes it, as she welcomes the lack of conscious intimacy with him, because she thinks it will grant her peace. If her craving for rest is understandable in terms of her history, the means by which she seeks to attain it are unpromising to say the least!

People have been so mystified by Kate's sexual experience with Cipriano that many theories have been proposed. The sober sort include a reference to the so-called vaginal orgasm which Freud took be the mature kind but whose very existence nowadays – without clitoral stimulus at any rate – is disputed. The wilder variants include Gerald Doherty's attempt to relate it to the Tantric maithuna ritual, which involves prolonged ecstasy without orgasm for either partner.[17]

Lady Chatterley's Lover belongs to the final period of definition or over-definition in Lawrence's art. The author's findings are snatched from the context of life to become the context against which life as we normally understand it is to be judged or defined. Lawrence's last novel is what Barbara Hardy called a "lapse into schematic fable".[18] It is, as it were, the victory of Birkin's "Salvator Mundi".

The themes we have so far considered are simplified. Existence is divided into two: the mental, represented by the crippled aristocrat in his motorized wheelchair, together with the social, intellectual and industrial systems he administers; and through Connie and Mellors the sensual or phallic, carrying with it a genuine and deep commitment to another person and through this to life itself. Lawrence's own pamphlet definitions are an apt enough summary of what the novel has to offer: we have the "two great ways of knowing ... knowing in terms of apartness, which is mental, rational, scientific, and knowing in terms of togetherness, which is religious and poetic".[19]

Compared with the previous novel, social reconstruction has dropped almost out of sight. There is a great deal of social criticism (see Chapter 2 above) and Mellors reflects this in the pessimism of a disillusioned Luddite, but no regenerative platform. The wish for an exclusively male purposiveness appears only wistfully in Mellors' hopes for a "natural physical tenderness" between men, "in a properly manly way".

In the sexual relations, much of the imbalance in *The Plumed Serpent* is redressed. The power struggle is muted and moves towards the balance and mutuality seen in *The Rainbow* and *Women in Love*.

17. See Doherty, "The Throes of Aphrodite", in *D.H. Lawrence: Critical Assessments*, eds David Ellis and Ornella De Zordo, III.
18. Barbara Hardy, *The Appropriate Form*, 9.
19. Lawrence, *Apropos of Lady Chatterley's Lover*, in *Lady Chatterley's Lover*, 331.

Although there is some emphasis on passiveness in Connie (as we will see) their physical reverence for each other is completely mutual, Mellors' tenderness is stressed much more than his power, and the detailed portrayal of the physical attests the closeness of the contact between them, as well as laying down its own definition of how this should be achieved. It is the insistence on a recipe (though a different one) that links the two novels.

The reader enters the story with Connie Chatterley, and her story, rehearsing that of the Brangwens, is more appealing than that of any of Lawrence's novel heroines since Ursula. The clearly marked stages of her development are in thematic terms similar. A limiting moral environment (at Wragby, married to Clifford) a self-defeating love-affair with a weak and self-enclosed lover (Michaelis) and a conflict between despair and hunger for life lead her to a readiness equivalent to Ursula's at the start of *Women in Love*. Of course, what the comparison shows up is the relative slightness of Connie. The amount of exploratory detail given is no more than that offered in *The Rainbow* about Tom Brangwen. The vivid pastoral component in it reminds us too: her response to Spring when she sits "with her back to a young pine-tree, that swayed against her with curious life, elastic and powerful rising up" and the whole function of the wood as the antithesis of what goes on at Wragby Hall, as well as her playing with Mrs Flint's baby and watching the pheasant chicks (a scene that in its tenderness recalls some of those with Tom). At the end of the story her pregnancy insists on the need, as in *The Rainbow*, to integrate with others, and the imagery of seed and womb from the dual novel reappears here, insisting on the continuities.

Lawrence was returning to the basics of the theme as he had presented them at the start of *The Rainbow*, and once more keen to stress the achievement more than the problems to be met on the way to it. Connie's self-discovery is based on lessons from her past but comes about like Tom's from the discovery of her true partner – and like his quite suddenly, in her case in the throes of sexual climax:

> Oh, and far down inside her the deeps parted and rolled asunder, in long, far-travelling billows, and ever, at the quick of her, the depths parted and rolled asunder, from the centre of soft plunging, as the plunger went deeper and deeper, touching lower, and she was deeper and deeper and deeper disclosed, and heavier the billows of her rolled away to some shore, uncovering her, and close and closer came the palpable unknown, and further and further rolled the waves of herself away from herself, leaving her, till suddenly, in a soft, shuddering

convulsion, the quick of all her plasm was touched, she knew herself touched, the consummation was upon her, and she was gone. She was gone, she was not, and she was born: a woman. (174)

The loss and rebirth of herself has the kind of wish-fulfilling quality seen in Tom's proposal scene, with the partner in shadow as it were and responding to her needs without our understanding exactly what is behind his ability to do so. Out of "his incomprehensible stillness" comes "the other power". He like Lydia is the controlling partner in the progress towards a culmination in which Connie reaches the "the real bed-rock of her nature" and feels totally revealed, accepted and given up.

In any comparison with *The Rainbow,* apart from the obvious sexual explicitness – which caused all the fuss for one generation, and for another was not explicit enough – the most important distinction is the domination of the didactic motive. In *The Rainbow* the reader has Tom's feelings of the new, alarming and demanding; Connie's feelings, on the other hand, are all of the desirable and prescribed; and the achievement is brought about not so much by individual effort and painful self-acknowledgment as by the magic wand of the phallus. The style of the rhythmic and verbal repetitions here strike a note of deliberation, which makes the passage slightly predictable.

The prescriptive motive becomes more obvious later, after the lovers' "night of sensuality":

> In this short summer night she learnt so much. She would have thought a woman would have died of shame. Instead of which, the shame died. Shame, which is fear: the deep organic shame, the old physical fear which crouches in the bodily roots of us, and can be chased away only by the sensual fire.[20]

The point that the lovers are free to have whatever sexual experience they want, which was implicit in the great dual novel, is here weakened by the explicitness. Moreover, whereas the sensuality of Tom and Lydia in *The Rainbow* is actively and equally shared – "She wanted his active participation, not his submission" – here the pleasure and release felt by Connie comes about from letting Mellors "have his way and will of her". The ghost of anxiety about male

---

20. *Lady Chatterley's Lover*, 247. Added in the final version. In the second version, the Mellors figure, called Parkin, is unashamed and reckless but there is nothing about the burning out of Connie's shame.

authority continues to haunt this fable in which the two figures move towards a slightly lopsided generalization.

Forms shorter than the novel often lend themselves more readily to fable. For example, Lawrence's tale "The Virgin and the Gypsy" (written during this last period) though it lacks the human detail and density of *Lady Chatterley's Lover,* is relatively free of its artistic problems. All the more acceptable as a fable on account of its moral centrality, unbedevilled by any off-centre dogmas, it shows a mastery of the stylistic poise necessary for its success. The vivid actuality of the flood, for instance, sits well with its symbolic function, and the human details of what happens between Yvette and the gypsy bring the scene to life without interfering with its meaning in the fable.

In the novel the surrounding detail is more naturalistically representative of normal human life and not symbolically representative as in the classic fable, and too many factors crop up that conflict with the simplicity of the general ideas. The dramatic reality of some of the other characters, for instance, however confined or minimal their presentation, sometimes claims our attention in a way that makes us object when the narrative brushes them aside. The dismissal of Clifford Chatterley, the first Mrs Mellors and Mellors' own daughter, along with most responses to (let alone claims from) any relationship outside the specifically sexual one between Connie and Mellors detrimentally affects one's view of the novel's achievement.

The central theme itself is uneasy because Mellors as he emerges after the initial lovemaking supplies details about his past (as Lydia Brangwen never does) which cast doubt upon the validity of his new sexual relationship. One gets only his version but there is enough in the bare facts of his relations with his wife Bertha to make his malice against her suspicious. Bertha, he says, has achieved her own sexual satisfaction after he has completed his, in spite of his willingness to "hold back" and he has felt victimized. Isn't this essentially the same situation as that between Michaelis and Connie in the early chapters? There Michaelis is portrayed as a man whose weakness and lack of outgoing concern compels the woman to insist on her own pleasure by her own efforts. The critical judgment which is applied convincingly to Michaelis is almost switched off in Mellors' case (Bertha's blockheaded, unregenerate selfishness is to blame, though Mellors does admit his wilfulness made things worse). The reader is expected on the whole to accept his self-exonerating verdict on his marriage, after the more dramatically convincing explanation of mutual responsibility in Connie's earlier affair. There are contradictions too between what he admits to being before – nervous, vulnerable, bad-tempered with his wife – and the calm, self-sufficient character he is now. Moreover, talking about his past, he seems to contradict what we have already seen in his lovemaking with Connie when he tells her: "I never could get my pleasure and satisfaction of her unless she got hers of me at the same time." Many would dismiss as naïve the endorsement of the ideal of simultaneous orgasms (simultaneous with which one? they might ask) but more baffling (and crucial to Connie) is Mellors' apparent unawareness of any responsibility on his part to ensure them. Can she rely on his tenderness and his stated need of her fulfilment? If she were to take the initiative in a "night of sensuality" would she become a Bertha in his eyes? These and other questions – ranging from Mellors' social prejudices to his whimsical use of the vernacular – are raised by the residual realism of the story and continually undermine it.

4

ENGLISH TRADITIONS

George Eliot, the Brontës and Dickens

This study now embarks on a search among the novels Lawrence read, piecing together the traditions that influenced the development of his thematic novels. In the English traditions they are to be found not so much in George Eliot and Charlotte Brontë as in Emily Brontë and Dickens.

Lawrence grew up at a time when George Eliot's reputation was at its height (she died five years before he was born). He was the second major novelist to respond strongly to her influence – the first was Henry James – but as we shall see the influence was limited by the direction his own art took.

In his late teens, according to Jessie Chambers, Lawrence read *Adam Bede, The Mill on the Floss* and *Romola*; he later mentioned *Silas Marner*. These are the books to be discussed here, with a glance at *Middlemarch*, since he may well have read that and it is difficult to clinch certain general points about her work without reference to it.

F.R. Leavis declared, "In Ursula we have the Maggie Tulliver theme"[1] and it is true that the affectionate and creative energy Maggie shows as a child in *The Mill on the Floss*, together with her conflict with the conventions of her environment may well have been a stimulus to the creation of Ursula Brangwen. She was certainly the "favourite heroine"[2] of Lawrence's late teens. There is a phase in Maggie's development when, made miserable by the family misfortunes, she subjects herself to a formula of self-renunciation and charity, inspired by reading Thomas á Kempis. It enables her, by suppressing all instinctive responses or sublimating them into noble ones, to escape from unwelcome conflicts in herself and others. At the same time the self-appointed martyrdom feeds her vanity. This

---

1. Leavis, *D. H. Lawrence: Novelist*, 132.
2. Chambers, *D. H. Lawrence: A Personal Record*, 98.

encapsulates an aspect of Lawrence's critique of idealism and may remind us a little of Ursula Brangwen's short phase of self-renunciation during her teens in *The Rainbow*. In the last part of Eliot's book – the part that disappointed Lawrence, according to Jessie Chambers – this clear focus on the psychology of the character is lost, when she is overtaken by other ideals: first her romantic infatuation with Stephen Guest and then, for the sake of her friend, her self-sacrificing renunciation of him. Lawrence was not the only one to find fault. F.R. Leavis and Joan Bennett, for instance, criticized the handling of the love affair and its renunciation.[3] Lawrence later recalled "slightly indecent" sexual "titillations" in the love scenes,[4] although the only truly embarrassing aspect of them is the author's self-consciousness, which is almost as acute as the lovers':

> Stephen was mute; he was incapable of putting a sentence together, and Maggie bent her arm a little upward towards the large half-opened rose that had attracted her. Who has not felt the beauty of a woman's arm? – the unspeakable suggestions of tenderness that lie in the dimpled elbow, and all the varied gently-lessening curves down to the delicate wrist, with its tiniest, almost imperceptible nicks in the firm softness.[5]

Elsewhere, George Eliot was as keen as Lawrence to criticize any kind of idealism that delimits human responsiveness. Adam Bede, for instance, lives by a set of moral rules which have removed him from the complex interaction, understanding and experience that a full life demands:

> Whenever Adam was strongly convinced of any proposition, it took the form of a principle in his mind: it was knowledge to be acted on, as much as the knowledge that damp will cause rust. Perhaps here lay the secret of the hardness he had accused himself of: he had too little fellow-feeling with the weakness that errs in spite of foreseen consequences.[6]

Even in this novel, which is unsubtle by her highest standards, George Eliot does not separate Adam's idealism from other features of his developing character. His suffering when his ideal is shattered eventually enlarges his sympathies and forces him out of his egoism.

---

3. See Leavis, *The Great Tradition* and Joan Bennett, *George Eliot: Her Mind and Her Art*.
4. Lawrence, "Pornography and Obscenity" (1929) in *Phoenix*, ed. Edward McDonald, 177.
5. *The Mill on the Floss*, ed. Gordon S. Haight, 388.
6. *Adam Bede*, ed. Carol A. Martin, 197.

His love of Hetty shows itself in the end to be not just an idealistic indulgence; it is still there when she needs it, even after the tragedy of her infanticide. The very strength of his idealizing feelings has registered his capacity to love.

This characteristic mixing of motives differentiates George Eliot from Lawrence, who most urgently wanted to separate out for analysis the various factors that lead to a creative or destructive outcome. She on the other hand wanted to mix them together in her characters so as to stimulate in her readers just that kind of regenerative sympathy she most valued. Even at the outset of her career she explained to her publisher: "My artistic bent is directed ... to the presentation of mixed human beings in such a way as to call forth tolerant judgment, pity, and sympathy."[7]

The results are most striking in *Middlemarch*, which explores, for example, the conflict in Bulstrode between his religious beliefs and his ruling desires for money and power – sometimes in alliance, "Bishop and Banker", but at times of crisis the one overpowering the other. Eliot's analysis of Bulstrode is quite as relentless as that of Thomas Crich in *Women in Love*, and more moving. We follow "the train of causes in which he had locked himself" into the near-murder of the enemy who could expose the lie on which he has based his life. A conclusion is drawn – "There is no general doctrine which is not capable of eating out our morality if unchecked by the deep-seated habit of direct fellow-feeling with individual fellow-men" – which might stand for a summary of a feature of Lawrence's thinking about idealism. But then the compelling analysis of Bulstrode's sin is capped by the scene where his wife accepts him in spite of it, and we see the false idealism as part of the developing life of an individual. Similarly, Dorothea's idealistic disillusion and frustration with Casaubon is overwhelmed in her pity of him. In Lydgate's story many general factors play their part as he moves from the immature idealism and egoism of his early attachment to Rosamond and to his career, through his moral isolation both from her and the townsfolk, to his growing sense of responsibility, but they are all part of the "process and unfolding" of his character.

Bulstrode's idealism, for all its baggage of genuine belief, is ultimately a reflex of his egoism. George Eliot's treatment of the enclosed ego itself ranged from the semi-indulgent irony applied to the Dodsons in *The Mill on the Floss* – "The religion of the Dodsons

---

7. George Eliot to John Blackwood, 18 February 1857, in *Letters*, II, 299.

consisted in revering whatever was customary and respectable" – to the relentless sifting of the motives that promote the treachery of Tito Melema in *Romola*. But the finest studies of the purest egoism occur later, in *Middlemarch* for instance, where Rosamond Vincy is assessed in a way similar to Lawrence's study of Gudrun, but without the pathos that attaches to her. Again the attention is on the individual, although her selfishness repels sympathy.

There were, of course, occasions when Eliot lapsed (as she put it) "from the picture to the diagram".[8] The most notorious was in the portrait of Daniel Deronda, as Henry James was the first to point out. One of these lapses was deliberate and successful, for it produced the fable of *Silas Marner,* in which the starved affections of a solitary weaver get fixated on his accumulating wealth, until for that is substituted real life and real affection when his gold is stolen and in its place appears an orphan baby girl: "As her life unfolded, his soul, long stupefied in a cold narrow prison, was unfolding too, and trembling gradually into full consciousness." The symbolism at the core of the novel is not unlike that in *The Scarlet Letter* by Hawthorne, whom Eliot called "a grand favourite of mine".[9] Lawrence in 1927 (prompted perhaps by his own interest at that time in the fable form) saw this as an acceptable form of "sentimentality".[10]

In *Romola* Eliot's enthusiasm for regeneration – pursuing the creative possibilities that were cut short in Maggie Tulliver's death – led her into a structure in which the pursuit of that theme is parallel to the development of the main character. Romola has Maggie's kind of responsiveness, "vivid and intense enough to have created a wide fellow-feeling with all that is human". Trapped by her "girlish simplicity and ignorance concerning the world" into a marriage with Tito Melema that brings disillusion and despair, she seeks escape and redemption. At every juncture in this pilgrim's progress the generalities of regeneration are underlined. She wants to break "an outward tie that no longer represented the inward bond of love" feeling that "there could be no law for her but the law of her affections". But her need to love is drawn, by Savonarola, whose preaching she admires, into an alternative channel, an equally passionate but wide-ranging sense of fellowship with the disadvantaged. Then, seeing Savonarola's mistakes and hearing "the

---

8. George Eliot to Frederick Harrison, 15 August 1866, in *Letters*, IV, 300.
9. George Eliot to Mrs P. A. Taylor, 19 August 1852, in *Letters*, II, 52.
10. Lawrence, *Phoenix*, ed. Edward McDonald, 224

ring of egoism" in his speeches, she turns her back on that allegiance too, calling it a "purblind delusion" – for "rebellion might be sacred too". She asserts (as Anna Brangwen does): "God's kingdom is something wider – else, let me stand outside it with the beings that I love." The climax of the theme comes when, having put to sea in a small boat so that it might carry her away, possibly to death, she is saved by a current that lands her near a plague-stricken village. Once there, she is impelled, by an instinctive reaction to a sick child's cry, to cope with its causes: "she had simply lived, with so energetic an impulse to share the life around her, to answer the call of need and do the work which cried aloud to be done." This latter sequence of scenes was deliberately adopted, Eliot said, "as romantic and symbolical elements" and she explained: "The various *strands* of thought I had to work out forced me into a more ideal treatment of Romola than I had foreseen at the outset."[11] Her word "strands" here corresponds in some ways to our themes. Referring to this uneasy coalition between theme and psychological development, K. M. Newton explained: "George Eliot is prepared to pay an artistic price to write a philosophical novel."[12]

In this novel's pattern of regeneration it is possible to make out a misty affinity with the abstracts associated with Ursula and Birkin: a commitment to "the nearest" in love and to others in some kind of passionate social responsibility, with a reliance on what is instinctive and a critique of the ready-made and egoistic. But Lawrence of course repudiated the terminology of "duty" and derided what he saw as George Eliot's version of "the chaste Beatrice ... the noble woman, the pure spouse, the devoted mother".[13] As he became more absorbed in his mature work he lost interest in George Eliot's, though towards her he was never quite as indifferent or dismissive as he was to the two other major nineteenth-century novelists, Jane Austen and Henry James, with whom Eliot shared a preoccupation with the development of individuals and the literary forms dictated by that. When Lawrence turned away from that type of novel he was in the company of every major English novelist in his generation except E.M. Forster.

Something like George Eliot's frame of mind existed in her lesser contemporaries. For example, the theme of egoism was turned by

---

11. George Eliot to Sarah Hennell, 23 August 1863, in *Letters*, IV, 104.

12. Newton, *George Eliot: Romantic Humanist*, 72.

13. Lawrence, "Give her a Pattern" (1928) in *Phoenix II*, 535.

George Meredith into the title of his most famous novel, in which Sir Willoughby Patterne demands "an adoring female's worship" to supplement his own: "Possession without obligation to the object possessed approaches felicity." (His Laetitia marries him with her eyes open, admitting that "he worships himself".) There is a whole gallery of similar figures in Trollope's books.

Meredith's direct influence might be detected, as we have seen, in *The White Peacock.* The strongest character in *The Egoist*, Clara Middleton, might be conceptually related to some of Lawrence's women, since she voices the feminism that runs through Meredith's work. These influences were not very important to Lawrence, but there was something special for him in William Hale White. Even after he had long grown out of him Lawrence still recommended him as "just and plucky and sound".[14] When White in his fifties began to write (under the pseudonym of Mark Rutherford) it was easy to spot Eliot's influence. His autobiography, which includes a meeting with her, advocates a "perpetual undying faith in principles". Nevertheless, like her, he offers in his novels both endorsement and criticism of them, in the dramatic opposition between what Irvin Stock called "the spontaneous life of feeling and intuition and the deliberate life of reflection and rule".[15] *The Revolution in Tanner's Lane* gives a largely uncritical portrait of its artisan hero, Zachariah, whose unsatisfactory marriage makes him all the more noble a lover of humanity and justice: "He was by nature a poet; essentially so, for he loved everything which lifted him above the commonplace." *Catharine Furze,* however, contains a picture of a zealous minister whose high-mindedness is seen as blindness when he neglects his well-meaning, unimaginative wife: "there were in her whole regions of unexplored excellence, of faculties never encouraged, and an affection to which he offered no response." The marriage is summed up in no uncertain terms: "He fell in love with himself, married himself, and soon after discovered that he did not know who his wife was." He is saved from further folly only by a higher idealism, his romantic attachment to the nobly self-renunciatory Catharine Furze – "a love of the soul, of that which was immortal, of God in her" – which Lawrence would hardly have endorsed.

Although these Victorian novelists undoubtedly affected Lawrence's thinking about the subjects of his major themes, their

---

14. Lawrence to Arthur McLeod, 2 December 1912, in *Letters*, I, 482.
15. Stock, *William Hale White*, 200.

influence on his handling of them did not endure into the thematic novels with which we are chiefly concerned here.[16]

The same is true of Charlotte Brontë, but with a significant difference. Like Eliot she was chiefly interested in (and now is most valued for) the psychology of her characters, although she did not have the same benefit of an admiration of Jane Austen, against whom her prejudice was as strong as Lawrence's: "Can there be a great Artist without poetry?" she asked G. H. Lewes when he told her to read her.[17] Her appeal to Lawrence was strongest when psychology *per se* was his chief interest also. At the time he was writing *The White Peacock* he paired *Shirley* with *Jane Eyre* as "two of my favourite English books".[18]

In *Shirley* Charlotte was mainly concerned with creating a quartet of main characters: two women who are sisters in mental outlook, and two men who are brothers in fact, together with a fine supporting ensemble. There is however a curious feature of its whimsicality, a symbol that fossilized in Lawrence's mind, enduring against all the odds of the revising process, right into *Women in Love* (in the "Excurse" chapter). It is the Genesis prophecy about the sons of God and the daughters of men, and appears in the five-page fable written by Shirley for Louis, her tutor (and future husband) and recited back by him as part of his oblique courtship of her. The coy irony with which it is offered (Shirley self-deprecatingly calls it "rubbish") is typical of this part of Brontë's novel. As Louis retells it, "Genius" marries Eva, who exclaims:

> "A Son of God! Am I indeed chosen?.... I receive a revelation. The dark hint, the obscure whisper, which have haunted me from childhood, are interpreted."[19]

Some of the minor figures in *Jane Eyre* show Charlotte to be almost as a keen critic of limited high-mindedness as George Eliot. The most lenient of the portraits of characters who sacrifice themselves and others to their ideals is that of Helen Burns, the girl at Lowood School, victim of the headmaster's persecution, who dies

---

16. It is an offshoot of the concern with power in human relationships, which Patricia Menon saw as the central interest in the novel: see her *Austen, Eliot, Charlotte Brontë and the Mentor Lover*, 2003.
17. Charlotte Brontë to George Henry Lewes, 18 January 1848, in *Letters,* II, 14.
18. Lawrence to Blanche Jennings, 4 November 1908, in *Letters,* I, 88. See Alison Hoddinott's study of Charlotte's influence on Lawrence, in *Brontë Studies,* XXVII.
19. *Shirley*, eds Herbert Rosengarten and Margaret Smith, 552.

meekly, a model Christian looking forward to heaven. Jane fervently admires her but implicitly rejects, at least for herself, that kind of passivity, "in which there was an alloy of inexpressible sadness". After Helen's death she has all the more reason to loath what she sees as its cause, Mr Brocklehurst, the Dickensian hate figure.

The most subtle and keenly observed negative idealist is St John Rivers, the minister who offers to marry Jane after she has left Rochester. "So much has religion done for me", he tells Jane, "pruning and restraining nature". But he confesses to a conflict of "propensities and principles" which makes him, he says, "almost rave in my restlessness". His sister says:

> "He will sacrifice all to his long-framed resolves .... It is right, noble, Christian; yet it breaks my heart!"[20]

He himself admits he is "a cold, hard, ambitious man .... Reason, and not feeling, is my guide". Jane senses a murderous ruthlessness in him: "I felt now, if I were his wife, this good man, pure as the deep sinless source, could kill me."

The chief interest for a reader of Jane Eyre lies in the unfolding of Jane's character. Rochester himself may be an unconvincing Byronic figure but what Lawrence could have found memorable in his encounters with Jane is her insistence on their personal equality and her own independence of spirit and judgment. This follows convincingly from her behaviour with her aunt and at Lowood School, and the craving she feels as she leaves it, for what she calls "liberty" – that is, an exploratory freedom for her mind and imagination, together with "more of intercourse with my kind" – is Ursula Brangwen's kind of ambition.[21] When she leaves Rochester after hearing about his first marriage and the subsequent adulteries, it is primarily (when we strip away the conventional trappings) because she fears that her hard-earned status of respect is threatened in a socially unsanctioned union. She needs the conventional props to allay her anxieties about it:

> If I were so far to forget myself and all the teaching that had ever been instilled into me, as – under any pretext – with any justification – through any temptation – to become the successor of these poor

---

20. Jane Eyre, eds Jane Jack and Margaret Smith, 455.
21. Heather Glen defined the theme as "aspiring, heroic... a restlessness to go beyond the restrictive limits ... [which] has the peremptoriness of 'nature' itself" (Charlotte Brontë: The Imagination in History, 101).

girls, he would one day regard me with the same feeling which now in his mind desecrated their memory.[22]

But for Charlotte, particularly in this book, there were other dimensions. It took its origins from a wide range of sources, including Gothic novels, ballads and folk-tales, and one result of these multiple influences is that, as Penny Boumelha pointed out, "Jane's inner life, whatever her modest demeanour, seems to range across heaven and earth in a kind of cosmic melodrama".[23] There is something even Lawrencian in Charlotte's insistence that a novel must take in "what throbs fast and full, though hidden, what the blood rushes through, what is the unseen seat of Life".[24] This brings into play in *Jane Eyre* general themes of passion and regeneration which may well have appealed strongly to Lawrence's nascent thematic interests. The interaction between the spiritual or intellectual and what the narrator calls "tenderness and passion" is more specifically sexual than with George Eliot – more, in that respect, like Ursula Brangwen's – and expressed in general terms through the imagery. On the night of Rochester's proposal to Jane, lightning strikes the great chestnut tree at Thornfield. On her wedding-eve, walking by the two halves of the divided tree (later an emblem of Rochester's disablement):

> It was not without a certain wild pleasure I ran before the wind, delivering my trouble of mind to the measureless air-torrent thundering through space .... As I looked up at them [the "monster-splinters"] the moon appeared momentarily in that part of the sky which filled their fissure; her disc was blood-red and half overcast; she seemed to throw on me one bewildered, dreary glance, and buried herself instantly in the deep drift of cloud.[25]

The moon recurs at crises, as it does in Lawrence's double novel. It is shining when she first meets Rochester on horseback (Chapter 12) and on the night his mad wife injures him (Chapter 20) and when he proposes (Chapter 23). More portentously, it appears on the night after the disrupted marriage ceremony, in a "trance-like dream" where it turns into a white mother-figure telling Jane to leave. It reappears on the night she hears the call to return: "the room was full of moonlight."

22. *Jane Eyre*, eds Jane Jack and Margaret Smith, 398.
23. Penny Boumelha, *Charlotte Brontë*, 76.
24. Charlotte Brontë to W.S. Williams, 12 April 1850, in *Letters*, II, 383.
25. *Jane Eyre*, eds Jane Jack and Margaret Smith, 348-49.

On the other hand, even the youthful Lawrence could hardly have endorsed the other aspect of the thematic structure, the workings of Providence: what Barbara Hardy called "imposing an ideology on to a realistic psychological pattern".[26] This climaxes in the telepathic message calling Jane back to her Master, now a blinded "Samson" who is both helpless and adoring. Lawrence during his own didactic phase dogmatically labelled "pornography"[27] this conclusion in which Jane finally acquires moral superiority.

In Emily Brontë's work (influenced from the same sources as her sister's) several master-themes were developed more strongly in themselves and aligned more strictly with the psychology of the characters. In *Wuthering Heights* Edgar's educated upper-class idealism is set against the brute lower-class egoism of Heathcliff, with Catherine caught between; and in the second half of the novel the answering theme, the potential for regeneration is worked out, chiefly in terms of character development, through the love of young Cathy (born as her mother dies) and her cousin Hareton Earnshaw. The novel's deployment of the social factors, its poetic quality and intense impersonality, and the sharp objectivity (obtained partly by placing the story within a story told by narrators who also figure in it) suggest affinities with Lawrence, quite apart from the themes themselves.

It was the tragic thematic development, stretching to the end of the novel in Heathcliff's grief that impressed Lawrence most, for that is what he later remembered. He read the book when he was twenty and never lost his admiration of it. The monomaniac passion that unites and destroys Heathcliff and Catherine, though it gets its expression through their domineering egos, is rooted deeper. It is unlike love; Edgar if anyone in the novel provides the norm for that. They indulge in no softening illusions about each other; they are as clear-sighted as if they were enemies. Many readers have been unwilling to think of the violent attachment, the obsessionalism and the irrationality as inherently human. Even Charlotte called it "fierce and inhuman". Some have romanced it into something else: for instance, by aligning it with a tradition of love that goes back to the troubadours. But as Lawrence pointed out, Catherine's feelings are without "any of the graces of sentiment". "Sheer female instinctive passion" he called it, "the ferocity of frustrated instinct ... bare and stark".[28] Emily shared

---

26. Barbara Hardy, *The Appropriate Form*, 68-69.

27. Lawrence, *Phoenix*, ed. Edward McDonald, 176.

28. Lawrence, *Phoenix*, ed. Edward McDonald, 265.

his kind of ambition to uncover the underlying, impersonal drives in human nature. However, although in his own work impersonal animal sexuality operates in diverse ways, any kinship with the passion of Heathcliff and Catherine is nominal. Between them the sexual itself is under a severe quasi-incestuous ban (they have slept together as brother and sister in the same bed until she is over twelve) and sublimated into something absolute. "Whatever our souls are made of, his and mine are the same", she says, and he, "I cannot live without my life! I cannot live without my soul!". Only when she is dying does an erotic element emerge:

> He neither spoke, nor loosed his hold for some five minutes, during which period he bestowed more kisses than he ever gave in his life before, I dare say; but then my mistress had kissed him first, and I plainly saw that he could hardly bear, for downright agony, to look into her face![29]

As in Lawrence's dual novel, these figures are identified with the theme, impersonalized by it, yet remain vividly individual. Theme and character are aligned, but not interpenetrative as they are in *Women in Love*. Their passion is a current that runs alongside the natural bent of their characters without altering them. She remains the wilful, marred child whose fancy for conventional comforts makes her marry Edgar, only to languish in that environment, though loving him well enough until he challenges her obsession with Heathcliff. He is a cruel brute whose "utter lack of sympathy" (Nelly spots the genetic trait in his son) is twisted by deprivation into ugly shapes of revenge and greed. The conflict between their mania and their normal life kills them. Like Gerald Crich Heathcliff is a "denier" of normal human feelings and manically given up to a single passion which is the only source of his vulnerability; but by comparison, the compulsion that destroys Gerald Crich is a cultured product, seeded by his environment and rooted in his ego.

Because it has been generated partly during their outings together in their early teens, "half savage and free" to the moors, their feeling for each other is associated with "the heather on those hills". As Catherine dies she imagines "my soul will be on that hill-top". The landscape is, as it were, "continued into their souls".[30] That kind of

---

29. *Wuthering Heights*, eds Hilda Marsden and Ian Jack, 194.
30. The phrase is taken from A.C. Bradley, who noticed that the two main characters in *Macbeth* are "never detached in imagination from the atmosphere that surrounds them and adds to their grandeur and terror. It is, as it were, continued into their souls" (*Shakespearean Tragedy,* Lecture IX, part 3).

intense conjunction of the human and non-human is something that Lawrence achieved in *Women in Love.*

Important as these influences were for Lawrence, in the creation of his thematic novels they were less so than Dickens. Reading his novels in his late teens – at least six of them – was "the entering into possession of a new world, a widening and enlargement of life".[31] The gulf between that world and George Eliot's can be instantly gauged by a glance at its simplest manifestation, in *A Christmas Carol,* whose structure is governed by two master-themes: on the one hand "the master-passion Gain" which has controlled Scrooge's life and made a misery of it both for him and everybody he affects, and on the other the powers that undertake what is called his "reclamation" to the generous enjoyment of life. The first is personified in Scrooge himself as the image of a miser, together with attendant figures (his colleagues at the Stock Exchange, the wretches who squabble over his belongings after his imagined death) and symbolic images of Ignorance and Want. The second theme is dramatically present in the pictures of the happy families of Scrooge's nephew, Fezziwig, and of Bob Cratchit, and in the imagery of Christmas merriment and benevolence, as well as in the ghosts who visit him. The details of the narrative are there not so much to produce the impression of everyday life as to explore the themes. In this context, by the time Marley's ghost appears it is as acceptable as Hamlet's father's.

This most popular of Dickens's works also suggests that some of their sources were among the popular theatrical traditions – stretching back to the medieval mystery and morality plays, and including Shakespeare – which he enjoyed so much in his youth and commemorated in the Crummles of *Nicholas Nickleby.* His relation to those sources and to the traditions of the picaresque and adventure novels was much like that explored by Mikhail Bakhtin in Dostoevsky's background.[32]

In his major novels there is the same kind of search as in Lawrence's for underlying processes in his people and an intentness on diagnosing the obstructive and creative factors. He was less interested in the niceties of psychological development than in the way the psychology of his people's personal impulses and conflicts

---

31. Chambers, *D. H. Lawrence: a Personal Record,* 96.
32. Bakhtin's theory of dialogism has frequently been applied to Dickens's novels. For a survey of this field, see Lyn Pykett, *Charles Dickens,* 2002.

are related to the sociology of their historical setting and their religious and moral ideology.[33] The moulding of these factors is brought about by a highly integrated and flexible narrative texture charged with a multiplicity of internal references and with poetic and comic effects gained from symbolism, analogy, parody and metaphor.

The quickest way of demonstrating the structural affinity with Lawrence is to examine one novel in detail. *Dombey and Son* is suitable for this purpose, in spite of the fact that it is not particularly strong in Lawrence's first theme, the critique of idealism, which figures prominently elsewhere in Dickens in prisoners of belief such as Gradgrind, William Dorrit and Mrs Jellyby. The second theme, however, appears powerfully in *Dombey and Son* in the sinister shape of a destructive monomania.

Self-isolating monomania, of course, is everywhere in Dickens. To mention only some of the books we know Lawrence read: there is Nell's grandfather in *The Old Curiosity Shop*, whose gambling, sanctioned by the idea of benefiting Nell, is like a demonic possession. There is Ralph Nickleby, in whom the personal hate-obsession, clearly emanating from his repressions, operates on a wide scale as the avarice that drives his successful business, and who ends with suicidal feelings that recall Gerald Crich's: "'Night after night comes and goes, and I have no rest. One night's unbroken rest and I should be a man again.'" There is Jonas Chuzzlewit, with "an imprisoned devil" in him, and Steerforth in *David Copperfield*, whose personal magnetism hides a restless destructive drive, "a torment to myself".

The analysis of Dombey is as relentless and consistent as Lawrence's of Gerald Crich. His obsession with the idea of self-advancement, of "Dombey and Son" has its roots in his environment. As a successful capitalist, like the Criches in *Women in Love*, his mentality is crucially representative of a phase of social history – the one to which Thomas Crich's father belongs. Relatives and employees alike want material advancement, and in so far as Dombey can be the source of this they respect and co-operate with his single-mindedness. Even such a representative of common sense and compassion as Mr Morfin honours him for his efficiency in this respect. He has the effective single-mindedness that generally they themselves have not.

---

33. Juliet John saw in him an aversion to "psycho-centred" thinking as a result of his profound belief in "communality and cultural inclusivity" (*Dickens's Villains*, 3).

He has both the personal power and the motives to apply ruthlessly the ideology that has formed him and that they all to some extent share.

Nevertheless the obsession expresses a personal neurosis. His basic dissociation from the business activity as anything other than an expression of will and a way of canalizing life is proved by the way in which he allows the detailed running of the firm to slip into the hands of the manager, Carker. He behaves like an "automaton" (often said of Gerald Crich) acknowledging only the fixed idea, inhibiting all contact with people:

> Towards his first wife, Mr Dombey, in his cold and lofty arrogance, had borne himself like the removed Being he almost conceived himself to be .... He had kept his distant seat of state on the top of his throne, and she her humble station on its lowest step; and much good had it done him, so to live in solitary bondage to his one idea.

It is the idea of "Dombey and Son" that permits and promotes his one affection, for Paul. In losing him he loses the element that has seemed to justify and give thrust to his monomania. The death causes him to seek support and furtherance of the experience he knows, and so (just as Gerald after his father's death turns away from Birkin) Dombey turns away suicidally from the sources of renewal offered through Florence, and chooses a woman bred to respect and need the same things he does and in whom pride and will are just as evident as the only motives left for action. The reasons she seems especially attractive are the ones that make her most dangerous to him personally. They are both dead to almost everything but the dictates of their own wills:

> He had imagined that the proud character of his second wife would have been added to his own – would have merged into it, and exalted his greatness. He had pictured himself haughtier than ever, with Edith's haughtiness subservient to his.[34]

She is not only one of his own kind, but as such, and as a powerful force in his life, she becomes a further challenge to his monomania. Victory over her becomes a necessity. But Edith, like Lawrence's Gudrun, sees the man solely as an antagonist in this respect. No other understanding comes through their own preoccupations, and so the fight is carried to the limits.

---

34. *Dombey and Son*, ed. Alan Horsman, 538.

As Gudrun turns to Loerke, so Edith turns to Carker, impressed and victimized by the feeling that he knows her as well or better than she does herself, but unlike Gudrun she repudiates what she sees, both in him and herself. Although she despises him she elopes with him as an act of vengeance against Dombey, against public opinion and against herself. In both cases, however, the liaison is a final act of despair.

Carker is the other leading representative of the enclosed ego in *Dombey and Son*. Totally irresponsible towards people, he works outside any code of morality or principle, acquiring and abandoning people and power as the urge arises. The repeated emphasis on his teeth as the only informative feature of his grins, and the image of him as a cat stress the impermeability of his self-interest and the dangerous predatoriness behind it. There is no underlying directive, no motivating force beyond the desire to gratify his wishes, which are keenest when vengefully conceived. The efficiency he shows in gradually gaining control of the firm of Dombey and Son is partly prompted by the urge to defy the social system in which he is labelled an inferior, in so far as it can be manipulated by him and he can achieve a position of control within it unattainable by those who are bothered by respect for the false ideology surrounding it. But it is also partly prompted by the instinct to be in a position of vantage. Cat-like he keeps alert to all the possibilities.

The lack of directive beyond these two factors is finally clear when he abandons all this effort in order to run off with his employer's wife – she representing at the time the opportunity to spite Dombey (and through him the system) and bring him down, and at the same time to enjoy a sensual retirement. Soulessness and moral anarchy, the idea that each acquisition or desire is of equal importance and value as it occurs (and best when operating vengefully) – these are the thematic factors underlined in the portrait.

Dickens provided a range and variety of studies of this kind of negativity unequalled even by Dostoevsky. Sometimes they are heaped together in a satirical farce and given names to suit: Ralph Nickleby's gang of cads, for example, Messrs Pike, Pluck and Snobb, with Lord Verisopht and Sir Mulberry Hawk. Sometimes they are deliberately grotesque, such as Quilp in *The Old Curiosity Shop*, his sadistic inhumanity given shape and convincing vitality in the ugliness of his behaviour and his dwarfish body; or Squeers and Creakle, with their sadistic "craving appetite" for punishing their pupils.

Bleak House mounts the richest variants on the theme, various ideologies there cloaking and sanctioning the greed and inertia. Like the fog in the opening scene, their alliance threatens to smother every manifestation of spontaneous life. Tulkinghorn, conspiring for power, operates a legal code which is a perversion of the morality it ought to uphold. The aristocratic code of behaviour, shared by Sir Leicester Dedlock and his comic parody Turveydrop pampers vanity and puts blinkers on the nobility to the detriment of the poor. The usurer Smallweed's economic creed accommodates a plentiful profit at the expense of his customers. The humanitarianism of Mrs Jellyby and Mrs Pardiggle – the "telescopic philanthropy" of the one and the "rapacious benevolence" of the other – provides charity at the expense of their nearest and dearest. Finally, Skimpole's aesthetic pretensions guarantee his own idleness at the expense of anybody. The viewpoint is not merely bifocal – the omniscient present-tense observer and the character-narrator – but shifts into many permutations, not unlike those to be found in a Dostoevsky novel.

The townscape shares the deformity – the fog in *Bleak House*, for example. Coketown in *Hard Times* is as blighting as Tevershall in *Lady Chatterley's Lover*. The imagery of water, focused on the Thames, is given its traditional (and Lawrencian) significance of the destroyer and also giver of life, as we see in the chapters where young Paul Dombey, his frail sensitivity overpowered by the demands of his father's regime, is dying: "How fast the river runs ..." towards "what the wild waves are saying". Later, with Florence's recovery, we hear "new voices on the waves". In such passages the dreamlike or mythic element is strong.

Although akin in conception, Dickens's regenerative theme lacks Lawrence's psychological detail. It is important and omnipresent but it is explored not so much as to its content as to its effect. The need to achieve a balance and a renewal – shown most explicitly in the characters who falter on the edge of failure and despair, such as Carton, Clennam and Wrayburn – is generally seen as a matter of exposing oneself to the benign influences of life rather than a matter of rigorous challenge and self-questioning. In Dickens's work the good influences are constants not only in nature but in people. So in the front rank are heroes like Nicholas Nickleby (always more convincing knocking down his opponents than uttering sentiments, but noble in any case) and heroines like Nell, Kate Nickleby, Agnes Whitfield, Florence Dombey and Esther Summerson, whose virtues are unvarying.

Lawrence was dismissive of what he called "the 'Virgin' conception of woman, the passionless, passive conception" in which he included Dickens's Agnes.[35] He was not ignorant of other kinds of women in the Dickens novels – the Rosa Dartles and Edith Dombeys – but was objecting to the cliché aspect of Dickens's thematic distillation of the essence of male and female relationships into the purely self-sacrificing on the one hand and the solely selfish on the other. Lawrence's own processes of distillation in this area were considerably more subtle. However, there are unexpected refinements in Dickens's handling of his heroines, such as the delicate tracing of Amy Dorrit's fixation on her two father figures, as she struggles with the humiliations and rewards of her devotion to William Dorrit (her real and unsatisfactory father) and the disappointments of her love for Clennam; and there are critical sidelights too, like her sister's calling her "Goody Two-shoes" and Mrs Chivery's send-up of her: "It is not my intentions to be a wife, it is my intentions always to be a sacrifice."

Besides, in all the novels there is a wonderfully generous supporting cast: people like Kit, the "shock-headed shambling awkward lad" with the big laugh in *The Old Curiosity Shop*, or Mark Tapley, the most admirable character in *Martin Chuzzlewit* (more convincingly so than Tom Pinch, his companion of the "simple heart") as well as pairs like the Garlands (in *The Old Curiosity Shop*) the Micawbers, the Bagnets and the Boffins, and whole families like the Kenwigs, Toodles, Peggottys and Plornishes, and groups of people, especially those on the fringes of the social system, such as the itinerant entertainers in *The Old Curiosity Shop,* the Crummles' theatrical troupe in *Nicholas Nickleby* and Sleary's circus in *Hard Times*. Sometimes the good, fine, sensitive characters are victims – either quenched by their burdens, like Smike in *Nicholas Nickleby* and little Paul Dombey, or holding their own in subjection, like Newman Noggs. All these are set up against monomaniacs like Dombey, Gradgrind and Mrs Clennam and the huge cast of characters throughout the novels who cripple the vitality of others and are themselves crippled.

Looking more closely at this aspect of *Dombey and Son*, the sources of regeneration centred in Florence Dombey (and initially Paul) are to be seen spread out in a cross-section of society and in widely differing characters. In the Toodles, in Miss Tox, Susan

35. Lawrence, *A Study of Thomas Hardy*, 105.

Nipper, Sol and Cuttle and in Cousin Feenix we have low, middle and upper-class representatives of survivors, just as we have a similar range of those whose natures, co-operating with their circumstances, have kept them negative and destructive: with Mrs Brown and Alice, Mrs Pipchin, Bagstock and Mrs Skewton. The width of coverage given to this line of interest takes the place of depth of analysis given to individual characters. This is not to suggest that there is a lack of psychological understanding, but that this understanding is at the disposal of the author's more general diagnosis before anything else.

Florence Dombey, for instance, develops but along simple lines. She is neither entirely passive nor entirely unchanging. Her love for her father alters in reaction to his increased animus: she tries "to love him rather as some dear one who had been, or might have been, than as the hard reality before her eyes". The main character change, however, is in her father. We have seen how in the first half of the book his every response is referred back to his obsession and the pride through which it operates. At each major crisis – Paul's death, Edith's desertion – his feelings refer to Florence, in jealousy and hatred initially, but with a slow infiltration of a new regenerative experience from the impact of these tragedies and her steady influence. His redemption is completed through his devotion to his grandchildren.

The processes of regeneration are not always as nominal, sweeping and to be taken for granted as they are in *Dombey and Son*, which was after all only the first of Dickens's great wholly integrated (rather than episodic) novels. For instance, Arthur Clennam's approach towards reclamation by Amy Dorrit's love is painfully slow and reaches, as Dickens himself put it, "a very quiet conclusion". And in *Our Mutual Friend*, Eugene Wrayburn's emergence from a condition of satirical cynicism is intriguingly spasmodic and tentative.

Dickens's regenerative theme comes closest to Lawrence's in the imagery that pervades the novels. For example, in the classroom in the first chapter of *Hard Times*, the sunlight falling on Bitzer – which "appeared to draw out of him what little colour he ever possessed" – falls on Sissy Jupe too, so that "she seemed to receive a deeper and more lustrous colour from the sun". It establishes not just the distinction between the two figures but one that runs right through the novel, between what Lawrence would have called "knowing in terms of apartness, which is mental, rational, scientific" and "knowing in terms of togetherness, which is religious and poetic".[36]

36. Lawrence, *Lady Chatterley's Lover*, 331.

In order to see how intricately the diagnosis of a general pattern, the analysis of an individual character, symbolism and direct authorial commentary are woven together, let us look at Dombey's journey after Paul's death. During this journey the train he travels in partly represents the process of death, and death itself: it is Dombey who sees it as such and in his eyes he is "hurried along headlong, not through a rich and varied country, but a wilderness of blighted and gnawing jealousies". It stands for death in its suddenness and single-tracked indifference to people and their works: "There are jagged walls and falling houses close at hand, and through the battered roofs and broken windows, wretched rooms are seen, where want and fever hide themselves in many wretched shapes." Nevertheless, "As Mr Dombey looks out of his carriage window, it is never in his thoughts that the monster who has brought him there has let the light of day in on these things: not made or caused them". The train represents change and progress as well as death, something that Dombey in his sealed condition cannot respond to. The death of Paul is a means by which "the light of day" is let in on him. On this journey the thought of his daughter Florence is "abroad in the expression of defeat and persecution that seemed to encircle him like the air"; but by the end of the story it has become "that which he could so easily have wrought into a blessing and had set himself so steadily for years to form into a curse".

When one remembers that Toodles is a train driver and that Carker is killed by a train, one sees the extensive work that such a symbol is doing. And it is only a fraction of the complex structure by which Dickens sustains the pursuit of the themes that interest him. The story is moreover packed out with direct and indirect comment. Indirectly the comment occurs of course in the comic or ominous slanting of the descriptions of the environment or of group activities – such as those of Dombey's wedding, or of Paul's christening, or even his house and street. Florence, alone after Paul's death and ignored by her father, sees "the blank walls looked down upon her with a vacant stare, as if they had a Gorgon-like mind to stare her youth and beauty into stone". The animation of the inanimate was a habit of mind with Dickens, and the comic is an essential ingredient, even in the ominous. Indeed, that kind of fizz is a *sine qua non* of the alertness, the pace and power of Dickens' style, which is champagne compared with the fine wine of

Lawrence's, and without which the flatness can lead to sentimentalism and didacticism.

Everything is complexly related within a structure that finally expresses life's indomitability. Funful exuberance is a necessary feature of the Dickensian regenerative, and in *Dombey and Son* the linking together at the end of all the natural representatives of "life" and the regenerated survivors, which is brought about by the marriages of Susan Nipper and Toots and of Florence and Walter, the joining of Miss Tox with the Toodles family and the reuniting of Florence and her father – all this, when coupled with the death or condemnation to single existence of the destructive characters, makes up the final analysis. It is an analysis accomplished not so much through individuals as by means of them.

In spite of its structural originality, the Dickens novel imposed itself on all and sundry immediately and ever since. His influence can be seen even on Charlotte Brontë (Mr Bocklehurst in *Jane Eyre*) and George Eliot (among many others, the Featherstones in *Middlemarch*). We shall soon be investigating his influence on Dostoevsky and Conrad, as well as Lawrence, but that (in amount) is an insignificant portion of his permeation of all subsequent literature.

5

AMERICAN TRADITIONS

Hawthorne and Melville

Lawrence's first contact with American fiction came in his teens, with James Fenimore Cooper. Perhaps it was partly because of his teenage enthusiasm for him that in his *Studies in Classic American Literature* he gave him as many chapters as Hawthorne. He had found the call of the wild in his yarns so attractive, as he wrote in the first version of his essays on him:

> The night-fishing on the teeming, virgin lake; the deer-hunting, the forests all green, the maple sugar taken from the trees – all this is given with a beauty and magnificence unsurpassable. It is rich with that pristine magic of futurity, like the Odyssey. (218)

In the final version written four years later he admitted "Fenimore puts in only the glamour" and "perhaps my taste is childish" – it is "wish-fulfilment". Lawrence pointed out similarities between Cooper's portrayal of women and Hardy's, but in Cooper the psychology is so slight as to make such affinities minimal. The theme Lawrence found most intriguing, the comradeship between the white dead-shot hunter and the Indian chief, he tried to rewrite in his own terms in his essay – "deeper than the deeps of sex". It operates, as he and other critics (such as Leslie Fiedler) have agreed, at the level of what is generally called "myth" – actually, Lawrence added, "an evasion of reality". He would have been better off writing about Mark Twain, who is truly "classic" and who himself wrote an essay on "Fenimore Cooper's Literary Offenses" which is both lethal and hilarious.

He read Hawthorne and Melville during the period when he was composing and revising *Women in Love*. They were important and in some ways crucial in their impact on that and subsequent work. They redirected into him the influence of Dickens's thematic art, which had so strongly affected them and lay in the background of his own development.

Nathaniel Hawthorne absorbed Dickens's influence in such a way that it combined with his own keen interest in folklore, myth and morality drama (as well as Shakespeare) to produce a hybrid quite as rare if not as powerful and prolific. For all the whimsicality, piety and ambiguity that Lawrence was quick to criticize in his work, Hawthorne was for him an important forerunner.

The Scarlet Letter was offered to his contemporaries ready-framed as if a document from a past age and carefully categorized (in the introduction) as occupying "a neutral territory, somewhere between the real world and fairyland, where the Actual and the Imaginary may meet, and each imbue itself with the nature of the other". That apparently apologetic comment puts its finger on a crucial feature of all the novels we are especially interested in, which establish a special relation between the particular actual and the universal imaginary.

The novel lacks, of course, the rich complexity to be found in Lawrence and Dickens but there is no doubt about the basic similarity of structure. Newton Arvin, pointing to "the thematic unity of Hawthorne's imaginative treatment of human life" used terms which suggest the affinity with Lawrence: "So constantly did he return to the question, What are the forces that abet, what are the forces that impede, a rich personal development?"[1] Hawthorne's novel is not, after all, like a fairytale, where everything is known beforehand, nor quite like a literary fable, where character equates with concept and we are taught a lesson either sanctioned by tradition, as in Eliot's *Silas Marner*, or given a twist by the author, as in *Lady Chatterley's Lover*. It is more tentative, exploratory and open-ended – more like the other great novels we are investigating.

Lawrence himself identified in Dimmesdale, the minister who repudiates his love for the sake of his calling, what he had portrayed in Thomas Crich: the Puritan ideal defeated by what it excludes. Dimmesdale hides the secret of his love affair with Hester Prynne, while she is publicly dishonoured for it. The psychology of their relationship is not closely explored; the tale begins with Hester's standing on the scaffold, with the main action in the past already, and there are no flashbacks, so our knowledge of it remains imprecise This refines our attention and concentrates it on the general significance.

Hawthorne made Dimmesdale's guilt his killer:

---

1. Arvin, *Hawthorne*, 201-202.

> And thus, while standing on the scaffold, in this vain show of expiation, Mr Dimmesdale was overcome with a great horror of mind, as if the universe were gazing at a scarlet token on his naked breast, right over his heart. On that spot, in very truth, there was, and there had long been, the gnawing and poisonous tooth of bodily pain.[2]

Dimmesdale is too ravaged to respond to Hester's wish that he start a new life with her in another country. He ends his public confession by what Lawrence called "dodging into death".

The element of dishonesty and weakness in the Puritan high-mindedness calls into being in Dimmesdale a perverse impulse of negation. The duplicity gives rise to a rare spate of ironic humour in the novel, After meeting Hester in the woods and being torn between keeping to his vocation and beliefs and going away with her, Dimmesdale has outbreaks of irreverence, including dropping into the ear of a devout parishioner "a brief, pithy, and, as it appeared to him then, unanswerable argument against the immortality of the human soul". This demonstrates "his sympathy and fellowship with wicked mortals and the world of perverted spirits". The Loerke-like theme of subversive malignancy – the outcome of neurotically suppressed life – is analysed further in Roger Chillingworth. He is a man of science and medicine who, having failed with Hester, appoints himself Dimmesdale's physician and hounds him with jealous malevolence towards a physical and moral breakdown:

> In a word, old Roger Chillingworth was a striking evidence of man's faculty of transforming himself into a devil, if he will only, for a reasonable space of time, undertake a devil's office. This unhappy person had effected such a transformation by devoting himself, for seven years, to the constant analysis of a heart full of torture, and deriving his enjoyment thence, and adding fuel to those fiery tortures which he analysed and gloated over. (170)

This theme shows itself in the other main characters: we are shown signs of the witch and sorceress in Hester, and of the demon in her daughter Pearl.

The duality between the high-mindedness and the answering malignity is explored in all the main characters, and a regenerative positive sought out. When Hester Prynne walking in the forest with Dimmesdale seven years after her public disgrace flings away the

---

2. *The Scarlet Letter*, Centenary edition, 148. Subsequent page references are to this edition.

stigma of adultery that is pinned to her breast and lets her hair fall down around her shoulders:

> The objects that had made a shadow hitherto, embodied the brightness now. The course of the little brook might be traced by its merry gleam afar into the wood's heart of mystery, which had become a mystery of joy.
>
> Such was the sympathy of Nature – that wild, heathen Nature of the forest, never subjugated by human law, nor illumined by higher truth – with the bliss of these two spirits! Love, whether newly born, or aroused from a deathlike slumber, must always create a sunshine, filling the heart so full of radiance, that it overflows upon the outward world. (203)

The scarlet letter itself stands for the glory as well as the sin of sexual sensuality. They are embodied in Pearl, who is, as Lawrence put it, "the scarlet letter incarnate".[3] Hester's potential is blighted, her beauty turns austere, but whatever creative outcome remains possible resides in her (and her daughter's) surviving the struggle and in her understanding and accepting her own and society's guilt, and her own and society's rightness. She eventually becomes one to whom

> people brought all their sorrows and perplexities, and besought her counsel, as one who had herself gone through a mighty trouble. Women, more especially – in the continually recurring trials of wounded, wasted, wronged, misplaced, or erring and sinful passion – or with the dreary burden of a heart unyielded, because unvalued and unsought – came to Hester's cottage demanding why they were so wretched, and what the remedy! Hester comforted and counselled them, as best she might. She assured them, too, of her firm belief, that, at some brighter period, when the world should have grown ripe for it, in Heaven's own time, a new truth would be revealed, in order to establish the whole relation between man and woman on a surer ground of mutual happiness. (263)

In spite of the fact that in the final version of his essay Lawrence debunked the piety with which Hawthorne invests his heroine, and stressed her destructiveness from Dimmesdale's point of view, the general pattern of Hester's experience, from her suffering at the hands of idealism to her final regenerative stance, is similar in design to features of *Women in Love*.

---

3. Lawrence, "Nathaniel Hawthorne", 1st version (1919), in *Studies in Classic American Literature*, 251. Most of Lawrence's best observations on *The Scarlet Letter* are to be found in the first version of his essay. The final version kept them but dished them up with scornful remarks about the American way of life.

These themes run throughout Hawthorne's other novels, which are structured in similar ways. The rigidity and isolation brought about through pride and egoism are contrasted with the need for belonging, and the ideologies supporting the former are brought under scrutiny. In *The Blithedale Romance*, for example, the theme of ruinous high-mindedness – the "inflexible severity of purpose" he admits to – is analysed in Hollingsworth, who is willing to sacrifice every other consideration to his scheme for the reform of criminals:

> He had taught his benevolence to pour its warm tide exclusively through one channel; so that there was nothing to spare for other great manifestations of love to man, nor scarcely for the nutriment of individual attachments, unless they could minister, in some way, to the terrible egotism he mistook for an angel of God.[4]

The Hester theme recurs in the sensuous Zenobia – her potential destroyed in the conflict with Hollingsworth. Her emblem is the rose, "exotic, of rare beauty" which she always wears in her hair. The shadowy, evil-minded Westervelt who makes the narrator's flesh creep, and the Pearl-like Priscilla, wayward "like a butterfly at play in a flickering bit of sunshine" but somewhat clinging and secretive, like what is called her "symbol," the silk purse she is making, and ultimately untrustworthy – these make up the rest of a structure we are familiar with from *The Scarlet Letter*.

In *The House of the Seven Gables* the parallels are not so close, but some of the same themes are pursued. There the malign human tendencies proceed from the ferociously acquisitive Colonel Pyncheon, founder of the family, and focus on the contemporary Judge Pyncheon, "a determined and relentless man, with the genuine character of an inquisitor". He dominates his sickly or enfeebled cousins Clifford and Hepzibah but has no effect on Phoebe, "graceful as a bird, and graceful in much the same way; as pleasant about the house as a gleam falling on the floor through a shadow of twinkling leaves" who not only brightens Clifford's and Hephzibah's lives but challenges the remote impersonality of the artist Holgrave and renews him in marrying him:

> And it was in this hour, so full of doubt and awe, that the one miracle was wrought, without which every human existence is a blank .... They transfigured the earth, and made it Eden again, and themselves the two first dwellers in it. The dead man, so close beside them, was forgotten. At such a crisis, there is no Death; for

---

4. *The Blithedale Romance*, Centenary edition, 55.

Immortality is revealed anew, and embraces everything in its hallowed atmosphere.[5]

As we have seen, Hawthorne can be said to have influenced George Eliot's *Silas Marner,* and we are about to see his impact on Melville. Henry James admired him, of course, and wrote a fine book on him, but he interpreted his work chiefly in terms of character studies. There is enough of that to justify the approach, but James neglected the poetic aspect, just as he had done with Dickens. Lawrence was the first major novelist after Hawthorne's death to appreciate the structure of his novels.

Herman Melville was Hawthorne's friend, and gratefully received his influence alongside that of Dickens, which was in the very air they both breathed – their families avidly following the current practice of reading his novels aloud as soon as they were published. It is fitting that something like the egomania of *Dombey and Son* (1848) should join forces with the religious fanaticism of *The Scarlet Letter* (1850) to contribute to *Moby Dick* (1851). That novel has all the features of the kind of thematic novel we are looking for, in a more striking form than Hawthorne's.

The centre of critical attention is again held by an incarnation of the Puritan consciousness – this time in a man more like Gerald Crich.[6] Ahab characterizes obsession and desperation. He spends his life almost totally isolated, with his normal responses suppressed. In the first two-thirds of the book one sees him sternly repudiating his human inclinations – he even throws his pipe overboard as a gesture of self-defiance – and only after the idiot boy, Pip, has awakened his sympathies does he vent his misgivings, which reveal in his past a wife abandoned the day after their wedding and a son he hardly knows. He admits that "the madness" that governs him has made him "more a demon than a man". The conflict within him provokes nightmares, visions of hell, and then:

> with glaring eyes Ahab would burst from his state-room as though escaping from a bed that was on fire .... For at such times, crazy Ahab, the scheming, unappeasedly steadfast hunter of the white whale; this Ahab that had gone to his hammock, was not the agent that so caused him to burst from it in horror again. The latter was the

---

5. *The House of the Seven Gables*, Centenary edition, 307.
6. For a comparison of Ahab and Gerald, see Richard Swigg, *Lawrence, Hardy and American Literature*, 323-27.

eternal, living principle or soul in him; and in sleep, being for the time dissociated from the characterizing mind, which at other times it employed for its outer vehicle or agent, it spontaneously sought escape from the scorching contiguity of the frantic thing, of which, for the time, it was no longer an integral.[7]

To Ahab the whale-hunt is a witch-hunt – the book in this matter depicts, as does The Scarlet Letter, a morbid Puritanism turning against natural response. Ahab's perverse crusade is in revenge not merely for losing his leg but for the inner torment he has created for himself. He projects his own destructive impulses on the white whale, which becomes "the monomaniac incarnation of all those malicious agencies which some deep men feel eating in them". Out of his fear and loathing he becomes a martyr in the devil's cause. His purpose, as Starbuck sees, is "heaven-insulting".

In association with Ahab's mentality, "whiteness" in the novel becomes representative (as it does at Gerald Crich's death) of

> the heartless voids and immensities of the universe .... There is such a dumb blankness, full of meaning, in a wide landscape of snows – a colorless, all-color of atheism from which we shrink. (195)

But of course whiteness in the great whale Moby Dick has opposite connotations. Dualism, ambiguity and opposition is as pervasive in the imagery of this novel (and in its entire structure) as it is in *Women in Love*, and the texture of the prose (at its best) as highly charged, metaphorically and rhythmically.

The association of Ahab's mentality with the non-human world is achieved as in *Women in Love*; the poetic association of the human and non-human as strong in this novel as in *Wuthering Heights*. It evokes, for instance, the fascination Ahab finds in "the horrors of the half-known life" of the sea, "all whose creatures prey upon each other, carrying on eternal war since the world began". And it gives vivid pictures of atrocities such as those of the sharks crowded around a whale's carcase and eating their own damaged entrails.

Ahab's power over his crew is achieved partly through arrogance and partly through a kind of mesmerism whereby he seeks to turn them into the instruments of his will; but the mesmerism is successful only in his drawing upon and utilizing (as Gerald Crich does) that part of their experience of life which is similar to his own: "my cogged circle fits into all their wheels, and they revolve .... The path to my

---

7. *Moby Dick*, Northwestern-Newberry edition, 202. Subsequent page references are to this edition.

fixed purpose is laid on iron rails." They acquiesce and the ship "freighted with savages, and laden with fire, and burning a corpse, and plunging into that blackness and darkness, seemed the material counterpart of her commander's soul".

In that microcosm traditional principle is pitched against the absence of principle and every exponent is vividly individual. The first mate, Starbuck, is a man of Christian principle and traditional pieties (he is also an expert killer of whales and guardian of the shipowners' commercial interests). He opposes Ahab's unholy crusade, but his powers are not strong enough to enable him either to persuade the rest of the crew to refuse Ahab's challenge or to stand alone in opposition. Ahab's denial of life is too potent: "My soul is more than matched; she is overmanned; and by a madman!" At the other end of the scale of values is the ghoulish crew Ahab has collected to man his own boat for the final hunt. At their head is the fire-worshipping, prophesying Fedallah – "the devil in disguise" Stubbs calls him – with his inscrutable face distorting occasionally into "sneering triumph" at Ahab's recklessness, while he reserves for himself a "fatalistic despair".

Melville's fascinated identification with Ahab evokes the "unexampled intelligent malignity" of the whale, but Moby Dick eventually appears in his natural majesty – "a grand god" – to defend his life against Ahab's attack:

> At length the breathless hunter came so nigh his seemingly unsuspecting prey, that his entire dazzling hump was distinctly visible, sliding along the sea as if an isolated thing, and continually set in a revolving ring of finest, fleecy, greenish foam. He saw the vast, involved wrinkles of the slightly projecting head beyond. Before it, far out on the soft Turkish-rugged waters, went the glistening white shadow from his broad, milky forehead, a musical rippling playfully accompanying the shade; and behind, the blue waters interchangeably flowed over the moving valley of his steady wake; and on either hand bright bubbles arose and danced by his side. (548)

It hardly needs the simile that follows, comparing Moby Dick with Jupiter carrying off Europa, to confirm the truth of Lawrence's observation that he represents "our deepest blood-nature" – or if that phrase appears too Lawrencian, some basic sensual (and specifically sexual) power which not surprisingly turns nasty when threatened. Melville, Lawrence continued, was "passionately filled with the sense of the vastness and mystery of life which is non-human" – life in which the creative eventually triumphs over the destructive, even in the act of destruction. There is an equally potent sense of wonder at people and their means of survival. We see it in the analytical vividness of the minor characters: a vividness sometimes Dickensian, as with Peleg the carpenter, "a pure manipulator; his brain, if he ever had one, must have early oozed along into the muscles of his finger" – or Bildad:

> When Bildad was a chief-mate, to have his drab-colored eye intently
> looking at you, made you feel completely nervous, till you could
> clutch something – a hammer or a marling-spike, and go to work like
> mad, at something or other, never mind what. Indolence and idleness
> perished before him. His own person was the exact embodiment of
> his utilitarian character. (74-75)

With these figures the writing penetrates to what Melville called their "unaccountable life-principle". And in what Lawrence called "the magnificent records of actual happenings" there is a strong sense of the insatiable and indomitable in the involvements of life, including the relish of exploration, discovery, even mere information – as also in specific relationships like the friendship of Ishmael and Queequeg, which begins by their sharing a bed in the Nantucket inn and ends when Queequeg's coffin becomes Ishmael's lifebuoy.

Lawrence praised *Moby Dick* as a book of "profound significance" but added, "and of considerable tiresomeness".[8] The mixture is found in Melville's other books, his full imaginative power operating more patchily. The themes identified here recur from first to last. For example let us to take only the first and the last. The values endorsed in *Moby Dick* surface first in the buoyant high spirits of *Typee,* which celebrates Melville's discovery among the Marquesans of the antithesis of his Calvinistic upbringing: the Typees' physical beauty and natural, spontaneous behaviour are pointedly contrasted with the changes the missionaries brought about in some of the other Pacific islanders. And at the end of Melville's career the same positives shine in the picture of Billy Budd, beautiful, innocent and dangerous like the white whale himself, likened as he is to the Greek gods and also to the "barbarians" who are "closer to unadulterated nature". In that last tale the answering theme of "malignity" appears in the master-at-arms, Claggart, whose enmity towards Billy is partly motivated by vulgar envy and suppressed homosexuality – "that glance would follow the cheerful sea-Hyperion with a settled meditative and melancholy expression, his eyes strangely suffused with incipient feverish tears" –

---

8. Lawrence, *Studies in Classic American Literature*, 146.

but activated also by the "mania of an evil nature". Like Ahab he is driven to hunt down and destroy the being whose very beauty and innocence is an offence to him. His alliance with the political anxieties and rule-book mentality of Captain Vere and his officers accomplishes Billy's death. Even in this comparatively slight tale, the various themes are tied in together as we have seen in the novels of Lawrence, Dickens and Hawthorne.

The impact of *Moby Dick* bypassed Henry James (who gave no sign of recognition) and Conrad (who was decidedly hostile) and fell on Lawrence. Reading it in February 1916, just before the first revision of *Women in Love,* was an inspiration (especially perhaps in the handling of Gerald Crich).

6

FRENCH TRADITIONS

Stendhal, Balzac, Zola and Flaubert

Lawrence's reading of the French novels that extend from Stendhal to Zola was not very extensive but was a vital contribution to that part of his literary development which led to the creation of his thematic novels.

Le Rouge et le Noir made a big impression on Lawrence when he read it in French while drafting the second version of "Paul Morel" which was later to become *Sons and Lovers*. He wrote: "I feel so much like Julien Sorel."[1] The two novels share the themes of spontaneous life thwarted and perverted by conscious preconceptions. Stendhal was, like Lawrence at the time of *Sons and Lovers*, equally interested both in the psychology of his characters and in his more general themes, and managed to correlate them more effectively than Lawrence.

He adopted an episodic structure with some abrupt transitions that reminds one at times of Dickens, and as in a Dickens novel the narrative directs the psychological mechanism of the scenes so as to highlight the themes, separating out the values as through a moral prism, though with a comparative paucity of the poetic dimension, which made Lawrence complain that "he misses out the religion, the philosophy if you like, of life ... he doesn't satisfy my sentimentality".[2] It was a complaint he might have made of the French tradition generally, as far as he knew it.

There may not have been much attraction for him in Stendhal's handling of the theme of "*l'âme commune*" as represented by figures like Valenod and M. de Rénal, in whom a mixture of insulated self-importance and craven conformism is satirized with a vehemence recalling Molière, nor for the variants that appear in high society and

---

1. Lawrence to Louie Burrows, 28 April 1911, in *Letters*, I, 262.
2. *Ibid*, 262.

in the church. But he undoubtedly reacted with interest to the other themes, which showed him some of the options available though a technique more integrated than his current practice. Stendhal explored them through the experience of the two major female characters, with Julien in the middle, the focus of their conflict.

Mme de Rénal, Julien's first love, offers "*le naturel et la vivacité de l'esprit*" and a truly spontaneous and unselfconscious affection which he eventually comes to value above all else. She is not only an embodiment of the theme, but also a closely observed psychological study with complications of her own. We see her, for instance, in the comedy and pathos of her falling in love with Julien, developing the selfish, obsessional aspects of *l'amour-passion*, and later she is driven by her training to acquiesce in the priest-dictated letter that denounces Julien and provokes the tragedy.

There is a complex portrayal of idealism in Mathilde. She is constantly posturing in the mirror of her own self-regard and measuring her simulated response against the ideals of nobility she derives from the medieval phase of her family's history: "This young girl of high society only lets her heart be moved when she has proved to herself by very good reasons that it ought to feel emotion." Like Hermione in *Women in Love* she is obsessed with what is due to her on account of this consciousness of noble feelings – obsessed, that is, with the will "to dominate all around her". Julien Sorel is a match for her in this respect, and the relationship works out some of the discrepancies between desire and action and the interplay of domination and submission that Lawrence was suggesting between Miriam and Paul in *Sons and Lovers* and later worked out between Hermione and Birkin. As with the latter pair, the conflicts are pointed towards the universals of the theme:

> Il n'y avait rien de tendre dans ses sentiments de ce premier moment. C'était le plus vif bonheur d'ambition ....
>
> A la vérité, ces transports étaient un peu *voulus*. L'amour passionne était encore plutôt un modèle qu'on imitait qu'une réalité.
>
> Mademoiselle de la Mole croyait remplir un devoir envers elle-même et envers son amant.[3]

---

3. *Le Rouge et le Noir*, in *Romans et Nouvelles*, ed. Henri Martineau, I, 541-43. In C.K. Scott Moncrieff's translation it runs: "There was nothing tender in his sentiments at this first moment. What he felt was the keen gratification of his ambition .... To tell the truth, their transports were somewhat deliberate. Passionate love was far more a model they were imitating than a reality with them. Mademoiselle de la Mole believed that she was performing a duty towards herself and

A see-saw of pride and lust, the one stimulating as well as distorting the other, sways within Mathilde, and between her and Julien, who is alternately adored as her master – "He is worthy to be my master, since he was just about to kill me" – and disdained as her servant: "Mathilde, sure of being loved, felt utter contempt for him." When his pride is most murderous she is most his "slave". Her erotic imagination needs the constant stimulus of histrionics or art. Like *Women in Love*, the novel scornfully depicts the conventions of "*l'amour de tête*" but it also develops a sympathetic appreciation of the lovers' predicament as "*l'amour-passion*" grows under its cover.

The last part of the story explores in Julien himself the irreconcilable features of the conflict – a path that Paul Morel does not take. Julien is not just a man "at war with society" but at war with himself: "*l'homme a deux êtres en lui*" he reflects towards the end. On the one hand is his pride, will and ambition – the man of power seeking the approval of his fellows if only to dominate them – and on the other his "kind-heartedness quick to sympathize [*la bonté facile à s'attendrir*]" with its need to love and be loved and the dreamer's love of beauty and truth: all those faculties that are suppressed in the concentration on his career. The catastrophe is brought on in a series of self-contradictory reactions that arrive with a shock, without premeditation, and are often too quickly succeeded by the next to allow much reflection. The focus is on his psychology and at the same time equally on the general human conflict represented. At the height of his worldly success, isolated, exhausted and frustrated by the role-playing and lies that have brought it about, Julien reacts like a madman to Mme de Rénal's letter of denunciation: he shoots and wounds her. It is a revolution in his psyche which brings the suppressed faculties uppermost, where they take a revenge that includes the suicidal (that is there in the shooting, since it carries the death penalty) as well bringing, in prison, the "happiness" of his sense of inner release, the freedom of "*le naturel*". He feels happy partly at the death of his old self and partly at the thought of death itself – the neurotic symptom of his breakdown and despair. Then the counter-revolution that the old Julien, hand-in-glove with the suicidal, stages in the courtroom, vindicating his actions, insulting the jurors and

---

towards her lover." For the reader's convenience, most of the other quotations from the novel are from this translation.

calling for the death penalty shows that the discord is inextinguishable except in the physical death to which it leads.

The ending of the novel forces us (in the words of the epigraph to Chapter 40) "to follow the underground workings of the passions" although the clues to them are given with extraordinary economy, for Stendhal wanted to say "things that are great or profoundly beautiful ... with the utmost simplicity, as if one were striving to prevent them from being noticed".[4] The book was not always regarded as a masterpiece, not even by Henry James, who held Stendhal otherwise in high esteem. Lawrence was the second major English novelist (after Conrad) to respond to it with enthusiasm.

The theme of *l'âme généreuse*, which is jointly represented in *Le Rouge et le Noir* by Julien and Mme de Rénal recurred of course in Stendhal's other writings. It involved pre-eminently, according to Margaret Tillett, a "capacity for intensity and range of feeling, and strength of imaginative sympathy".[5] In his diaries we see Stendhal struggling towards the kind of complex balance that eludes Julien Sorel. That struggle permeates the action of *La Chartreuse de Parme.* Idealising "divine love" persists there also, most memorably as an element in Fabrice's genuine passion for Clelia, when all he can do is gaze at her through a hole in his prison shutters. However, in this novel Stendhal was less concerned with underlining his general themes (though he regularly ticked them off in passing) than with working out the complicated relations of four complex characters in whom the tendencies are intertwined. Lawrence, immersed in the final didactic phase of his own work when he reread it in 1927, was in no mood to do the book justice.[6]

Lawrence read only two novels each by Balzac and Zola during his formative period, as far as the evidence shows.[7] There is no call here

---

4. Stendhal to Pauline Beyle, 20 August 1805, in *Correspondance*, eds Martineau and del Litto, I, 213; translated by Norman Cameron, *To the Happy Few*, 68.
5. Tillett, *Stendhal: The Background to the Novels,* 4. In such natures, according to Stendhal, generosity is not a principle but an impulse as spontaneous as self-interest. They need constant energetic change, but also solitude and *"la rêverie tendre".*
6. Writing to Aldous Huxley on 2 September 1928 (*Letters*, VI, 543) Lawrence called *La Chartreuse de Parme* "so good historically, socially and all that – but emotionally rather empty and trashy".
7. Lawrence read at least the two Balzac novels we mention. In 1916 he said he knew of Zola only *Germinal,* in spite of having five years before offered Louie Burrows copies of *L'Assommoir* and *La Débâcle.* All three were available at that time in the Vizetelly translations reprinted by Chatto.

to rehearse all the themes of *La Comédie Humaine* and the Rougon-Macquart series. They were not themselves a powerful direct influence on his work, but their influence on other novelists was so wide-ranging that they became an important part of the tradition Lawrence inherited.

Balzac's novels are driven by themes but focused on individuals. Character studies are combined into a story which reveals the people's virtues and maladies and searches out causes and effects, both psychological and social. In the extraordinary variety of these figures and the detail of their setting we see what his admirer, Henry James, called the "historian's impulse" to record and his skill in "putting people on their feet, planting them before us in their habit as they lived".[8]

There were enough compatibilities of response to make Lawrence declare him "vastly sympathetic .... Balzac can lay bare the living body of the great Life better than anybody".[9] At the age of twenty-three, when he made this statement, he might well have enjoyed the vigorous Dickensian endorsement of unanalysed goodness and nobility to be seen, for example, in Goriot, a monolith of "noble passion" in stark and pathetic contrast to the egoists in that novel, including the daughters he adores. And in *Eugénie Grandet* – "one of the finest novels out of the heart of man" – one might spot a germ of Ursula Brangwen. When Eugénie is in love, "It was as though the distant hopes that had begun to bud in her heart had suddenly burst into bloom like a great mass of flowers" – though her romantic aspirations with her equally naive young man are trampled underfoot by her father. Frustrated, she begins to show signs of some of his traits, though not his meanness, and ends a rich, lonely, charitable old maid. When Lawrence came (in *The Lost Girl*) to re-envisage Arnold Bennett's portrait of Sophia Baines (in *The Old Wives' Tale*) whose promise, taking a different course, ends in a similar state of resignation, he may have had Eugénie's fate also in mind.

He liked Balzac well enough to continue reading novels like *La Lys dans la vallée* into the late nineteen-twenties. John Collier, a social worker who met Lawrence in New Mexico around 1922, recalled evenings at Mabel Luhan's when Lawrence read out loud a translation of Balzac's tale *Seraphita* and the "kindly satire and irony"

8. James, *Selected Literary Criticism*, 194.
9. Lawrence to Blanche Jennings, November 1908, in *Letters*, I, 89-91. He was reading the translation of *Eugénie Grandet* by Ellen Marriage, which we quote. It retained its place in the Everyman Library throughout the following century.

of his reading "made of this Balzac writing the supreme example of sentimentalism, triumphant and unashamed".[10]

Much of Zola's best work consists, like Balzac's, of character studies with social connotations: the long process of Gervaise Macquart's degradation in *L'Assommoir*, for instance, relentlessly detailed yet unfailingly sympathetic. It might well have appealed to Lawrence's sympathies, although his acquaintance with that novel is uncertain. The appeal of both novelists was strongest in that phase of his writing (off our designated map) which includes the early tales and *Sons and Lovers*. As his thematic drives took over it lapsed.

Germinal was perhaps an exception. It was one of those later novels of Zola's where he was moving away from the documentary style into another which in its distortion of actuality has been likened to post-impressionism in painting. Wider universals are emphasized, often in poetic terms, and this brings these novels closer to the kind of thematic structure we are investigating. For example, in *Germinal* there is a symbolic correlation between the underground mine, the oppressed lives of the miners, and their repressed instincts, which are liable to break out violently.

The theme of egoistic greed is explored partly in terms of its effect on the industrial scene. Zola's abomination of the squalor shows as strong as Dickens's or Lawrence's. The place is another Coketown or Tevershall:

> To the right the view was impeded by the colossal mountain of shale, resembling a barricade thrown up by giants, and already covered in some of its older parts with sprouting grass, while at the other end internal fire had been smouldering for the last twelve months, emitting dense columns of smoke, and leaving long tracks of blood-like rust on the surface .... There remained of the night's vision the incessant puffing of the pumping-engine, ever panting with the same long hoarse gasp, the breath of an insatiable ogre.[11]

There is also a critique of idealistic responses to the industrial set-up, which would have struck a chord in Lawrence. The hero of the book, Etienne Lantier starts by idealising the proletariat, enjoying the vanity of leadership over them and manifesting the "obsession of the fanatic". He ends in disillusion with the mob, detesting the bourgeoisie as much as ever (though Zola retained his admiration of

---

10. J. Collier, in Nehls, *D.H. Lawrence: A Composite Biography*, II, 198.
11. *Germinal*, Part I, Chapter 6. The edition used here is the one Lawrence probably read, edited and partially translated by Ernest Alfred Vizetelly and published by Chatto in 1901. This passage appears on pages 59-60.

ordinary good-hearted people, middle-class or not, such as the Gregoires).

Zola's regeneration theme is strongly felt, but its terms were too broad to have much to offer Lawrence. After the high melodrama and sentimentalism of the scenes in the mineshaft when he kills his rival, consummates his love and then watches her die, Etienne's despair is tempered by his remembrance of her and of his comrades. Zola's faith in renewal, which has been grimly voiced at the spectacle of teenagers making love in the ruins of a disused pit – "the powers of creation were taking their revenge" – gets Etienne's endorsement on the last page of the book:

> The April sun was now high in the sky, radiant in all its glory, warming the pregnant earth. From her nourishing flanks life sprang forth once more, buds were breaking into leaf, fields throbbed with sprouting grass.

It has a Hardyesque flavour which may have appealed to Lawrence.[12]

Gustave Flaubert too was an influence in Lawrence's phase of social and psychological realism, but his impact was more profound and enduring, for in spite of his concentration on circumstantial exactitude he was essentially a thematic novelist. His standing among Lawrence's older contemporaries, including James and Conrad, was high. Particularly admired was his stance of impersonal detachment – "The author in his book must be like God in the universe, present everywhere and visible nowhere"[13] – which was particularly crucial to him when he made this statement because of his effort to stand clear of Emma Bovary's predicament. Some of the next generation resisted and repudiated. Joyce put into the mouth of Stephen Dedalus an ironic parody of Flaubert's dictum. Lawrence's first responses have not survived, but four years later, in 1910, he was standing out against the pretensions of the "impersonal, like Turgenev or Flaubert. I say no".[14] By 1913 he was diagnosing in Flaubert a "loathing of himself": he

---

12. The resurgence of human vitality under the stimulus of nature is a note often sounded by Giovanni Verga, who was called the Sicilian Zola. He does not figure as a formative influence on Lawrence, since he did not read him until 1922. Lawrence praised "the great picture of poor life in Sicily" and liked the portrait of Gesualdo, whose decline is monitored with a relentlessness and sympathy that recalls Gervaise in Zola's *L'Assommoir*.
13. Flaubert to Louise Colet, 9 December 1852, in *Correspondance*, ed. Jean Bruneau, II, 204; translated by Francis Steegmuller, *Letters*, I, 173.
14. Lawrence to Louie Burrows, 9 September 1910, in *Letters*, I, 178.

"stood away from life as from a leprosy".[15] This may sound a far cry from the pages of the novels, though it is explicit enough in *The Temptation of Saint Anthony*, which Lawrence may have read by then.

Lawrence's interest in Flaubert focused primarily on *Madame Bovary*, and in that novel on Emma herself. In her are explored the themes of idealism and egoism – interactive as they are in Lawrence – in such a way that (partly through the intensity of the author's identification with her and his corresponding effort of impersonality) she is fused with them, her psychological malady offered as a universal or at least all-pervasive one.

The handling of its other themes was not likely to have attracted Lawrence's admiration. Flaubert's absorption in Emma's fate leaves little room for the portrayal of what is sacrificed. The positives in the novel are weakened by the invasive cancer of egoism, the dominant theme of the novel from which no part of it is immune except one slight figure that is *ex machina*. Charles Bovary, of course, is the chief victim of the tragedy and the only character with continuous and developing affectionate responses: the only one to love Emma, suffering at her illnesses, mourning her death and forgiving her adultery, and the only one to look after their daughter. But his affections are disqualified by his stupidity, which functions for most of the novel (in Emma's eyes) as one of the features of a sordid and insentient environment. His right feelings, combined with his blindness, complacency and incompetence, only make them the more "wrong" for Emma. Good intentions without understanding appear, from the viewpoint that prevails in the book, to be yet another kind of egoism, locked in itself. The only untainted positive moral standpoint in the book (for young Justin is merely an embryonic Emma) appears in the final death scenes in the shape of Dr Larivière, "one of a now-vanished generation of philosopher-healers who cherished their art with fanatical love and practised it with zeal and sagacity".

The other subsidiary theme, the aspect of egoism named *"le vulgaire"* – the unimaginative preoccupation with what can be felt, measured and added to the self – has its purest embodiment in Homais, the self-important and avaricious chemist. But the obsessive virulence of Flaubert's contempt towards that kind of mentality Lawrence did not entirely share.

---

15. Lawrence, "Thomas Mann" (1913), in *Phoenix*, ed. Edward McDonald, 312.

Emma's, however, is a type of egoism that always interested Lawrence, who portrayed it in various forms, pre-eminently in Gudrun Brangwen in *Women in Love*, though he never gave it the central position it has here. For Emma the pettiness, meanness and stupidity of the life she leads and the people she lives with seem to justify an intense self-involvement and withdrawal. The idealism or *"lyrisme"* that obsesses her is, like Gudrun's, partly the result of the entrenched ego's sealing off normal contacts with others. From the beginning (even her girlish religious fantasies are required to "absorb her soul and swallow up her entire being") each attempt to escape from reality provokes a more desperate successor. She moves like Gudrun from one dreamworld to another, the role-playing more important than any reality. Even for her lovers her responses are for the images she can superimpose upon their inferior material. The affair with Leon, after the romance of "constructing an ideal of themselves" has lapsed, leaving her "sick of him as he was weary of her" finally makes clear (like Gudrun's with Gerald) her desperate disengagement and the neurotic function of their love-making.

> She still was not happy, she never had been. Whence came this insufficiency in life?.... Nothing was worth the trouble of seeking it; everything was a lie.[16]

It is a thought echoed by Gudrun. But Gudrun does not destroy herself.

Flaubert took the condition to the limit. Emma's failure to make sympathetic contact with the reality of anyone, husband, child or lover, is repeatedly shown, accompanied by spates of nervous illness which are the result of this frustration of her own vitality and her inability to go out of herself. Illusions and fantasies are sensitively invoked by the author and ruthlessly shed by a dissociative irony. The most radical of them is the glamour of Emma's femininity, which, at

---

16. *Madame Bovary*, Part III, Chapter 6. The translation is by Eleanor Marx-Aveling (1886, reprinted 1906) chosen here as the best of those available to Lawrence in 1906 (although he may have read it in French). He may have had access at some time in his life to a somewhat inferior anonymous translation published in 1902 with an introduction by Henry James. In his Introduction to *Mastro-Don Gesualdo* (1927) Lawrence seems to be echoing James's notion of a flawed discrepancy between author and subject in the novel. Compare Lawrence, "people such as Emma and her husband are simply too insignificant to carry the full weight of Gustave Flaubert's sense of tragedy" (*Phoenix*, ed. Edward McDonald, 226) with James: "Our complaint is that Emma Bovary, in spite of the nature of her consciousness and in spite of reflecting so much that of her creator, is really too small an affair" (James, *Selected Literary Criticism*, 222).

times indulgently handled, moves inexorably towards its demolition. The intensifying confinement generates further destructiveness. The obviousness and desirability of suicide is forced upon her. The consciousness that takes over in the end is that of Emma the suicidal, disappointed dreamer, finally isolated in death as she has always been essentially in her life.

The figure of the doctor in the last scenes (and its dramatic unreality) highlights the desperation which centres on Emma but pervades the entire texture of the writing with what Lawrence generously called Flaubert's "deep and bitter tragic consciousness". By the time Lawrence wrote that (1927) Flaubert had regained his respect. He was now a "great soul" whose "joy in its own consciousness ... is itself a refutation of the all-is-misery doctrine".[17]

---

17. *Phoenix II*, 281.

7

RUSSIAN TRADITIONS

Turgenev, Tolstoy and Dostoevsky

Lawrence's reading of the Russians, in the years when Constance Garnett's translations were making them available to English speakers, "meant", he said, "an enormous amount to me, Turgenev, Tolstoy, Dostoevsky – mattered almost more than anything, and I thought them the greatest writers of all time".[1]

Ivan Turgenev may well (like his friend, Flaubert) have led Lawrence part of the way towards adopting a thematic organization of his materials. Turgenev's novels are character-based, but as each of his characters is based on one or two concepts, the result is much like a neatly constructed small-scale thematic novel. Jessie Chambers reported that Lawrence liked them "immensely" in 1909.

Was he keen on the satirical portraits? – liberals like Rudin, whose death while waving a red flag on the barricades is virtually a suicide from the sense of the ineffectuality of his life, and ladies like Liza in *The Home of the Gentry*, who after falling in love with somebody else's husband renounces him and retires to a nunnery. These relate to Lawrence's as well as Turgenev's critical interest in liberal idealism. So too does Pavel Petrovich Kirsanov in *Fathers and Sons,* who survives on his position, elegance and good taste – "his fastidiously dry though passionate soul, with its touch of French cynicism" – making a discreet espousal of progress and principles while entrenched in his aristocratic position. Pretension, vanity and materialism among the Russian upper classes are treated by Turgenev with contempt, tinged with a cynicism more genial than Flaubert's.

His attention to an ideological variant brought his influence to bear on the evolution of at least one of Lawrence's major themes. *Fathers and Sons* is dominated by its one main character, Bazarov, and he is

---

1. Lawrence to Catherine Carswell, 2 December 1916, in *Letters*, III, 45.

dominated by his ruling passion, which makes him resemble
Crich in *Women in Love*: "I like to reject, my brain's made that way."
He has something too of the same dismissive scientific materialism
about people: "Human beings are like trees in a forest: no botanist is
going to occupy himself with each individual birch tree." His
intermittent enthusiasms for scientific study are succeeded by "dreary
boredom or vague restlessness". He is uncertain about his powers,
switching from assertive arrogance ("I am a giant") to his dying
comment on his parents' hopes for him: "That's all nonsense." Partly
as a result of their pressure and his reaction against it, he has become a
mistruster of human ideas, institutions and emotions – most of all the
latter. The resultant outlook on life – "What a monstrous business!
What futility!" – seeks justification in the current ideology of nihilism:
"We repudiate everything."

Like Gerald he falls for a woman (Anna) whose whole energy goes
in keeping her own balance safe, insulated against any shock that
might upset it. She is incapable of escaping from a neurotic
dependence on routine. She tells Bazarov: "I love what you call
comfort, and at the same time I have little desire to live."

Turgenev was demonstrating in Bazarov what he regarded as an
important social and moral theme, associated with the current
philosophy of nihilism, but was content with a sketch which leaves
several questions hanging. Is his affair with Anna simply promoted by
unlucky fate, or is it driven by the same sense of isolation, defeat and
rejection that motivates him elsewhere? Does that also relate to the
fatal carelessness of cutting himself whilst doing a post-mortem on a
typhus patient? The author sometimes even pointedly refuses to
interpret a situation:

> Was the truth, the whole truth to be found in their words? They could
> not themselves have said, and much less could the author.[2]

In the end he simply underlined the pathos of the outcome with a
picture of the parents, in "their hallowed, selfless love" tending their
son's grave. In the last words of the novel:

> However passionate, sinning and rebellious the heart hidden in the
> tomb, the flowers growing over it peep serenely at us with their
> innocent eyes; they tell us not of eternal peace alone, of that great
> peace of "indifferent" nature; they tell us too of eternal reconciliation
> and of life without end.

---

2. *Fathers and Sons*, Chapter 25, in Constance Garnett's translation, which Lawrence
probably used. This passage appears on page 307 of the Traveller's Library reissue.

Lawrence's later comments generally show exasperation with this kind of "pathos and bathos".[3]

He was not the only one to feel exasperated. In Dostoevsky's *The Possessed* Stepan Verhovensky exclaims: "'I don't understand Turgenev. That Bazarov of his is a fictitious figure, it does not exist anywhere.'" Stavrogin in that novel shows so close an affinity with Bazarov that he might be called Dostoevsky's attempt to do Turgenev's job better, especially as the novel also presents a satirical caricature of Turgenev himself, in the figure of Karmazinov. Many of Bazarov's features, such as the spoilt child/great man background, the association with nihilists, the fruitless love-affair with a self-contained woman, are there in Stavrogin, and all except the erotic are developed more richly and without the glamorous pathos. The suicidal trend is underlined, not passed over.

Admiration for Turgenev was high among Lawrence's older contemporaries, including James and Conrad, but faded among his peers in his own generation, such as Joyce: "a little dull … at times theatrical."[4] It was overshadowed of course by his two great compatriots.

Lawrence's profound response to Tolstoy was complicated by developments in his own art and in his personal life. When he first read *Anna Karenin* in 1905 he was deeply moved. May Chambers remembered many years later how "he sympathized to such a point of suffering".[5] Her sister Jessie reported that it was for Lawrence "the greatest novel in the world".[6] Nobody can doubt that it powerfully shaped his understanding of many of the subjects he was to explore in his work. But some ten years later he saw in it chiefly an attitude he repudiated, an approval on Tolstoy's part of the social condemnation that promotes the tragedy, a siding "with the community in condemnation of the aristocrat ... with the average against the exception".[7] He and Frieda had recently been in a predicament similar to that of Anna and Vronsky – she abandoning her husband and children to live with him in Italy – and they were fiercely fighting the

3. Lawrence to Lawrence Pollinger, 20 July 1929, in *Letters*, VII, 382.
4. James Joyce to Stanislaus Joyce, 18 September 1905, cit. Ellmann, *James Joyce*, 209.
5. May Chambers Holbrook, in Nehls, *D H. Lawrence: A Composite Biography*, III, 593.
6. Jessie Chambers, *D.H. Lawrence: A Personal Record*, 114.
7. Lawrence, 1915, in *A Study of Thomas Hardy*, 49.

negative aspects of the situation (although Vronsky of course creative genius and Frieda was made of tougher material than Anna).

In any case, by that time the kind of novel he needed to write was not Tolstoy's.[8] The distinction to be made between their artistic aims is parallel to that we have made between Lawrence and George Eliot. Tolstoy was ultimately interested more than anything else – more than any of the universals suggested by his ideas and symbols – in individuals, their development and relations. That, at any rate, is what is most valued in his work: the finest understanding (in the novel genre) of the most complex subject.

Broad subject-themes resembling Lawrence's do inhabit Tolstoy's novels, and sometimes, when the people are not strongly developed, one is aware of theme and character running alongside each other, with roughly equal attention being given to both. For example, something like Lawrence's critique of an idealistic mentality appears in the portrait of Sergius Koznishev, the "celebrated Moscow intellectual" in *Anna Karenin*, who sees his half-brother Levin as "full of contradictions" so that argument with him seems "too easy a victory". His categorical style of thinking often wins him, with the help of some careful dodging of the main issues, the arguments they do have, which bring up many of the questions raised in *Women in Love:* nationalism, democracy, education, productivity. On every one Koznishev offers self-important abstractions divorced from first-hand experience.

Towards the end of the novel, after Levin's marriage to Kitty, this middle-aged bachelor discovers Varenka, the high-minded woman whom Kitty, during her revulsion against life after being jilted by Vronsky, has come to admire. Varenka, like Sonya in *War and Peace*, is an adept at suppressing her feelings and attaining an altruistic nobility which the reader has to admire while suspecting in it a way of dodging life and embracing failure. She and Koznishev might seem to offer each other a way out of their self-enclosure.

> "Mlle Varenka, when I was very young I set before myself the ideal of the woman I loved and should be happy to call my wife. I have lived through a long life, and now for the first time I have met what I sought – in you. I love you, and offer my hand."

---

8. For a full-length discussion of parallels between the two novelists (regardless of structural distinctions), see Dorthe Engelhardt's *L.N. Tolstoy and D.H. Lawrence*, which is especially interesting on the technique of repetition in the two authors.

Koznishev was saying this to himself while he was ten paces from Varenka.[9]

He never says it to her, and it is clear that finally she does not want him to. The comic misfire – the way they both dally with the issue, funk it and relapse into their sterile inertia and separateness – comments upon the mentality they share and the supportive idealistic ideology they subscribe to. The scene draws our attention equally to the individuals and the mind-set they share with others.

But when we move into the same area in the mind of Anna's husband, Alexey Karenin, idealism and conscientiousness find a much deeper context. However much he merits his wife's accusation – "as for those lofty ideals of his, his passion for culture, religion, they are so many tools for advancement" –   he draws on our sympathy in unexpected ways.

> When returning from the races Anna had informed him of her relations with Vronsky, and immediately afterwards burst into tears, hiding her face in her hands, Karenin, for all the fury aroused in him against her, was aware at the same time of that emotional disturbance always produced in him by tears. Conscious of it, conscious that any expression of his feelings at that minute would be out of keeping with the position, he tried to suppress every manifestation of life in himself and so neither stirred nor looked at her. This was what had caused that strange expression of deathlike rigidity in his face which had so impressed Anna.[10]

Our attention moves away from the process of withdrawal itself into the individual in whom it is taking place. This of course is a trivial incident compared with the profound and overwhelming tumult of his contradictory feelings when Anna is dangerously ill with puerperal fever. For a while it forces on her and the reader not just a different view of him but radically enlarged sympathies. What emerges is not the desiccated Christian idealism of the senior civil servant but a child's longing:

> He suddenly felt that what he had regarded as nervous agitation was on the contrary a blissful spiritual condition that gave him all at once a new happiness he had never known. He did not think that the Christian law

---

9. *Anna Karenin*, 547. The translation is Constance Garnett's, which was known to Lawrence, and which was reissued for many years. Page references are to the one-volume Heinemann edition of 1972. The names of the characters used here for both *Anna Karenin* and *War and Peace* are those adopted by Louise and Aylmer Maude because they are more familiar to most readers.
10. *Ibid.*, 275.

that he had been all his life trying to follow, enjoined on him to forgive and love his enemies; but a glad feeling of love and forgiveness for his enemies filled his heart. He knelt down, and laying his head in the curve of her arm, which burned him as with fire through the sleeve, he sobbed like a little child.[11]

Later, his habitual mentality returns, and this new "feeling of tender sympathy" (strong enough to prompt a life-saving solicitude for the newborn girl, Vronsky's daughter) later becomes atrophied within a newer self-defensive and self-deceiving ideology derived from Lydia Ivanovna, which gives him a "tranquil elevation, thanks to which he could forget the things he did not wish to remember". Out of this comes the *volte-face* refusal of a divorce that precipitates Anna's suicide.

It is the range and depth of the attention given to the variables of individual development that distinguishes this study from anything similar in Lawrence's novels, such as Thomas Crich.

The same must be said of Levin. He is shown, like Birkin in *Women in Love*, to be full of ambitious idealism infused with generous sensitivity (though Levin's ambitions are more practical than Birkin's and his generosity warmer). His understanding parallels Birkin's to some extent. He is equally obsessed with generalities, but like Birkin he regards marriage as "the chief thing in life" and his longings for a more coherent way of life crystallize into his desire to marry Kitty: "In the whole world there was only one being able to unite in itself the universe and the meaning of life for him." However, whereas we find in Lawrence's novel the emphasis thrown on the factors whereby a balance is to be achieved – a blueprint of the necessities – the best central scenes of Tolstoy's actually give us the experience of it. Levin's mowing with the peasants, for example, creates for him the kind of harmony between mind and body and between the individual, the collective and the natural that Birkin is only striving to reach.

In the main story of Anna and Vronsky any thematic issues are overridden by the attention to complex individuals. Vronsky could be seen at first as someone trapped in the folly of living according to the Officer code. He is also in the early chapters diagnosed as one whose insensitivity (in the first place to Kitty, whom he flirts with and blithely abandons, and then to Froufrou, the mare whose back he clumsily break in the steeplechase) is a dangerous liability for anyone in a close connection with him. But his love of Anna drives him into an area where his nature is tested against hers, and sympathy for his

---

11. *Ibid.*, 404.

difficulties, and eventually his suffering, over-rules any categorical judgment of him.

Anna herself is altogether too many-sided to function as the embodiment of a theme, but what she tells her sister-in-law Dolly Oblonsky at the start – "I should so like you all to love me as I love you" – is the keynote of her nature. We are always on her side in her struggle for more life, more interchange, than people will give her. Her capacity for love is stifled: that is the tragedy. She is crushed by other people's legitimate human needs. Vronsky needs to belong to people, to have a "position" and settle into a social context, so he wants the divorce. Karenin needs to preserve his mask, so he refuses it. Her son too (whom she loves at least as much as Vronsky) insulates himself to save himself from more hurt. Respectable people need to preserve their own relationships by keeping Anna at a distance and repudiating what she has done. All her lifelines are cut. Her suicide is a wild act of revenge on people for withholding their love. For the main story of Anna and Vronsky there is no equivalent in Lawrence. It evokes tragic sympathies beyond the range of his novels.

In *War and Peace* the searching out of universals is more to the fore, especially of the regenerative kind, and occasionally in poetic terms. The widower Prince Andrew, for instance, visiting the Rostovs, overhears the sixteen-year-old Natasha expressing her youthful aspirations, feels rejuvenated, and on his departure notices a tree which only a few weeks earlier he had identified with himself as "finished":

> The old oak, utterly transformed draped in a tent of sappy dark green, basked faintly, undulating in the rays of the evening sun. Of the knotted fingers, the gnarled excrescences, the aged grief and mistrust – nothing was to be seen.[12]

But this image is not so much the articulation of a broad theme, like those in Dickens and Lawrence, as part of the psychological map of a character. It is difficult of course to assess the poetic quality of such a passage through a translation, but it is clear that its focus is on the individual.

Natasha herself is a vividly realized individual rather than a touchstone of regeneration. She shares with Andrew's sister (who is superficially plain) the spontaneous, self-escaping sympathy which gives them both their beauty, and is the only creative power that can

---

12. *War and Peace*, Book VI, Chapter 3. The translation is Constance Garnett's (probably the one known to Lawrence) in the edition of 1904.

match the destructiveness that rages through the story
surface parallels with Ursula Brangwen. She has a fierce hunger for
life that drives her, like Ursula, into a sensual entanglement (with
Anatole Kuragin) and subsequent shame and breakdown. Her
experiences, like Ursula's, produce an enlargement of her sympathies
which makes her eventually ready to become Pierre's wife. But the
focus throughout is on the total development of a specific individual.

It is Pierre who has an abundance of generalities: "I desire
regeneration" he says to the Masons, and whole chapters are devoted
to his fruitless search among them for blanket answers to his particular
problems. Later, coping with the horrors of his experience of the war,
he engages in a series of ideological manoeuvres necessary for his
psychological survival, latching on to the wise passivity he sees in the
peasant, Platonov Karataev, who "loved and lived affectionately with
everything life brought him". He seizes on a vision of the wholeness
of nature that seems to compensate for the loss and suffering of so
many lives (his thoughts growing more simplified and ironically more
optimistic as the dangers increase). So that when he returns to Natasha
as a prospective husband he carries as much intellectual baggage of
the "Salvator Mundi" kind as Birkin when he meets Ursula in *Women
in Love*. Nevertheless, like Birkin, the central, saving focus of his life
remains the woman: "That terrible question: Why? what for? which
had till then haunted him in the midst of every occupation, was not
now replaced by any other question nor by an answer to the old
question; its place was filled by the image of *her*."

And the focus is always on the unfolding of his capacities. He
steadily grows in passional power and understanding throughout the
novel. By the time of Natasha's abortive elopement and disgrace,
when he confronts Anatole, contemptuously pays him off, and
afterwards declares his love for Natasha, he shows himself superior in
moral stature to everyone else in the book. In spite of the time and
energy expended on Pierre's theories Tolstoy in his case too is finally
more interested in the individual than the universals.

It looks as though Lawrence failed to appreciate the value of
Pierre. In 1925 he condemned him as "dull .... fat, diluted".[13] Was he
simply remembering Pierre in the epilogue, where he appears
diminished in his married happiness? Or was it a habit of hostility he
had acquired towards Tolstoy? Lawrence was ready at times to throw
at him the accusation often levelled at himself: "a marvellous sensuous

---

13. Lawrence, 1925, in *A Study of Thomas Hardy*, 183-86.

understanding, and very little clarity of mind".[14] However, he did praise in him "a true artist [who] worshipped every manifestation of pure, spontaneous, passionate life".[15]

That compliment is less applicable to the last phase of his writings. Even in the last few chapters of *Anna Karenin* – when Levin determines to "live only by virtue of the beliefs in which he had been brought up" – it is possible to detect a rise in the valuation of generalities. There is no mistake about it in *Resurrection*. Lawrence read it, "for the first time" in 1924, at the onset of his own final prophetic phase. He had no high opinion of the novel, however: "That would-be-expiatory Prince is as dead as lumber." He was generally contemptuous of the elderly Tolstoy, especially his "very nauseating Christian-brotherhood idea of himself".[16]

Nevertheless, in structure *Resurrection* resembles nothing in Lawrence's novels so much as the one with which that last phase of his culminated, *Lady Chatterley's Lover*. Both books are unashamedly didactic, concerned with the kind of salvation that involves the individual's subordination to larger forces in life, although of course they are diametrically opposed in their conception of those forces. The opposing principles that govern *Resurrection* are dogmatically traditional:

> In Nehludov, as in every man, there were two beings: one the spiritual, seeking only that kind of happiness for himself which tends towards the happiness of all; the other, the animal man, seeking only his own happiness, and ready to sacrifice to it the happiness of the rest of the world.[17]

As in Lawrence's novel, most of contemporary conventional life is consigned to the hell of the rejected mode. The opening paragraph, while announcing the theme of regeneration with the arrival of spring – "the birches, the poplars and the wild cherry-trees were unfolding their sticky, fragrant leaves, and the swelling buds were bursting on the lime-trees" – insists that it is only for "the plants, birds, insects and children" because the "grown-up people" are preoccupied with "wielding power over each other".

At the beginning of the book Nehludov has come to the conclusion that he has spent most of his life living for himself. That didactic

---

14. Lawrence, 1915, in *A Study of Thomas Hardy*, 92.
15. Lawrence, 1927, in *Phoenix*, ed. Edward McDonald, 246.
16. Lawrence, 1925, in *A Study of Thomas Hardy*, 184.
17. *Resurrection*, 57. The translation is by Louise Maude, in the edition of 1912.

summation is not quite accurate, for he later reveals (as Oliver
does in *Lady Chatterley's Lover*) a complicated history more like his
author's, including the distribution of his father's property to the
peasants. However, he now looks for regeneration in the total service
of others. Looking back, he identifies his youthful seduction of his
maidservant, Maslova, as the start downhill for both of them, she into
prostitution and he into a life of selfish pleasure (at least as far as
women are concerned). His offer of marriage Maslova refuses – out of
a loving concern for him, he thinks, although the terms of her first
reaction have a stunning finality: "You want to save yourself through
me .... I'd rather hang myself."[18] It is much like Louisa's response in
Lawrence's "Daughters of the Vicar" to the prospect of marrying the
new vicar, who "lacked the full range of human feelings" but was "a
perfect Christian": "I'd walk the streets barefoot first."

However, Nehludov has set in motion a new way of life, as he
announces to himself on the concluding page: "And so here it is – the
business of my life. Scarcely have I finished one task, and another has
commenced." His concepts are as far away from Mellors as you can
get, but he is still, like him, the standard-bearer of a long-meditated
programme of regeneration. The fable is less successful than Eliot's
Silas Marner chiefly because, although, like hers, the message is
based on traditional moral concepts, the twist he gives it is off-centre.

Tolstoy's influence bypassed Henry James, who was famously
dismissive of his novels – the "loose, baggy monsters" – and also
Conrad, but flourished in Lawrence's own generation (when
Constance Garnett's translations appeared). Lawrence himself was for
his own special reasons, as we have seen, equivocal, but Joyce (for
example) made no bones about it: "magnificent ... head and shoulders
over the others."[19] Of course, eminence does not guarantee influence.
As with Shakespeare, the magnitude of the achievement forbids
emulation. Besides, the Modernists of Lawrence's generation and the
next chose not to adopt that type of novel.

Lawrence came upon Dostoevsky chiefly 1913-16, when his own art
was beginning to assume its mature shape. He reacted to the novels
with unusual intensity and personal involvement, fiercely rejecting
aspects of their content even while adopting a similar structure for his
own. He called them "great parables ... but false art" because, he said,

18. *Resurrection*, 187.
19. James Joyce to Stanislaus Joyce, 18 September 1905, cit. Ellmann, *James Joyce*, 209.

Dostoevsky was using the characters "as theological or religious units" – a criticism often levelled against thematic writers, including himself.[20]

It is fairer to say of Dostoevsky's novels what we have said of Lawrence's, that the characters and the ideology are combined in a special way that illuminates both. This is one of the chief points made by Mikhail Bakhtin:

> The image of the hero is inseparably linked with the image of an idea and cannot be detached from it. We *see* the hero in the idea and through the idea, and we *see* the idea through him.[21]

And in case we assume that "idea" here means something narrowly intellectual, he added: "The idea is a *live event*, played out at the point of dialogic meeting between two or several consciousnesses."[22] His people, like Lawrence's have a strong individuality that coalesces with the ideas with which they are associated. Dostoevsky spoke of his own novels as a "great dialogue" and Bakhtin explored the meaning of this remark, revealing "a plurality of consciousnesses, with equal rights and each with its own world" producing "a polyphony of battling and internally divided voices".[23]   His chief characters, like those in Lawrence's double novel, are constantly challenging and subverting each other's values and tenets: "Everything in his world lives on the very borders of its opposite."[24]

Bakhtin demonstrated that the kind of novel Dostoevsky devised had its origins, like those of Dickens, in popular adventure tales and drama with traditions going back to medieval times at least. He was also, of course, following the example of Dickens himself. Although evidence of Dostoevsky's actual reading and responses is scanty, that kind of evidence is not essential to establish the kinship we are interested in here. As Loralee MacPike put it: "Whatever Dostoevsky

---

20. Lawrence to Middleton Murry and Katharine Mansfield, 17 February 1916, in *Letters*, II, 544.
21. Bakhtin, *Problems of Dostoevsky's Poetics*, 87.
22. *Ibid.*, 88.
23. *Ibid.*, 6 and 250.
24. *Ibid.*, 176. Nina Perlina effectively corroborated some of Bakhtin's observations, for instance about Ivan Karamazov and Father Zossima, defining the purpose of "polyphony" in such cases as the achievement of "the utmost polarization of moral spheres in the novel" (*Varieties of Poetic Utterance*, 157).

read of Dickens he internalised, ma
the fabric of the lives he created in his own novels."[25]

There is in his novels the same sort of search for underlying
processes in the people:

> With utter realism to *find the man in man* .... They call me a
> *psychologist; this is not true* .... I portray all the *depths of the human
> soul*.[26]

This parallels, in his own style, Lawrence's statement quoted in our
introduction. It involves a diagnosis of wider-than-individual
destructive and creative tendencies. The psychology of his people,
their social setting and their religious and moral ideology are all
brought together in a narrative whose cohesion and multiplicity
resembles Lawrence, Dickens and (as we shall see) Conrad.

The quickest way to demonstrate the existence of the parallels is to
examine in a little detail one particular novel, as we did with Dickens.
The choice falls on *The Brothers Karamazov* because there the driving
obsessions of Dostoevsky's entire career are explored and elaborated,
and show the most remarkable correspondence with those of *Women
in Love*. It is possible to identify there (though in very different
formulations) all of Lawrence's basic themes. The structure of the
book is based on their relationship.

Let us look first at what Lawrence himself made of Dostoevsky's
basic tendencies in his letter to Middleton Murry and Katharine
Mansfield in 1916. There is, he said, a will "to be self-less, a pure
Christian" which he identified in Myshkin (in *The Idiot*) and in
Alyosha Karamazov; and secondly, "to be a pure, absolute self, all-
devouring and all-consuming" which he saw in Rogozhin, Stavrogin
and Dmitry Karamazov; and thirdly, the "unemotional *will*" to be seen
in Ivan Karamazov.[27] We will take these in the reverse order.

But first note that Lawrence in his summary missed Dostoevsky's
equivalent of one of his own themes, the critique of idealism. It was as
important to Dostoevsky as it was to Lawrence to explore those who
have their natural outgoing responses dammed up and altered by a

---

25. MacPike, *Dostoevsky's Dickens*, 200. See also N.M. Lary, *Dostoevsky and
Dickens* (1973); and Albert J. Guerard, *The Triumph of the Novel* (1976) which
compares Faulkner as well. These studies are not as much concerned with questions
of structure as we are here.

26. Dostoevsky, quoted by Bakhtin, *Problems of Dostoevsky's Poetics*, 60.

27. Lawrence to Middleton Murry and Katharine Mansfield, 17 February 1916, in
Letters, II, 543.

passionate adherence to ideologically evolved standards of behaviour, and in whom the resulting chaos is so great as to be dangerous. Katrina in *The Brothers Karamazov*, with her alternating needs to dominate and be dominated, comes under a scrutiny not unlike that given Hermione in *Women in Love*. Dried up and tortured with ideals of life and behaviour, she attempts to act them out one after another, desperately trying to drain from each falsified situation an emotional reality. She does not really venture her sensibilities but regards them and measures them up against a mental prototype. The desire to control, to have the measure of others and use them in her incidentally self-glorifying and self-promoting schemes is shown in her attempts to seduce Grushenka (who is also her rival) to obedience to her will through flattery and close, oppressive attentions, just as Hermione does Ursula. Alyosha is an embarrassed witness of her raptures over the beauty and essential innocence of Grushenka. She attempts to whitewash Grushenka's behaviour and show implicit trust in the future nobility of her actions in order to direct her in the way she wishes her to go. Grushenka calls her bluff. Dmitry's love-hate response to Katrina reminds one of Birkin's early feelings about Hermione. Dmitry she wants to "save" – or vengefully ruin. He claims: "She loves her own virtue, not me." The battle between them brings out the same destructive, even murderous instincts, once the unbalanced idealist has been pushed too far, insulted and hurt: "for hers is an infernal nature" he says, "and she's a woman of great wrath". She proves the truth of this at his trial when she reads out the letter in which he has expressed anxiety and guilt at his father's murder (which he did not commit) and thereby brings about his conviction.

The critique of idealism is carried on vigorously in Dostoevsky's other novels. In *The Possessed* for example, Varvara Stavrogin and Stepan Verhovensky form a pair of carefully related studies in the vanity behind idealism. Stepan is a pretentious liberal humanist and a failure as a man – "innocent" at fifty – though refined and generous. His whole consciousness has been virtually "invented" for him by Varvara, "a tall, yellow, bony woman with an extremely long face suggestive of a horse" who is his possessive patroness. She is a "noble" lady with *idées fixes:* "it was characteristic of her to attach herself doggedly and passionately to any dream that fascinated her, any idea that struck her as noble." She protests, "There's no greater happiness than self-sacrifice". Not only the vanity of these two characters is disclosed but their failure as parents. Their ideologically

supported insulation or inflexibility is
the rootlessness and lack of faith of their sons, Peter Verhovensky and
Stavrogin.

Lawrence's definition of Ivan Karamazov reminds one of Gerald
Crich, and Ivan's monomaniac mental regulation is as tragically
extreme as Gerald's. Disastrously insulated, his sickness is at the
centre of the book. He is presented as gravitating towards death, a
mental magnate hollowed out in the course of extending his
intellectual empire, the need for which is stimulated partly by recoil
from his father's sensuality and partly by the desire to have a
semblance of personal control and social prestige. But mainly it serves
as cover and weaponry for his destructive and vengeful feelings
against life. Generally under the strictest control, such feelings erupt
in small acts of sudden repudiation, as when he strikes Maximov in
the chest as he takes his place in the carriage with his father after the
fiasco of the family visit to Zossima; or when, near the end, on his
way to meet Smerdyakov for the last time, totally preoccupied with
fear, guilt and disgust, he meets a drunken peasant:

> Ivan felt an intense hatred for him before he had thought about him at
> all. Suddenly he realised his presence and felt an irresistible impulse
> to knock him down. At that moment they met, and the peasant with a
> violent lurch fell full tilt against Ivan, who pushed him back
> furiously. The peasant went flying backwards and fell like a log on
> the frozen ground. He uttered a plaintive "O-oh!" and then was silent.
> Ivan stepped up to him. He was lying on his back, without movement
> or consciousness. "He will be frozen," thought Ivan, and he went on
> his way to Smerdyakov's.[28]

The scenes with the mare and the rabbit are similar acts of violence in
Gerald's story.

Like Gerald (and also Turgenev's Bazarov) he gives his love to a
woman (Katrina) incapable of returning it, and (again like Gerald's) it
veers into hate: "Ivan loved her madly, though at times he hated her so
that he might have murdered her .... They were like two enemies in
love with one another." In the end the underlying destructiveness of
his concepts comes home to roost in him when Smerdyakov forces
him to face the fact that he is responsible for his father's murder, in
that Smerdyakov, who did the deed, believed it to be both desired by

---

28. *The Brothers Karamazov*, 657. The translation is by Constance Garnett (1912)
which Lawrence read. The page reference, and those which follow subsequent
quotations from this novel are to the reissue of 1951.

Ivan and ideologically sanctioned by the argument put forward by him earlier that if there was no God then everything was lawful.

Ivan uses his intellect to justify and sustain his negative view of life, just as Gerald uses the industrial system. In his fable of the Grand Inquisitor he assesses life totally without trust in it. Lawrence's essay on this fable, written in the last year of his life, made the assumption that the Inquisitor "speaks Dostoevsky's own final opinion about Jesus" and judged the whole episode to be "the final and unanswerable criticism of Christ".[29] He missed the sharp irony of the episode. As Peter Kaye put it: "The Grand Inquisitor needs to be understood in terms of Ivan's tragedy."[30] The story shows in Ivan, less "the thinking mind of the human being in rebellion, thinking the whole thing out to the bitter end" as Lawrence imagined, than the urge to reduce, to control, to use and at the same time to be oneself used. The fable attempts to raise this to the level of compassion. The Inquisitor argues that people cannot accept responsibility for themselves: they want, beyond everything, material wellbeing and are happiest when subject to those who devote themselves effectively to that end. It is an argument for an equality in submission to the lowest common factor of mankind that resembles Gerald's idea of an equality in submission to a rational system. Both express fear of life.

Behind Ivan's words is a growing dissociation. He denies even the sense of commitment expressed by the very fact of his writing the fable:

> "Why! It's all nonsense, Alyosha. It's only a senseless poem of a senseless student, who could never write two lines of verse. Why do you take it so seriously? Surely you don't suppose I am going straight off to the Jesuits, to join the men who are correcting His work? Good Lord, it's no business of mine. I told you, all I want to do is to live on to thirty, and then ... dash the cup to the ground!" (270-01)

In his conversations with Alyosha – where, as Bakhtin pointed out, Alyosha's main function is to intervene in Ivan's internal dialogue – he comes closest to self-betrayal. He reveals compassion for human defeat, but what affects him most is the defeat of a mental concept. Life must satisfy his idea of what it should be:

---

29. *Phoenix*, ed. Edward McDonald, 283-7.
30. Kaye, *Dostoevsky and English Modernism,* 58.

"What comfort is it to me that th
follows effect simply and directly, and that I know it? I must have
justice, or I will destroy myself." (250)

He appraises the victimization of humanity with no sense of awe at its
adaptability, strength and urge to grow. Individuals do not interest
him: "For anyone to love a man, he must be hidden, for as soon as he
shows his face love is gone." Never able to lapse out towards others
and towards life in general – "Another can never know how much I
suffer, because he is another and not I" – he feels only the insularity of
everybody, and this is the basis of his final insanity. It is a similar
sense of emptiness that produces Gerald's downward rush to suicide.
Ivan keeps at bay (as Gerald does with Birkin) the possibility of help
and change that he is made aware of through his affection for
Alyosha.

Like Gerald he wills his father's death. In each case the father
represents the living proof of the mess created by a dedicated self-
indulgence. In Thomas Crich's case the mess is caused by attempts to
defeat the flesh and its preoccupation with selfish acquisition, in order
to promote that sense of harmony to be gained from working beyond
the self and towards a general good. In Fyodor's case it is caused by
the attempt to defy in himself and in others the urge towards a
working harmony because he feels it has cheated the flesh. After the
death of the fathers, in both Gerald and Ivan there is a speedier
degeneration. Some of the driving power of their activity is removed
and they feel themselves vicarious murderers. In Ivan's hallucinations
at the end (those of the devil visiting and plaguing him) he has the
devil say: "Before time was, by some decree which I could never
make out, I was predestined to deny." His unconscious awareness of
the "denial" in him reminds us of what is said of Gerald, the "denier".

The association with Smerdyakov is the final shock to Ivan's
system because he represents, as Loerke does to Gerald, a kind of
moral anarchism that even he is loath to admit in himself. Smerdyakov
is a minor but crucial figure whose maimed morality and
understanding comes across sharply and succinctly. The hardship of
his growing up is etched: a bastard son of Fyodor Karamazov and a
beggar-woman, he has been brought up by a religious bigot. By means
of this background the reader is put sympathetically in touch with the
processes of sealing off that have taken place in him. It is a rounded
study, with some compassion in it, besides sharpness (like that of
Loerke) and more than just the map of a psychology. In the spurious
logic of Ivan – "everything is lawful" – Smerdyakov finds expression

for the anarchy he feels; and coming as it does from Ivan, the respected intellectual, it offers both refuge and an opportunity for vengeance. As Bakhtin explained, their conversation prior to the murder is "between Smerdyakov's open and conscious will (encoded in hints) and Ivan's hidden will (hidden even from himself) taking place, as it were, without the participation of Ivan's open and conscious will".[31]

Ivan's movement from the love of Katrina to the spiritual fathering of Smerdyakov maps the degenerative in *The Brothers Karamazov*. Lawrence, perhaps misremembering slightly a novel he had read three years before, mistook Dmitry's position, and linked him with Rogozhin (of *The Idiot*) and Stavrogin of *The Possessed*, who were fresher in his memory. His definition of the tendency "to be a pure, absolute self, all-devouring and all-consuming" fits both of them well enough. Rogozhin has a devouring love of Nastasya, which, Myshkin points out, "cannot be distinguished from hate" and which ends with his knifing her in bed. Stavrogin's atrophied sympathies – "a crippled creature" his girlfriend calls him – his boredom, the wanton aggression, the craving for sensation and excitement, the fruitlessness of his affair with the self-contained Lisa Tushin, all suggest both Steerforth in *David Copperfield* and Gerald Crich in *Women in Love*, as does the inner conflict, suppressed though acknowledged at the end. Such figures in Dostoevsky's novels are often associated with the insect motif, which, as R.E. Matlaw pointed out recurs in Dostoevsky's writings (as it does in Lawrence's) to indicate a preoccupation with the insulation of the self.[32]

But Dmitry belongs, with Grushenka, in the area of regeneration, which is explored on several levels, including (surprisingly) his father, Fyodor, as well as Zossima and Alyosha.

The study of Fyodor looks (from our point of view) like an inverted Birkin theme: a warped lust for life. In many respects he has greater vitality, or at least demands more from life, than those around him who appear content with halves – half-truths and half-desires. His sensuality and buffoonery are in equal proportions, and indicate not only exacting desires but an exacting need to have these desires, or the energy that feeds them, accepted and understood. He too demands a passional integration, and it is his inability to get it or escape from the

---

31. Bakhtin, *Problems of Dostoevsky's Poetics*, 259.

32. See R.E. Matlaw, "Recurrent Imagery in Dostoevsky", in *Harvard Slavic Studies*, III. For similarities between Loerke and Svridrigailov (in *Crime and Punishment*) see George Panichas, *Adventure in Consciousness*.

defiant, perverse indulgence of the sensual vitality he generally denied, that is at the root of his buffoonery – as in his comment on the "woman of loose behaviour":

> "perhaps holier than you are yourselves, you monks who are seeking salvation. She fell perhaps in her youth ruined by her environment. But she loved much, and Christ Himself forgave the woman 'who loved much.'"
>
> "It was not for such love Christ forgave her," broke impatiently from the gentle Father Iosif.
>
> "Yes, it was for such, monks, it was! You save your souls here, eating cabbage, and you think you are the righteous. You eat a gudgeon a day, and you think you bribe God with gudgeon." (71)

Fyodor sends up conventions, duties and ideas that make nonsense of his vitality, as well as sending up himself for being unable to come to terms with them. He sneers at the pretences or defences of others, like Miusov, or even Zossima – "Is there room for my humility beside your pride?" – who has achieved a sense of harmony by not joining the scrum. The vigorous sensual life that others seem to defend themselves from or to condemn he uses, often to spite all comers, sometimes to spite himself, always in mockery. His actions in company are calculated to disconcert to the extent that the company should realize their basic similarity with himself:

> "For sin is sweet; all abuse it, but all men live in it, only others do it on the sly, and I openly. And so all the other sinners fall upon me for being so simple." (175)

It is his undeniable representativeness that makes his life and his buffoonery so loathsome to the others. At the same time he is credulous enough to suspect that somewhere they are right and he is wrong, because, compared with his, their lives seem to have some order. Unable to break out of the circle of revenge and his childlike desire to be accepted, alienating almost all others, he is thrown back on himself, and this contributes further to the desperate violence of his debauchery. What he says about his skirmishes with the monks speaks for the rest of his life as well:

> "Well, there is no re-habilitating myself now. So let me shame them for all I am worth. I will show them I don't care what they think – that's all!" (84)

He is unthinking generally, except in shafts thrown out by the passionate need to get under the guard of his listeners. His abuse of innocence, his own and others', in fact destroys him: he is murdered by the son he fathered by rape on the innocent idiot Lizaveta. Yet, trapped in his bewilderment and misery, with his warped craving for more life, he functions in both hemispheres of the novel, the right vehicle for some of the keenest insights it has to offer on the pre-requisites for regeneration.

Both the lust for life and some of the vengeful spite are passed on to Dmitry. But Dmitry, though often at sea among his own responses, oscillating wildly between extreme guilt and whole-hearted indulgence in what he considers to be his worst tendencies, makes a laborious but persistent progress towards an objective understanding of himself.

Part of his problem at first is that he identifies the most destructive leanings of his nature with the obvious representative of them, his father, and this creates the murderous tension between them. Like Fyodor he can see the insufficiency of the ideals he flies in the face of, and the insufficiency of some of those who uphold them, but in reaction against his father's example he holds confusedly to the objective of an orderly life as seen in conventional moral terms. Early in the novel he speaks to Alyosha of his confusion:

> "What's still more awful is that a man with the ideal of Sodom in his soul does not renounce the ideal of the Madonna, and his heart may be on fire with that ideal, genuinely on fire, just as in his days of youth and innocence. Yes, man is broad, too broad, indeed. I'd have him narrower." (106)

He has to learn by experience to re-define what goodness means for him. Like Birkin in *Women in Love* he knows his sensuality is a source of growth, or at least an inescapable manifestation of his vitality:

> "For when I leap into the pit, I go headlong with my heels up, and am pleased to be falling in that degrading attitude, and pride my self upon it. And in the very depths of degradation I begin a hymn of praise." (105)

The need to discover afresh for himself the sources of life – "I always liked side-paths, little dark back-alleys behind the main road – there one finds adventures and surprises, and precious metals in the dirt" – is as strong as the need to belong to his fellow men and be accepted and respected by them. He shoulders his way through his experience towards an understanding whereby the two can operate together, mutually enriching, though doubting all the time:

"I go on and I don't know whether I'm going to shame or to light joy. That's the trouble, for everything in the world is a riddle! .... The boundaries meet and all contradictions exist side by side." (105-106)

As Zossima sees when he kneels to him, not only must he because of his unconquerable vitality take part in life to the full but he must experience to the full the suffering resulting from the struggle to adapt and achieve a balance.

He finally achieves the prospect of his balance and his regeneration with Grushenka, the woman he has sexually loved throughout the novel. At first, using the conventional moral measure, he undervalues this love, even though and even because he knows it to be obsessive. It is his consuming interest and the source of his greatest joy as well as misery, and he treats it suspiciously as if it testified to a form of helplessness on his part, as if he were in the grip of his own sensuality that has made a fool and a slave of him. He is anxious about it in spite of the fact that he feels he genuinely understands and sympathizes with Grushenka – far more naturally and readily than with Katrina, with whom he temporarily shares an "ideal" love.

Grushenka too has to approach an understanding of herself and her needs slowly, the way Dmitry does. She undervalues herself in some ways but refuses to be underestimated in others (as we see in the scenes with Katrina). She has to discover the mixture of personal pride and false romanticism that led to bitterness and disappointment at the end of her affair with the Polish officer. Meeting him again after the experience of Dmitry's love, she realizes the falsity of many of her motives and the position she has adopted. Like Dmitry she doesn't know where she is going nor what she really wants until the experience swallows her up. The processes in her that have dictated action (often bitter and vengeful) for so many years have been the product of attempting to reconcile a need for passionate self-surrender with the presence of dishonesty in others and reciprocally in herself.

Grushenka and Dmitry discover their deepest need and understanding of each other under the stress of his arrest and imprisonment: their underlying commitment is made clear to them and tested by the murder charge. During his imprisonment Dmitry realizes:

> The past was nothing! In the past it was only those infernal curves of hers that tortured me, but now I've taken all her soul into my soul, and through her I've become a man myself. (629)

He feels a new commitment to people and to life:

> "I may find a human heart in another convict and murderer by my
> side, and I may make friends with him, for even there one may live
> and love and suffer .... Oh yes, we shall be in chains and there will be
> no freedom, but then, in our great sorrow, we shall rise again to joy,
> without which man cannot live nor God exist." (625-26)

He identifies his achievement so strongly with exposure to experience
and suffering that he is afraid if he escapes from prison he will lose it.

Father Zossima, withdrawn from life yet vividly concerned with it,
articulates the general directives behind growth and renewal: "He
carries in his heart", says his pupil Alyosha, "the secret of renewal for
all". Through him is explored (as Lawrence did through Birkin) the
necessary factor of reflexion and crystallization of experience.
Zossima knows himself to be inferior to those who live a full life in
the world. He recognizes that to a great degree he protects himself
from the suffering and uncertainty involved: "I entered upon the safe
and blessed path." It is his knowledge and full admission of this
inability to risk his balance that lies behind his falling on his knees to
Dmitry. It makes him love "the greatest sinners the best" since their
sin measures their exposure to the onslaughts of life. Of the directives
he offers, honesty is the first:

> "Above all, avoid falsehood, every kind of falsehood, especially
> falseness to yourself. Watch over your own deceitfulness and look at
> it every hour, every minute. Avoid being scornful, both to others and
> to yourself. What seems to you bad within you will grow purer from
> the very fact of your observing it yourself." (53)

The next is the necessity of living a full and satisfactory life. The
difficulty of the struggle is life itself. His advice, often shocking to the
recipients, takes its effect from his intuitive understanding of their
needs. To Madame Hohlakov he says: "Love in action is a harsh and
painful thing compared with love in a dream." To a penitent: "How is
it possible to pray for the peace of a living soul?" To Alyosha: "In
sorrow seek happiness." He tolerates people's near-worship of him as
useful because they need to feel that the forces of good are accessible
and interpretable. The stinking of his corpse – where Bakhtin found
evidence of the influence of carnivalized Menippean satire – serves in
its ironic irreverence to offset the worship of Zossima and remind us
of that aspect of his humanity which has been unused and negated.
But there is a service to be done in the acquirement of wisdom in
isolation, and Zossima does it.

Lawrence denied any genuine regenerative theme in Dostoevsky,
insisting instead on a kind of hypocrisy in him: "professing love, all

love. But his nose is sharp with hate."[33] Whatever truth there m
in this diagnosis of Dostoevsky himself, nevertheless to apply it to
Alyosha would be perverse.

When Alyosha is sent by his Elder away from the monastery to
take part in life – "You will have to bear all before you come back" –
he remains for the duration of the novel an innocent – that is,
monkishly limited in his responses. In the scenes with Grushenka for
instance he seems, especially in comparison with his brother Dmitry,
out of touch, as if like a child he lacks the equipment for fully mature
understanding. But his sympathy is real enough, and constant:

> He did not care to be a judge of others ... he would never take it upon
> himself to criticise and would never condemn anyone for anything.
> He seemed, indeed, to accept everything without the least
> condemnation, though often grieving bitterly: and this was so much
> so that no-one could surprise or frighten him even in his earliest
> youth. (14)

His total venturing of sensibility is contrasted with Ivan's sealing off,
his faith in and love of humanity is in marked contrast with Ivan's
mistrust and dislike. Through Alyosha the emphasis is put on that
openness and sense of "the wholeness of things" he feels even in his
grief after Zossima's death:

> His soul, overflowing with rapture, yearned for freedom, space,
> openness .... The silence of earth seemed to melt into the silence of
> the heavens. The mystery of earth was at one with the mystery of the
> stars. (378)

The vivid individuality of the characters associated with the
regenerative theme gives life to their statements, however solemn and
high-flown they may sound (in this translation at least). That aspect of
the writing is not enough to account for Lawrence's reservations.
These, however, were scarcely more vehement than Conrad's. And
they were the two English novelists with the strongest artistic kinship
with Dostoevsky. In both of them, surely, Lawrence's reason was
paramount: "We have to hate our immediate predecessors, to get free
from their authority."[34]

---

33. Lawrence to Ottoline Morrell, 24 March 1915, in *Letters*, II, 311.
34. Lawrence to Edward Garnett, 1 February 1913, in *Letters,* I, 509.

8

OLDER CONTEMPORARIES

Hardy, Wells and Conrad

Is it a failing in Lawrence that he did not learn more from Henry James? There is an affinity between Lawrence's kind of artistic discipline and James's determination to make everything – action, idea, image and sentiment – totally relevant. Some of his themes, such as the self-delusive idealism of Isabel Archer, contrasted with the cynical aestheticism of Osmond (in *The Portrait of a Lady*) resemble Lawrence's. Some of his tales show a comparable structure as well. In "The Beast in the Jungle" for example, the theme of the imprisoned self embedded in the main character moves straight towards its appointed target, the revelation of John Marcher's destiny, to be denier, when he flings himself in misery and guilt on the tomb of the woman he might have loved. James's concern with the split psyche achieves an intense focus in "The Jolly Corner" which is the only one of James's works we can be fairly sure Lawrence read, since it appeared in the first number of *The English Review*. Lawrence's disinclination to read any more or even to refer to him later in correspondence may have had something to do with the lamentable dismissiveness James showed in his review of *Sons and Lovers* in 1914. James later confessed to having merely "trifled with the exordia".[1] But in any case, James in his novels gave priority to the fullest possible development of his chief characters; they belong, with George Eliot's, to a type that Lawrence turned away from.

In Hardy's, on the other hand, the obsession with broad subject-themes, often resembling Lawrence's, runs alongside the psychological development of his characters and is sometimes given priority over them. At the time of Lawrence's essay on them (Autumn

---

1. James, in Edith Wharton, *A Backward Glance,* 324.

1914) he was looking for ways to broaden his own writing beyond the psychological that had prevailed up to *Sons and Lovers,* which he had just finished. He seized on the thematic features of Hardy's, sometimes redefining them in ways that foretold his own. In that rambling, digressive and unfinished essay we have the rare case of a writer consciously assimilating and transcending another's influence. In rethinking Hardy's novels Lawrence was indicating the direction of his own thought towards a clearer and more inclusive integration of these themes.

One of them was idealism, conceived by Hardy (as Lawrence partly did) as an obstruction to mutual affection between the sexes. In Clym Yeobright's face in *The Return of the Native* is seen "the mutually destructive interdependence of spirit and flesh" and in that context thought itself is pronounced "a disease of the flesh". Lawrence in his essay was quick to point out that in Clym's case the "un-ease" (Lawrence's term) is due to the fact that he is "emotionally undeveloped ... within his limited human consciousness".[2]

Angel Clare in *Tess of the d'Urbervilles,* like Thomas Crich in *Women in Love,* owns "the will to subdue the grosser to the subtler emotion, the substance to the conception, the flesh to the spirit" – as well as being "a slave of custom and conventionality". His love for Tess is "ethereal to a fault:" he sees in her "a visionary essence of woman". When he learns that the girl he took for "a new-sprung child of nature" is not "pure" the ideal kills his love, until revived (too late) by guilt.

In *Jude the Obscure* Sue Bridehead is the most extreme expression of the idealistic obsession. A "Voltairean" free-thinker, devoted to intellectual and aesthetic pleasures, she wants in relation to a man (she tells Jude) "a delight in being with you of a supremely delicate kind". She suppresses with apparent ease the specifically sexual in herself. She has lived platonically with a consumptive man whose death, she feels, might have been accelerated by the stress of sexual suppression. She accepts marriage with her head-teacher Phillotson without allowing him to consummate it, and then leaves him for a relationship with Jude which Phillotson calls "Shelleyan ... to share each other's emotions, and fancies, and dreams". The narrative confirms this: "That complete mutual understanding, in which every glance and movement was as effectual as speech for conveying intelligence between them, made them almost the two parts of a single whole."

---

2. *A Study of Thomas Hardy,* 27.

In the account of their love there are several analogies with Paul and Miriam in *Sons and Lovers*. In his essay on Hardy, Lawrence said of Sue what Paul Morel says of Miriam: "She asked for what he [Jude] could not give – what perhaps no man can give: passionate love without physical desire." Resemblances between the scene in *Jude the Obscure* where Sue and Jude admire the roses at the Agriculture Show (V, 5) and the one in *Sons and Lovers* (195) when Miriam shows Paul a wild rose bush are suggested by Lawrence's gloss on the former: "this trembling on the verge of ecstasy, when, the senses strongly roused to the service of the consciousness, the things they contemplated took flaming being."[3] It is only to secure Jude that Sue (like Miriam) sacrifices her body to his physical desire.

Jude himself is almost equally given up to the pursuits of the mind, but this dominant bent is in conflict with a normal sexuality already matured in his marriage with a coarse country girl, Arabella. The portrait of Jude lies shadowily behind that of Will Brangwen, not only in this central conflict between spirituality and sensuality but also in circumstantials. Jude, for example, craves the medieval in religion and art and he is as fond as Will of repairing churches, even after he has similarly lost his faith under the onslaught of rationalism from a wife who holds sway over him.

Lawrence took less interest in the theme of animal egotism, arguing that the self-contained sensualists, such as Troy, Wildeve and Alec D'Urberville, who are significantly less devastating in their destructiveness than the idealists, are comparatively "non-individual" and "fragmentary".[4] Arabella in *Jude the Obscure* was for him a special case. She is a pig-sticking barmaid with an eye to the main chance as far as men are concerned and an absolute minimum of human sympathy. The narrative occasionally puts her down as a "complete and substantial female animal – no more, no less". Lawrence pointed out critically that she remains considerably more – "amazingly lawless, even splendidly so" – and accused Hardy of

---

3. *A Study of Thomas Hardy*, 118-19.

4. Henchard in *The Mayor of Casterbridge* is perhaps the least "fragmentary" of Hardy's villains. Parallels have been suggested between Henchard's wrestling match with Forfrae in Chapter 38 of *The Mayor of Casterbridge* and that of Gerald with Birkin in *Women in Love*, in spite of the flimsiness of resemblance between the characters – especially between Forfrae and Birkin. See H.M. Daleski, *Thomas Hardy and the Paradoxes of Love*, 119-24. He refers back in this matter to Showalter, Garson and others.

being offended by her coarseness, "because he is something of an Angel Clare".[5]

The third major theme, that of "Life ... the great pulse of existence" (as he called it in *Tess of the d'Urbervilles*) is registered by Hardy, like Lawrence, chiefly in the sexuality of his heroines – Bathsheba, Eustacia, and Tess – and finally of Jude. But it is also present, as Lawrence noted admiringly, in "the great background, vital and vivid". He associated Hardy generously in this respect with Shakespeare and the ancient Greek tragedians.[6] Hardy's descriptions of the countryside often reveal the hand of the fine poet in the sometimes clumsy glove of the novelist. He regularly insisted on its symbolic status in the drama. In *The Return of the Native*, for instance, he explicitly associated Egdon Heath positively with Clym (it is his "heart") and negatively with Eustacia, who hates it. He constantly drew parallels between the countryside and the characters' responses. Tess's recovery after the death of her baby is conceptually similar to Ursula's in *The Rainbow* after her abortion:

> and some spirit within her rose automatically as the sap in the twigs. It was unexpended youth, surging up anew after its temporary check, and bringing with it hope, and the invincible instinct towards self-delight.[7]

In the account of her early relations with Angel the way her feelings are linked with the springtime – "a season when the rush of juices could almost be heard beneath the hiss of fertilisation" – stresses the inevitability of their attraction. They are "almost impregnated by their surroundings".

Hardy was as interested as Lawrence in what in *Tess of the d'Urbervilles* he defined as the "organism called sex": the unpremeditated "gravitation of the two into one". He achieves at times a sensuality that reminds us of the early Lawrence: when, for example, Angel lightly kisses Tess's arm and her pulse is "accelerated by the touch, her blood driven to her finger-ends, and the cool arms flushed hot".

There are several circumstantial resemblances between Hardy's love scenes and Lawrence's. In *The Return of the Native,* for example,

---

5. *A Study of Thomas Hardy*, 101-102.

6. Lawrence retracted the compliment by criticizing Hardy for narrowing the tragedy down to the conflict between individual inclinations and social conventions. See *A Study of Thomas Hardy*, 28-30.

7. *Tess of the d'Urbervilles*, New Wessex edition, 128.

in one scene Eustacia dances in the moonlight with Wildeve (like Ursula with Skrebensky in *The Rainbow*) and in another she sees Clym behind her, glaring at her, as she sits in front of a mirror (like Gudrun with Gerald in *Women in Love*). Sometimes Hardy, attempting to suggest underlying feelings, moved towards a kind of symbolism that recalls Hawthorne in one direction and Lawrence in the other. Angel's sleep-walking scene in *Tess of the d'Urbervilles,* for instance, when after renouncing her on account of her impurity he carries her tenderly across the fields to lay her in an ancient stone coffin, reveals his unconscious feelings, both positive and negative, about her. The scene on the downs in *Far from the Madding Crowd,* where Bathsheba stands in front of Troy while he does his sword-practice symbolizes their undeclared sexual attraction:

> He flourished the sword by way of introduction number two, and the next thing of which she was conscious was that the point and blade of the sword were darting with a gleam towards her left side, just above her hip; then of their reappearance on her right side, emerging as it were from between her ribs, having passed through her body .... Beams of light caught from the low sun's rays, above, around, in front of her, well-nigh shut out earth and heaven – all emitted in the marvellous evolutions of Troy's reflecting blade, which seemed everywhere at once, and yet nowhere specially.[8]

More blatant symbolic effects often recall Dickens and are sometimes, as Lawrence pointed out, "very badly suggested, exaggerated". Little Father Time in *Jude the Obscure* is a grotesque inversion of Tiny Tim in *A Christmas Carol*, and Jude's critical illness accompanied by excerpts from the Book of Job recalls Jo's death in *Bleak House* (although the social message is nearer Flaubert's). In such situations, Lawrence declared, "Nothing is so pitiable as his clumsy efforts to push events into line with his theory of being".[9]

It was not just the stylistic crudity of the emphasis, but this particular overshadowing theme of fatality and loss itself that was uncongenial (in Hardy's terms) to Lawrence's mind. He disliked his imposition of a fatalistic plot and the victimization of the main characters to prove the cruelty of Nature as well as society. He accused Hardy of endorsing their capitulation to social pressures even while explicitly blaming "the arbitrary law of society" often for events more attributable to deficiencies in the characters themselves.

---

8. *Far from the Madding Crowd*, New Wessex edition, 203-204.
9. *A Study of Thomas Hardy*, 93.

However, Lawrence was the first (and last) great writer to take Hardy seriously as a novelist. Henry James had been half-dismissive, mocking his awkward attempts in *Far from the Madding Crowd* to imitate George Eliot's rustics, and commenting to Robert Louis Stevenson about *Tess of the d'Urbervilles*: "chock-full of faults and falsity and yet has a singular beauty and charm."[10] Conrad took little notice of him, Joyce respected but rejected him; Woolf, after a long acquaintance with his work, and some personal respect, remained ambivalent: "he had genius and no talent."[11] Forster saw him as "essentially a poet".[12] Lawrence's own grateful generosity towards him did not last. His last comment on him was:

> What a commonplace genius he has – or a genius for the commonplace, I don't know which .... But better than Bernard Shaw.[13]

Hardy's influence was strong among the minor novelists of the next generation, but others – Orwell, for instance – were unenthusiastic.

Brief mention should be made here of several older contemporaries who influenced Lawrence's writing chiefly in the years before he embarked on his thematic novels (and which are therefore outside our designated area of exploration).

George Moore is a link in the chain of influence that connects George Eliot, Hardy, Arnold Bennett (whose *Old Wives Tale* was inspired by Moore's *A Mummer's Wife*) and Lawrence. He was in sympathy with Lawrence's reaction against Hardy's tragic emphasis enough write, in *Esther Waters*, a kind of repudiation of *Tess of the D'Urbervilles*. Like Tess, Esther is seduced into pregnancy by a man without scruples, is loved by a man of principle and later lives with her seducer. Unlike Tess she raises her child: "Hers is an heroic adventure ... a mother's fight for the life of her child against all the forces that civilization arrays against the lowly and the illegitimate" (Chapter 20). Her Salvation Army captain does not disown her and her old lover becomes a reliable partner. The compassionate realism of the novel owes something to Moore's admiration of Zola, and some of the scene-setting reminds one of Lawrence's early stories. Moore was

---

10. James to Stevenson, 19 March 1892 in *Letters*, ed. Lubbock, I, 190.
11. Woolf, 7 January 1936, in *Diary*, V, 5.
12. Forster, *Aspects of the Novel*, 125.
13. Lawrence to Martin Secker, 24 July 1928 in *Letters*, VI, 471.

alert enough to the merits of *Sons and Lovers* to call it "the best novel
... of modern times".[14]

Lawrence's relation to James Barrie was perhaps based on the
parallels between their early lives. They were both from poor families;
and Barrie, like Lawrence, after the death of his mother's favourite
elder son, spent years of "incessant and unalterable devotion to her".[15]
There were perhaps biographical roots for the persistent interest both
Barrie and Lawrence took in the predicament of a man who finds it
difficult to love a woman as she needs and wants to be loved, although
the handling of the problem in the novels is (to say the least)
dissimilar. Barrie in his novels of the 1890s was fond of portraying an
effeminate hero enjoying the devotion of a pure, strong heroine whom
he loves like a brother or a son. One of them, *Tommy and Grizel,*
became useful to Lawrence in 1910, as John Worthen pointed out[16] as
a vehicle for explaining to Jessie Chambers in what ways he could not
love her. A connection could be made out between the sensitive,
whimsical, self-conscious isolation of Tommy and that of Cyril in *The
White Peacock.*

No such rapport existed between Lawrence and John Galsworthy
in spite of an agreed verdict between the two writers on what
Lawrence called "the social being in all its weirdness": the Forsytes,
that is, in Galsworthy's novels, a race whose emotions are dominated
by greed and lust while their minds are occupied by conventions.
Their portrayal was for Galsworthy "the criticism of one half of
myself by the other".[17] Lawrence in his *Scrutinies* essay of 1927
registered chiefly his disappointment that the honest effort "fizzles
out". Galsworthy was one of those contemporaries who detested
Lawrence. When they met in 1917 the feeling was mutual.

Arnold Bennett was more congenial and more of an influence in
Lawrence's early years. He was nearly twenty years older than
Lawrence, but like him provincial in origin, though middle- rather
than lower-class. He struck a defiant pose (in that era of aesthetes) of
commercial priorities: "I am a writer just as I might be a hotel-keeper,
a solicitor, a doctor, a grocer or an earthenware manufacturer", he
said, and bragged about his productivity. At the same time he was a
serious, self-critical novelist, student of French Naturalism and

---

14. Moore to Werner Laurie, 16 April 1920 in *George Moore on Parnassus: Letters*,
ed. Helmut E. Gerber, 461.
15. Denis Mackail, quoted by Janet Dunbar, *J. M. Barrie*, 23.
16. See Worthen, *D. H. Lawrence: The Early Years*, 264-65.
17. Galsworthy to Edward Garnett, quoted by Dudley Barker, *Man of Principle*, 12.

admirer of George Moore and Henry James. James in return admired the way in Bennett's novels "the canvas is covered, ever so closely and vividly covered, by the exhibition of innumerable small facts and aspects, at which we assist with the most comfortable sense of their substantial truth".[18]

An instance of direct influence on Lawrence is the effect of *Anna of the Five Towns*. In that novel a girl wavers between the middle-class Mynors, under whose caresses she feels a "dispassionate frigidity" and the lower-class Willie Price who rouses more generous feelings. She settles for a respectable marriage to Mynors, reflecting on "the profound truth that a woman's life is always a renunciation, more or less". "I hate Bennett's resignation", Lawrence declared[19] and a year later, when he came to rewrite the tale that became "Daughters of the Vicar" – in which Louisa, the vicar's daughter marries her young miner – some of the changes he made to it, making their union more deeply felt and convincing, could be seen partly as a rejoinder.

Lawrence was able to lift features of Bennett's work and deliberately rework them, even (as we have seen) into the thematic structure of *The Lost Girl*. Rewriting of this kind shows respect; it is better perhaps than being patronized in a kindly fashion by James and Conrad or superciliously by Virginia Woolf. The respect was mutual: Bennett called *The Rainbow* "beautiful" and regarded Lawrence as "the strongest novelist writing today".[20]

After the realism of the four novelists just mentioned, Wells's writings came as a welcome antidote, for they had greater intellectual and comic (Dickensian) dimensions and were essentially thematic in structure.

The biographical parallels between Lawrence and Wells are interesting. They were both third sons of poor and ill-matched parents, worked their way towards a university degree via teaching, associated with socialists and suffragettes and had severe problems in their youthful love affairs (Wells married a girl he later described as frigid). There were similarities as well as obvious divergences in their lifelong dissatisfactions with the conventional sexual code and in their partiality for messianic social remedies. Wells would speak of himself at times, somewhat as Lawrence did, as "a creature trying to find its

18. James, *Selected Literary Criticism,* 321.
19. Lawrence to Arthur McLeod, 4 October 1912, in *Letters,* I, 459.
20. Arnold Bennett, cit. Lawrence in *Letters,* II, 479; and *Evening Standard,* 7 June 1928, cit. Lawrence in *Letters,* VI, 438.

way out of a prison into which it has fallen" and of his writing "to get my soul and something of my body out of the customs, outlook, boredoms and contaminations of the current phase of life".[21]

Wells's rebellion against the mental fashions of his time was, however, like Shaw's, chiefly a matter of combating one topical contemporary notion with another, of shocking his public without disturbing their really deep-seated convictions. He was by nature and by experience drawn to that kind of thematic writing which escapes the complications of personal relationships. What his biographers, the Mackenzies, called the "fugitive impulse" was one of the main motives of his life and an equally a strong motive for writing. Rebelling against one idea of perfection and falling for another was the story of his work as well as his life. Some of his work borders on the wider popular reaches of thematic fiction, the chief aim of which is to simplify the complexities of life. In his long career he was to move from the fantasy of scientific romance for its own sake to the didacticism of science fiction with a message. It was in the middle of his life that he managed to inject into his writing the greatest reality of observation and experience.

Satire was incorporated into the longer early scientific romances. The portrayal of the Eloi, for example, in *The Time Machine* – the comely, leisured, artlessly inoffensive beings who inhabit the earth 800,000 years hence but who are merely the cattle of the ugly underground Morlocks – can be read with ironic reference to then-current dreams of aestheticism and pastoralism. Anthony West commented: "It is with something of a shock that one finds that what has brought about their debasement is precisely the complete success of mankind in establishing a technological society and world order of the kind to which Wells is supposed to have given his unqualified endorsement."[22] In fact, he was the father of both of the most celebrated twentieth-century dystopias.

When the Sleeper Wakes is an attack on the utopia of a perfected social organization. It contains a vision of the systematic enslavement of organized labour under a police state, "a nightmare of Capitalism triumphant". Later Wells dismissed it (in his Preface of 1921) as "a fantastic possibility no longer possible" but Orwell was to explore its potential.

---

21. Wells, 1924, quoted by Norman and Jeanne Mackenzie, *Life of H.G. Wells*, 338.

22. Anthony West, 1957, in *H.G. Wells,* ed. Bergonzi, 13.

The First Men in the Moon depicts a state brooded over by the enormous brain of The Grand Lunar, in which everybody is a factory-made component of a social machine. One of its scenarios is worth quoting because it is so close in outline to one in Huxley's *Brave New World* which we will be looking at later. The narrator Cavor reports:

> I am still very much in the dark about it, but quite recently I came across a number of young Selenites confined in jars from which only the fore-limbs protruded, who were being compressed to become machine-minders of a special sort. The extended "hand" in this highly developed system of technical education is stimulated by irritants and nourished by injection, while the rest of the body is starved. Phi-oo, unless I misunderstood him, explained that in the earlier stages these queer little creatures are apt to display signs of suffering in their various cramped situations, but they easily become indurated to their lot; and he took me on to where a number of flexible-limbed messengers were being drawn out and broken in. It is quite unreasonable, I know, but such glimpses of the educational methods of these beings affects me disagreeably. I hope, however, that may pass off, and I may be able to see more of this aspect of their wonderful social order. That wretched-looking hand-tentacle sticking out of its jar seemed to have a sort of limp appeal for lost possibilities; and it haunts me still, although, of course, it is really in the end a far more humane proceeding than our earthly method of leaving children to grow into human beings, and then making machines of them.[23]

Towards the end of the first phase of romances, in 1904, came "The Country of the Blind" which Wells thought his best short story. It was the only one to get a compliment from Lawrence, on "how beautiful is Wells' conception".[24] It is worth inspection because it brings one or two of the problems that bother Birkin in *Women in Love* into a focus that is unusually sensitive for Wells. It is a subtly two-sided parable of the need for and the possible effects of social acceptance

When the explorer, Nunez falls into a sealed-off valley inhabited by people who have been blind for generations he discovers that his gift of sight sets him painfully apart from them. The story conveys with sharp irony the sense of puzzlement and outrage on both sides, as Nunez and the blind people struggle to persuade or force each other to

---

23. *The First Men in the Moon*, Everyman edition, 169-70.
24. Lawrence to Edward Marsh, 24 May 1914, in *Letters,* II, 176.

"see" the truth. It is the ideal or mental preoccupation that impedes their understanding, and this is based on their unalterable make-up. Nunez is confronted with the choice of either losing his "deviant" power of sight and belonging to the community or else facing the perilous escape route out of the valley. Rebelling against the "perfected" order they offer in the trap of their giant "casserole" he escapes. The uncertainty about his survival is an effective expression of the story's ambivalence.

The revision of the story's ending throws into relief the trajectory of Wells's development. He itched to make the situation more cut-and-dried. He had already discarded a version in which Nunez returns to the valley to submit to the surgeons: "Down there in the valley was life and love, tender hands and a dear heart, down there was a sort of honour, a sort of consolation and a soul that stood in need of him, and above – solitude, and a fading dream, and a guideless struggle and death."[25] Then in 1939 he looked back, and stamping a narrow interpretation on the existing conclusion ("the visionary dies, a worthless outcast, finding no other escape from his gift but death") he discarded it and provided a new one in which Nunez and his chosen girl leave the valley just in time to avoid an avalanche which destroys it. Wells saw this as "something altogether more tragic" because here "the visionary sees destruction sweeping down upon the whole blind world".[26] Obviously provoked by the author's gloomy view of world politics at that time, the new ending is artistically uninspired. The whole process of revision demonstrates how a fine fable can be knocked off balance by dogma.

Lawrence was less interested in the science fiction than in the novels of Wells's second phase (1905-10) which are more realistic in style, though essentially thematic (that is, in his case, didactic) in conception.

Even the least ideological, *Kipps* and *The History of Mr Polly,* have a didactic purpose, as Wells himself pointed out: to show Kipps and Polly as victims of prevailing social conditions. Kipps is a born victim whom Wells the narrator has to interpret and excuse and cannot help patronizing: "The stupid little tragedies of those clipped and limited lives!" Polly on the other hand is a fun-loving hero with fight and imagination (to both of which his inveterate word-play is a clue)

---

25. Wells, quoted by Patrick Parrinder, "Wells's Cancelled Endings for 'The Country of the Blind'", in Science Fiction Studies, XVII, 72.
26. *Complete Short Stories of H.G. Wells*, ed. John Hammond, 880.

who earns Wells's and our respect and friendly appreciation. The tone adopted towards him is one of camaraderie: he has "a capacity for joy and beauty at least as keen and subtle as yours or mine". The book consists of a series of farcical set-pieces – his father's funeral, his wedding, his quarrels with his neighbours, the big fire, his fight with Jim the bully – in which we have no time to inquire into responses, we are kept so boisterously entertained with the author's "bluffing vivacity" as Henry James called it. E.M. Forster's comment on Wells's characters is most appropriate for this novel: "flat as a photograph" they may be, "but the photographs are agitated with such vigour, that we forget their complexities lie on the surface".[27] They embody simple concepts, and the effect is that of an uncomplicated thematic tale. The end does not simplify because the issues raised have been simple and the conclusion passes apt comic comment on Polly's previous troubles. Moreover, he rebellion against the problems of everyday life does not just resolve itself into an escape into a sleepy utopia, it involves the discovery of fresh perspectives.

Tono-Bungay was altogether more ambitious: to write a full-scale integrated novel in which the development of the characters would combine with wide social themes, so as to constitute what the narrator calls an "extensive cross-section of the British social organism". When it came out in 1909 Lawrence called it "a great book".[28] He was perhaps responding to the ambition behind it rather than its achievement. It actually fails in the attempt at what Lawrence was to achieve several years later. Its structure remained governed by the characters' biographical development, with the generalities superimposed. It is a failure of creative realisation that Lawrence put his finger on four years later:

> His folk have no personality – no passion. The feeling in the book wanders loose – like a sauce poured over it.[29]

The social and ideological portrait of late Victorian and Edwardian England in the novel begins in well-documented typicalities, with a flavour of Dickensian pastiche. George Ponderevo, the narrator, as a child is given situations that are echoes of Dickens's *Great Expectations*, and these extend to his relationship with Beatrice, which recalls Pip's with Estella. However, as the author leaves behind him the necessary authentication of his hero's childhood, so he feels more

---

27. Forster, *Aspects of the Novel*, 99.
28. Lawrence to Blanche Jennings, 8 May 1909, in *Letters*, I, 127.
29. Lawrence to Henry Savage, 15 September 1913, in *Letters*, II, 74.

and more free to elaborate on his real interest, which is the birth of his opinions. The tendency to categorize grows more insistent: "It is all one spectacle of forces running to waste, of people who use and do not replace, the story of a country hectic with a wasting aimless fever of trade and money-making and pleasure-seeking." This is the main theme of the book, and is conceptually and structurally comparable with aspects of Lawrence's theme of self-imprisonment.

George's uncle Edward Ponderevo exemplifies "the process of disintegration". There is some resemblance between him and James Houghton in Lawrence's *The Lost Girl*, in his "incurable, irresponsible childishness ... [his] imaginative silliness". He is less a businessman than an enthusiast who gets addicted to fraud on a grand scale, making millions out of a worthless patent medicine by the inspired lies of his advertisements. The reader catches his progress from shopkeeper to millionaire and eventually back to bankrupt in glimpses which present his increasing sense of direction in the world together with a dwindling inner directive, while his loving wife is left with less and less to love. The description of the enormous house he is prevented from finishing by his financial ruin is offered as equally apt of him and his epoch: "the compactest image and sample of all that passes for Progress, of all the advertisement-inflated spending, the aimless building up and pulling down, the enterprise of my age."

By this time the particularity in the earliest scenes of the book has given way to a generalized gloom in the picture, "one vast dismal spectacle of witless waste" with the muddled futility of "dingy people, wearing shabby second-hand clothes, living uncomfortably in shabby second-hand houses, going to and fro on pavements that always had a thin veneer of greasy, slippery mud". Lawrence in 1909 commented on this aspect of the book: "it makes me so sad .... he is on the whole so true."[30] It had struck a chord that was to sound through his own work whenever it pictured the contemporary urban scene. This includes Ursula's view of Wiggiston and Gudrun's of Beldover, although they are too complex psychologically to be compared with *Tono-Bungay*. Closer in some respects is Connie's of Tevershall in *Lady Chatterley's Lover*. Even there, however, Lawrence's pessimism is one of pain or anger rather than self-pity and disdain.

The theme of destructive waste in Wells's novel is linked with deceptive ideals, a juxtaposition explored in George's development, which consists of a pursuit of false trails. His love affairs are wish-

---

30. Lawrence to Blanche Jennings, 6 March 1909, in *Letters*, I, 119.

fulfilments gone wrong. In some externals they resemble Paul Morel's. He falls in love with girl whose conventionality and frigidity – "for her my ardour had no quickening fire" – make their marriage a failure. There are several characters like this in Wells's fiction – Ethel in *Love and Mr Lewisham*, for example – creatures with few responses besides those sanctioned by their middle-class training. They carry much of the blame for what goes wrong in their marriages. Remington's first wife in *The New Machiavelli*, Margaret, is a little like Miriam in *Sons and Lovers*, in her pathetic desire for self-sacrifice: "All I want in the world is to give my life to you" she tells him.

George's two subsequent love affairs are daydream fulfilments, even more than Paul's with Clara. The second one

> glows in my memory like some bright casual flower starting up amidst the debris of a catastrophe. For nearly a fortnight we two met and made love together. Once more this mighty passion, that our aimless civilization has fettered and maimed and sterilised and debased, gripped me and filled me with passionate delights and solemn joys.[31]

At the end of the novel he is left alone and disillusioned – again, (partly) like Paul.

He flirts with or pursues various ideals besides:

> All my life has been at bottom *seeking*, disbelieving always, dissatisfied always with the thing seen and the thing believed, seeking something in toil, in force, in danger, something whose name and nature I do not clearly understand, something beautiful, worshipful, enduring, mine profoundly and fundamentally, and the utter redemption of myself; I don't know – all I can tell is that it is something I have ever failed to find.[32]

He discovers at last the image of his heart's desire in, of all things, a naval destroyer:

> stark and swift, irrelevant to most human interests. Sometimes I call this reality Science, sometimes I call it Truth .... This thing we make clear is the heart of life.[33]

In this portentous image David Lodge found an irony that is "double-edged".[34] Lucille Herbert, on the other hand, disputed Lodge's

---

31. *Tono-Bungay*, Everyman edition, 338.
32. *Ibid.*, 182.
33. *Ibid.*, 352.
34. Lodge, *Language of Fiction*, 242.

Challenge and Continuity

discovery of a structural coherence in the novel as a whole and found instead a "notional coherence" imposed on it by the final image, in which she saw an attempt to stamp on the novel the author's currently favoured notion of "quasi-religious collectivism".[35] Most readers' responses have been less than complimentary. As Mark Schorer put it: "Of all the kinds of social waste which Wells has been describing, this is the most inclusive, the final waste."[36]

The failure, after *Mr Polly*, to create vivid individuals in his novels belies their lip-service to the value of individuality. This is true of *Ann Veronica*, which Lawrence read soon after *Tono-Bungay*. There are items in this novel, however, that provide a remarkably clear (though minor) instance how a young novelist reading suggestive hints in another's work may several years later weave them into the fabric of his own. For Ann Veronica's story has several obvious external resemblances to Ursula Brangwen's. She is a young student with an "innocent and audacious self-reliance":

> wildly discontented and eager for freedom and life .... All the world about her seemed to be – how can one put it? – in wrappers.[37]

Like Ursula she is keen on Biology and finds in its study a general purpose she can identify with her own. When she meets Capes, a lecturer, their relationship is for her "the dawn of a new life". He declares (like Birkin):

> "I'm making a mess of my life – unless you come in and take it. I am. In you – if you can love me – there is salvation."[38]

Like Birkin and Ursula they go to the Swiss Alps together:

> "We've deserted the posts in which we found ourselves, cut our duties, exposed ourselves to risks that may destroy any sort of social usefulness in us .... That wrappered life, as you call it – we've burnt the confounded rags!"[39]

In his later novels Wells's didacticism took more obvious forms. In *The New Machiavelli* Remington declares (like Ben Cooley in *Kangaroo*, but without irony or criticism) that people must recognize

---

35. Herbert, *"Tono-Bungay*: Tradition and Experiment", in *H.G. Wells*, ed. Bergonzi, 144. She went on to argue (as we have done) that *Tono-Bungay* is "a failed experiment in a fictional mode that Lawrence practiced, in *The Rainbow*, with infinitely greater delicacy" (*Ibid*, 155).

36. Schorer, *The World We Imagine*, 11.

37. *Ann Veronica*, Everyman edition, 5.

38. *Ibid.*, 221.

39. *Ibid.*, 238 and 244.

leaders such as himself who realize that the mind is the "hinterland ... in human affairs generally, the permanent reality". Wells became the prophet of that ideal of human perfectibility by applied science and social engineering to which he has given his name. Conrad said to him: "You don't care for humanity but think they are to be improved. I love humanity but know they are not!"[40]

Lawrence's final comment went further along the same lines, detecting in *The World of William Clissold* "a peevish, ashy indifference to everything except himself, himself as centre of the universe".[41] His verdict corresponds with several others on Wells at this time. "He has become a sort of 'little God,' demanding payment in flattery" wrote Beatrice Webb in her diary for July 1923, and on one occasion a year earlier, Rebecca West, who knew him very well, called him "enormously vain, irascible and in a fantasy world".[42]

It is easy for us now to spot in Wells's work what Henry James called "the loose, the improvised, the cheap and the easy" or to diagnose the processes by which he simplified or magnified experience into the stereotype or the ideal. His own retort when challenged by James was, "I had rather be called a journalist than an artist".[43] He and Bennett were close friends, but other major contemporaries were either patronizing or lukewarm. Conrad was friendly enough personally but poles apart in mentality, though he did call him "the Realist of the Fantastic". Joyce respected the man but not his work. Woolf lumped him together with Bennett and Galsworthy as the "materialists" of fiction. Lawrence was the one who took Wells seriously enough to learn from him, as he did from Hardy and Bennett. Although Wells did not return the literary interest, there was some friendly interchange between the two men at the very end of Lawrence's life when they were living near each other in the South of France.

In the next generation, readers as different as George Orwell and V. S. Pritchett enjoyed the feeling of wonder Wells provoked, and the "exhilarating sense of personal freedom".[44] So much so that Orwell felt it was "a kind of parricide" to find fault with him.[45]

---

40. Conrad, qoted by Hart Davis, *Hugh Walpole*, 168.
41. Lawrence, 1926, in *Phoenix*, ed. Edward McDonald, 349
42. Webb and West, quoted by Mackenzie, *Life of H.G. Wells*, 335 and 339.
43. Leon Edel and Gordon Ray, eds *Henry James and H.G. Wells*, 128 and 264.
44. Pritchett, *The Living Novel*, 117.
45. Orwell, 1941, in *Collected Essays*, II, 170.

Conrad claims special attention among Lawrence's contemporaries by the nature of his genius. His years (28 years older) and his Polishness set him apart, yet he is the essential link in the chain of influences and affinities that binds Dickens and Dostoevsky to Lawrence. It is not certain how much Lawrence read of him, but it included some early stories, *Lord Jim* (by 1909) and *Under Western Eyes* in 1912. Those are the main items to be considered here, together with a look at *Nostromo* because of its centrality in Conrad's work.

In English Conrad's literary debt was chiefly to Dickens and James. Conrad recalled reading Dickens in his youth – his father had published a translation of *Hard Times* – so the influence, as with Lawrence, remained relatively subliminal but no less powerful than that resulting from conscious study. He often made passing references in his letters to *Bleak House*, *Our Mutual Friend* and others, which show a close and easy familiarity with them. In his work there are some specifically Dickensian features – the scene with Winnie Verloc's mother and the cabbie in *A Secret Agent*, for instance, or the trio of villains in *Victory* – but these are sometimes weaknesses rather than virtues in his art. The more important kinship went deeper and is to do with the structure of the novels, as we intend to show. On the other hand, James's novels were encountered just as Conrad was preparing himself for a career as a novelist himself, so it was a matter of conscious learning – he always addressed him as *"cher maître"* in his letters – and he was rewarded with some fine object-lessons in the manipulation of the narrative point of view, as well as a kindred intensity of artistic discipline.

The deeper background was, of course, Polish – he was, according to Zdzislaw Najder, by the age of 17 "well-read, particularly in Polish Romantic literature".[46] Then there was Russian (translated into Polish, French or English). Of the great Russian novelists, Conrad had some praise for Turgenev, but none for Tolstoy and Dostoevsky. In 1912 (when he was 55, with most of his work behind him) we get the first reference in his letters to Dostoevsky. He read *The Brothers Karamazov* in Constance Garnett's translation of 1912 and told her husband: "It's terrifically bad and impressive and exasperating …. too Russian for me."[47] There is little other evidence of his reading or response. Is it conceivable, even allowing for his nation's and family's well-grounded antagonism towards all things Russian, that he had no

46. Najder, *Joseph Conrad,* 38.
47. Conrad to Edward Garnett, 27 May 1912, in *Letters,* V, 70.

knowledge of Dostoevsky's novels during his formative years? Some readers of *Under Western Eyes* have found good reasons for detecting Raskolnikov (of *Crime and Punishment*) behind Razumov, and aspects of *The House of the Dead* in the portrait of Peter Ivanovitch.[48] The kinship suggested in our study is (as with Dickens) not a matter of specifics. The effect of such an early influence is not like considered study, but more like a vaccine: it leaves potential themes and motifs, together with clues to their handling, available in the creative unconscious.

The French tradition of the novel – as far back as Stendhal and Balzac, both of whom he regarded as touchstones – was in the forefront of his mind when he began his writing career. Hence his praise of Maupassant, with the insistence in his Preface to *The Nigger of the Narcissus* in 1997 on the way "all art appeals to the senses". He later denied the influence of Flaubert's *Madame Bovary,* but it is evident enough in the work.[49]

Nearly all of Conrad's early work, like Lawrence's, was focused chiefly on psychological studies. As in Lawrence's, the thematic interests that were later to control the structure lay dormant or awkwardly protruding. An early experiment in the injection of thematic material into a psychological context is the tale (which Lawrence probably read) called "The Return" (1898). A city businessman who considers himself "well-connected, well-educated and intelligent" and is preoccupied with his appearance in the "mirrors" of opinion, is married to a woman equally conventional, inwardly fixed in an attitude of disillusion and resentment against him. Their house represents the moral prison in which they live: images of imprisonment recur, and their statuesque behaviour together recalls that of Dickens's Dombey and Edith. Some of the other imagery in the tale foreshadows Lawrence: "They skimmed over the surface of life hand in hand, in a pure and frosty atmosphere – like two skilful skaters cutting figures in thick ice for the admiration of the beholders, and disdainfully ignoring the hidden stream, the stream restless and dark; the stream of life, profound and unfrozen." The darkness-water-ice motifs that Lawrence developed – the two former with their ambiguity, both dangerous and life-giving, regressive and renewing, source of chaos and of regeneration – continue through Conrad's work

---

48. See Keith Carabine, "From Razumov to *Under Western Eyes*", in *Conradiana*, XXV, 3-29.
49. See Yves Hervouet, *The French Face of Joseph Conrad*, 64-69.

as they do through Lawrence's. The husband moves from despair (after his wife's infidelity and departure) to the realisation of a conscience:

> There can be no life without faith and love – faith in a human heart, the love of a human being! .... It was an awful sacrifice to cast one's life into the flame of a new belief ... the cruel decree of salvation.

If this was one of the stories Lawrence felt to be "so good" it was pointing a direction for him to take. But the thematic material is somewhat self-consciously superimposed on the psychological analysis.

The next year, in the first part of *Lord Jim*, the two coalesced. In the first thirteen chapters of that novel we see Conrad diagnosing the destructive and the creative factors in the situation and highlighting the profoundly ambiguous dynamic interaction between them, in a narrative texture which with its insistence on the primacy of the point of view (both the characters' and the narrators') underlines the moral relativity of the whole experience. Marlow the narrator (with most of the narrative in inverted commas) puts us sympathetically into touch yet critically detached. Conrad had learned from Henry James to master this feat which Flaubert had agonized over. It is a triumph of imaginative identification and scrupulous focusing, brought about by an impassioned criss-crossing of observation and analysis assisted by juxtapositions which dissect and reassemble time in order to reveal the essence of things. Conrad once said, "all my concern has been with the 'ideal' value of things, events and people".[50] The statement does not of course signify an allegiance to conventional liberal ideals, but rather an attention to the kind of generalities we have seen operating as controlling interests in the novels of Dickens, Dostoevsky and Lawrence.

Lord Jim resembles *Madame Bovary* in several ways, one of which is its concentration on a single character who is also the main theme, the two indissolubly fused. Another is the characters themselves, and the way they became for their authors an exercise in self-criticism. Jim is a diseased idealist, like Emma, although the balance in him of the desire to insulate and the need to belong is closer to Will Brangwen's. And just as Emma took on (and minimized) some of the romantic fantasies that had belonged to her author, so Jim for Conrad represented many of the positives he associated, especially in his early tales like *The Nigger of the Narcissus, Youth* and *Typhoon*, with good

---

50 Conrad to Colvin, 1 March 1917, quoted by Jocelyn Baines, *Joseph Conrad*, 439.

seamanship and the life-preserving values of mutual fidelity in that little kingdom, the ship at sea. He is also, or seems to be, like any young man who is full of energy and the desire to do well – "one of us" as Marlow says. But his ideals of heroism and service are essentially an expression of his insulation from others. His conscious life consists largely of a romantic affair between himself and his self-enhancing ideal. Living vividly in the dreamworld where he idealizes his responses, his first personal disaster – the desertion of the *Patna*, abandoned in the middle of the Indian Ocean with its 800 Asian pilgrims because of fears about a leaky bulkhead – comes upon him while he is gazing at the opportunity for heroism. "I knew nothing about it till I looked up", he says about his jump from the ship.

His egoism sustains his idealism, which interposes itself like a mirage between self and reality, treacherously separating its owner from the people it ostensibly serves. But Conrad is intent not only on analysing the psychological mechanism (though that is meticulous) but also exploring its general significance, and this involves judging Jim and what he stands for against a whole range of other people and the moral positions they represent: the wide context of the kind of thematic novel we are investigating.[51]

On one side of the scale is rampant egoism: the cowardice of the other whites in the *Patna* crew, the rapacity of people like Chester and Robinson, and the empty perfectionism of Captain Brierly, that paragon of seamanship who commits suicide after hearing Jim's case in court and is remembered tenderly only by his dog and a man who in his life could not stand him:

> "The posthumous revenge of fate for that belief in his own splendour which had almost cheated his life of its legitimate terrors. Almost! Perhaps wholly. Who can tell what a flattering view he induced himself to take of his own suicide?"[52]

On the other side are those like Bob Stanton – he "got drowned trying to save a lady's maid in the Sephora disaster" – whose sympathetic responsiveness operates spontaneously. Bob in this instance expects to live and sees the situation as involving immediate

---

51 For an application to this novel of some of Mikhail Bakhtin's notions about narrative structure, see Gail Fincham, "The Dialogism of Lord Jim", in *Conrad and Theory*, eds Andrew Gibson and Robert Hampson. For a more sceptical view see Cedric Watts, "Bakhtin's Monologism and the Endings of *Crime and Punishment* and *Lord Jim*", in *The Conradian*, XX (2000).
52. *Lord Jim*, Collected edition, 64. Subsequent page references are to this edition, which has the same pagination as the earlier Uniform and Medallion editions.

practical issues with little or no idea of his role. The clownish awkwardness and accident that enters into a natural and unpremeditated act is in evidence. We see Bob, a short man trying to get a tall hysterically immobilized woman off a sinking ship. He looks, to one of his shipmates, "for all the world, sir, like a naughty youngster fighting with his mother".

In the middle are those who demonstrate the social and survival value of a faith or a code, like the pilgrims and the Malay helmsman on the *Patna*. Somewhere near the centre too, close to Marlow himself is the French Lieutenant who at the risk of his own life supervises the towing of the abandoned ship. He reacts to Jim's case with fellow-feeling and admits that "one's courage does not come of itself". However:

> "'And what life may be worth when'... he got on his feet with a ponderous impetuosity, as a startled ox might scramble up from the grass ... 'when the honour is gone – *ah ça! par exemple* – I can offer no opinion. I can offer no opinion – because – monsieur – I know nothing of it.'" (148)

The way he cuts short the conversation betrays the potential insecurity of an obsessive leaning upon the code. His lack of imagination – at any rate, of what gives Jim his fatal "forestalling vision" on the Patna – is turned into a strength.

As these details show, the minor characters in this part of *Lord Jim*, for all their structural functionality, are not merely symbolic or illustrative figures but vividly individual. The human reality even of the anonymous *Patna* pilgrims is individualized in the man who just before the desertion clings to Jim's leg crying for water. Even the white *Patna* crew, though regarded by Jim with an almost Flaubertian detestation, sometimes grab at our fellow feeling in unexpected ways. In the lifeboat after they have abandoned ship:

> "they were suddenly and unanimously moved to make a noise over their escape. 'I knew from the first she would go.' 'Not a minute too soon.' 'A narrow squeak, b'gosh!' He [Jim] said nothing .... He noticed that they talked as though they had left behind nothing but an empty ship." (115)

The reader is almost brought to sympathize with their ordinary humanity. There is for them at least a sense of failure beneath the self-assertion, while Jim, with his desperate disregard for his own life as well as theirs – standing with the tiller in his hand ready to kill anyone who goes for him – may well seem at this juncture the more dangerous as well as the more complex threat.

But Marlow guesses deeper impulses:

> "I believe that, in this first moment, his heart was wrung with all the suffering, that his soul knew the accumulated savour of all the fear, all the horror, all the despair of eight hundred human beings pounced upon in the night by a sudden and violent death, else why should he have said, 'It seemed to me that I must jump out of that accursed boat and swim back to see – half a mile – more – any distance – to very spot ...?'" (113)

We can see an effort in him (which hardly exists in Emma Bovary) towards self-liberation and a deeper, more natural relationship with others, in the reaction of his conscience against becoming (not just appearing to be) like the Patna crew. The need to understand and relate is expressed as a near-hysterical mental activity

> He wanted to go on talking for truth's sake, perhaps for his own sake also; and while his utterance was deliberate, his mind positively flew round the serried circle of facts that had surged up all about him to cut him off from the rest of his kind; it was like a creature that, finding itself imprisoned within an enclosure of high stakes, dashes round and round, distracted in the night, trying to find a weak spot, a crevice, a place to scale, some opening through which it may squeeze itself and escape. (31)

His relationship with Marlow – confessing, wanting reassurance and guidance – testifies to the struggle. "He was not speaking to me", says Marlow, "he was speaking before me, in a dispute with an invisible personality, an antagonistic and inseparable partner of his existence – another possessor of his soul". The conflict constitutes what Marlow calls "a subtle and momentous quarrel as to the true essence of life". It is one in which he himself is crucially involved, sharing as he does Jim's attachment to certain ideals and the disillusion that must accompany their pursuit: "If he had not enlisted my sympathies he had done better for himself – he had gone to the very font and origin of that sentiment, he had reached the secret sensibility of my egoism."

The final vision of Jim in this part of the book is of tragic desperation:

> "And then at the moment of taking leave he treated me to a ghastly muddle of dubious stammers and movements, to an awful display of hesitations. God forgive him – me! He had taken it into his fanciful head that I was likely to make some difficulty as to shaking hands. It was too awful for words. I believe I shouted suddenly at him as you

> would bellow to a man you saw about to walk over a cliff; I
> remember our voices being raised, the appearance of a miserable grin
> on his face, a crushing clutch on my hand, a nervous laugh .... He got
> himself away somehow. The night swallowed his form. He was a
> horrible bungler. Horrible. I heard the quick crunch-crunch of the
> gravel under his boots. He was running. Absolutely running, with
> nowhere to go to. And he was not yet four-and-twenty. (155)

At this point Conrad's aim stands accomplished, with Jim essentially
more tragic than Emma Bovary because of the wider range of
sympathies involved, the sense of worth lost, and the universals
explored on the pulses.

The rest – two thirds of the book, spun out for many more issues
of *Blackwood's Magazine* than originally intended – is a bonus.
Nobody would complain if its literary quality were as high, but it is
not. At the end of January 1900, while writing Chapter 18, Conrad fell
ill: "Malaria, bronchitis and gout. In reality, a breakdown."[53] Perhaps
the physical breakdown accounts for the artistic one at this point in the
novel. Perhaps the physical breakdown itself was caused by the
sustained critical and self-critical effort of the first third of the book.
However we speculate, it is clear that all the issues raised in such a
challenging way by the early chapters are afterwards simplified. Not
equally so, however. Whereas nearly every critic has noted the
weakness of the Patusan chapters, the later episodes, after the arrival
of Gentleman Brown, have a higher reputation. Albert Guerard, for
instance, claimed that they "recover the authenticity in depth of the
first part of the novel".[54] Even if one does not agree with that, it is
easy to see a distinction in quality between the middle fifteen chapters
and the last nine.

Since the first part of the book ranks along with the kind of
thematic novels we have been most interested in, and as a whole
belongs with them, the nature of the failure is worth a little study,
because it illustrates some of the pitfalls of this kind of thematic
fiction.

The first thing one notices in the Patusan chapters is that the
universals are no longer fused with the character and action but
separated out, in poetic and abstract terms. Symbols and concepts
proliferate without particularity:

---

53. Conrad to Cunninghame Graham, 13 February 1900, in *Letters*, II, 248.
54. Guerard, *Conrad the Novelist*, 168.

"At the first bend he lost sight of the sea with its labouring waves forever rising, sinking and vanishing to rise again – the very image of struggling mankind – and faced the immovable forests deep in the soil, soaring towards the sunshine, everlasting in the shadowy might of their tradition, like life itself." (243)

The sustained intensity is gone. Marlow is no longer exploring an emotional crisis at first hand but relating episodes, sometimes from hearsay. He lapses occasionally into platitude: "Felicity. felicity – how shall I say it? – is quaffed out of a golden cup in every latitude." His friend Stein adds his quota: "To follow the dream and again to follow the dream and so – *ewig – usque ad finem*" – a statement which has provoked endless exegesis but as Ian Watt politely put it, "resists any consensus of interpretation" adding that in Conrad's revision of it "the logic of his sea metaphor then led to the confusing notion that man should 'follow the dream' by trying to keep out of it, but not too hard".[55] Some people have even seen Stein, with his talk of that day when he "had nothing left to desire" because he had bagged three natives and a rare butterfly, as a Polonius with a killer instinct.

Of course, neither Stein nor Marlow can be regarded as Conrad's spokesmen. Marlow dissociates himself from Stein's ambiguous romanticism, and his own man-of-the-world bluffness and garrulity dissociate him from Conrad. The ambiguous status of Marlow – neither reliable as authorial spokesman nor objectively focused as an independent character – makes unrewarding any attempt, such as Ian Watt's, to shift the centre of attention in the novel from Jim to the "personal relationship" between them.[56] The generality that pervades this part of the novel is of course performing one of the functions of Jim's idealism, which is to simplify the full flux of experience and separate oneself from it. Its extent suggests the degree to which Marlow (and at one remove, Conrad) share the tendency.

The temptation to conceptualize the living context was of course Lawrence's also, as we have seen in *Kangaroo*, for instance, although more dangerous for him was the dogmatic version of the tendency, to be seen in *The Plumed Serpent*: a trap Conrad did not fall into.

The second thing one notices in Patusan is that the good people on the map are less than convincing. The stock natives – the dignified Dain Waris, the statuesque Doramin and the crafty Rajah – are no more real than those in Conrad's first novel, *Almayer's Folly*. And the

55. Watt, *Conrad in the Nineteenth Century*, 327-9.
56. See Watt, *Conrad in the Nineteenth Century*, 337.

affirmation of what Marlow calls the "wonderful" and "amazing" adventure of Jim's salvation in Patusan, qualified ironically as it is by our previous knowledge of his problems, allows no clear focus, centred as it is on a love affair between Jim and Jewel that is like "knight and maiden meeting to exchange vows amongst haunted ruins". This kind of sentimentalism was less of a temptation for Lawrence than it was for Dickens and Dostoevsky; and the same is true of the next feature.

There is something theatrical in the villains. When Gentleman Brown is introduced in Chapter 37 an effort is made to provide him with a few appealing human frailties: his fear of imprisonment and that episode in his past when he adored some woman, lost her and cursed life the more. But it is a portrait bolstered with explicit statement: "an undisguised ruthlessness of purpose, a strange vengeful attitude towards his past, and a blind belief in the righteousness of his will." It is supplemented with stage gestures: "he fell back, clawing the air with skinny fingers, sat up again, bowed and hairy, glared at me sideways like some man-beast of folklore." The rest of his crew are stock cut-throats, dead shots and ruffians. There is no room here for the uncomfortable fellow feeling roused by Jim's fellow-deserters of the *Patna*, nor the boisterous bitter humour that brought those earlier scenes to life.

In the last nine chapters we have Jim, not as before via Marlow's narrative, but third-hand: somebody else's account, relayed by him. The most important scene, when Jim faces Brown across a creek to negotiate his departure or destruction is retold from Brown himself many years later. In his distorting mirror we have to imagine Jim preoccupied with his dream of himself and the reality of self-mistrust, and glimpse Brown's sensing this enough to play off one against the other, so winning his escape and a bloody reprisal. We may re-invent Jim as he was on the *Patna,* spellbound by a heroic vision of himself, making his decision to let Brown go while still rapt in the pride of his noble and merciful act, for we know from the past his incapacity to judge people – part of the dangerous simplicity born of his self-concern. But this is all guesswork, given only two observations about Jim by Brown – "looking black as thunder" and "thinking and switching his leg" – one generalization from Marlow, "These were the emissaries with whom the world he had renounced was pursuing him in his retreat" and a few boyscoutish pronouncements Brown quotes from Jim, culminating in: "You shall have a clear road or else a clear fight." It is not surprising that readers are divided about the significance of what happens. To some, Jim's leniency is excusable – to Ian Watt, for instance, on the grounds that "the extermination in cold blood of any human being – whatever their colour – would be morally offensive to anyone raised in the Western Christian tradition, even if he were not, like Jim, the son of a parson".[57] Others, such as Arnold Davidson, draw from the same evidence conclusions that condemn Jim's "obtuseness"[58] especially in contrast with some of the natives' clear-sightedness about Brown.

Conrad felt it necessary to defend the style chosen for the ending of the novel (which he said had been "thought out" before the story was begun):

> The end of *Lord Jim* in accordance with a meditated resolve is presented in a bare almost bald relation of matters of fact. The situation – the problem if you will – of that sensitive nature has been already commented upon, illustrated and contrasted. It is my opinion that in the working out of the catastrophe psychologic disquisition should have no place .... In the light of the final incident, the story in all its descriptive detail shall fall into its place – acquire its value and significance.[59]

This purpose is attained to a limited degree. Jim goes to his execution, after the disaster of Brown's revenge, out of shame but with a histrionic flourish of nobility, confirming that "an exalted egoism" has been the dominant motive in all his altruism, as it is now in this "pitiless wedding with a shadowy ideal of conduct". But because of the generality of treatment and the reticence of Jim's responses – "I have no life .... There is nothing to fight for .... There is no escape" – no consensus is possible about the significance of what is being offered. Ted Boyle, for example, concluded: "Jim has rid himself of his hollow romanticism, but he has not forsaken his dream."[60] Arnold Davidson, on the other hand, pointed out that his suicide is in one respect more reprehensible than Brierly's, for he deserts Jewel whereas Brierly at least makes careful provision for his ship and his dog![61] Linda Dryden pointed out: "Jewel's claim that he was 'false' and Stein's rejoinder, 'No! no! Not false! True! true! true!' are

---

57. Watt, *Conrad in the Nineteenth Century*, 342.
58. Davidson, *Conrad's Endings*, 19.
59. Conrad to William Blackwood, 19 July 1900, in *Letters*, II, 283; and 31 May 1902, in *Letters*, II, 417.
60. Boyle, *Symbol and Meaning in the Fiction of Joseph Conrad*, 84.
61. See Davidson, *Conrad's Endings*, 25.

opposing views of Jim that the narrative refuses to reconcile."[62] There
is not enough substance in the immediate situation to make an attempt
at reconcilement worthwhile. If we look back, as Conrad expected us
to, at Jim as he appeared in the first part of the novel, we are faced
chiefly with a discrepancy: this Jim is a ghost of his former self. We
have seen this kind of attenuation – the reduction of complex issues to
a skeletal diagram – in the novels Lawrence wrote soon after *Women
in Love.*

On the last page Marlow cannot help flinging a primadonna's
bouquet: "the alluring shade of that extraordinary success! ... the face
of that opportunity which, like an Eastern bride, had come veiled to
his side." If we need an antidote to this kind of romanticism, what
better than that provided by Conrad himself in "The Secret Sharer"
which was written twelve years later but actually conceived while he
was finishing *Lord Jim.* In this tale the narrator in his first command at
sea begins like Jim with "that ideal conception of one's own
personality every man sets up for himself secretly" and is forced to
recognize the real: the latent potentialities in himself that make him
uncannily resemble his strange visitor, Leggat, who has killed a man.
Leggat, a man of exemplary courage and seamanship, justifies the
murder in terms of provocation – the victim mutinied during an action
in which Leggat saved his ship from sinking in a storm – and his own
state of exhaustion at the time. With a clear-sightedness matched by
the style of the narrative, he accepts the fate that tortures Jim: "the
'Brand of Cain' business .... I was ready to go off wandering on the
face of the earth." The narrator is not only convinced by him but
imagines for him a positive outcome: "the secret sharer of my cabin
and of my thoughts, as though he were my second self, had lowered
himself into the water to take his punishment: a free man, a proud
swimmer striking out for a new destiny." The topic of "doubling"
touched on in the relationship of Jim and Brown is here dovetailed
into the portrait without artifice. The tale is written with perfectionist
skill, vivid, lucid and funny.

Some aspects of the handling of Jim's idealism appealed to
Lawrence – Jessie Chambers reported that he liked the book when he
read it in his twenties – but it is unlikely he would have been entirely
pleased. He would have been more so perhaps with the portrait of
Charles Gould in *Nostromo.* In that next novel the themes are

---

62. Dryden, *Joseph Conrad and the Imperial Romance*, 193.

developed on a scale that begs comparison with the major novels of Dickens, Dostoevsky and Lawrence.

All kinds of idealism are here incorporated into a dense political set-up. This ranges from those who have sacrificed their lives for simple political formulas, to those for whom ideals are the weapons of their egotism. The former include the outdated and displaced idealists of the old school. Don Jose Avellanos, for example, is "overtaxed by so many years of undiscouraged belief in regeneration" but made "ecstatic" by the sight of the "new deadly rifles" in the hands of his soldiers. The old Garibaldi fighter, Viola Gambetta keeps "his spirit of self-forgetfulness, the simple devotion to a vast humanitarian idea". But in the flocks of political vultures who infest the country, greed, barbarism, cowardice, sadism or megalomania are covered by a pretence to social good so crude that ordinary people go along with it only out of fear of its power or else wanting to share the spoils.

The analysis of negative idealism centres on Charles Gould, who is, like Lawrence's Thomas Crich, a capitalist with dreams of becoming a great benefactor. His idealism operates in the same way, hiding and abetting the basic defect of his nature. The catastrophe in his life comes upon him not out of the blue like Jim's but gradually, insidiously. It takes a lifetime and looks to most people like success. His materialism is a different form of escapism. A visionary rapt, as Martin Decoud says, in "a moral romance derived from the tradition of a pretty fairy tale" he dreams of making good his father's political and financial failure by using the wealth of his silver mine to bring order and justice to Costaguana, attracting other "material interests" – from Holroyd the powerful idealistic American financier down to the local gangsters – which parody, pervert or sully his enterprise.

As Gould becomes imprisoned in his obsession the vague, inarticulate bluntness of his responses hardens. His ideals become fixed ideas, and "a man haunted by a fixed idea is insane". When he succeeds materially the success mocks the original aspiration. Even his wife has to admit in the end that she sees the mountain with its silver "hanging over the Campo, over the whole land, feared, hated, wealthy; more soulless than any tyrant, more pitiless and autocratic than the worst Government; ready to crush innumerable loves in the expansion of its greatness". The machine he has built, like Gerald Crich's, absorbs the individuality of master and men alike.

The analysis is subtle, balanced and far-reaching, even if it lacks some of the intensities of the "trial" of Jim. The portrait is made up largely of observation and report but it becomes intimate and subtle though his relationship with his wife and her responses to him. We see their separational thinking in the roles they have allowed or allotted to themselves and each other: for instance in the scene where she, having seen through Holroyd's "religion of silver and iron" asks "Charley" for his feelings about it, and he, after offering a platitude, fobs her off with, "The best of my feelings are in your keeping" – said tenderly, for "theirs was a successful match". The irony in that comment is gentle because his genuine affection for her is his saving grace. But he steadily refuses to "discuss the ethical view" with her, and the separative reticence between them goes on eroding the freedom and fullness of their lives.

In *Nostromo* the villains and megalomaniacs have the same vivid reality as the Patna crew but are on a grander scale. The three uglies, General Montero, Pedrito his brother, and Sotillo show an undeniably human pleasure in destroying whoever gets in their way. The General is particularly memorable visually: "The white plume, the coppery tint of his broad face, the blue-black of the moustaches under the curved beak, the mass of gold on sleeves and breast, the high shining boots with enormous spurs, the working nostrils, the imbecile and domineering stare." One of the highs in this kind of drama comes when poor Hirsch, being tortured for information about the silver consignment, spits in Sotillo's face, provoking him to shoot him – the victim revenged and released in one.

Nostromo himself is a curious variant, believing in his ideals though they are simple reflexes of the ego. He is in love with a vision of his own glory: "To be well-spoken of" as he says. "Embodied vanity of the sailor kind" Conrad called him.[63] At least it is not hypocritical, for he sees glory in terms of service of the great and good, until the last episodes, when he turns thief, with the excuse that the great have not been good to him, they have failed to live up to his idea of what it behoved them to do for him. After the death of his idealism the ego remains, undiminished, disgruntled and dangerous.

The most challenging and complicated of all the self-imprisoned egos in the novel is Martin Decoud. He is distinct enough in his assertion that he does without ideals or convictions of any kind. "What is a conviction?" he asks: "A particular view of our personal advantage either practical or emotional." If he espouses any it is entirely in the spirit of the rogues in the book, for personal gain, in his case of Antonia Avellanos – or so he says. The interesting aspect of

---

63. Conrad to Cunninghame Graham, 31 October 1904, in *Letters*, III, 175.

his case is suggested by the fact that neither Antonia nor Emilia Gould really believe him. Emilia detects "tremendous excitement" under his "cloak of studied carelessness". Talking politics to Antonia, Martin himself is "surprised at the warmth of his own words". They and we are intrigued and eventually moved by the contradictions that exist in him between his professed moral nihilism and "the genuine impulses of his own nature" to which he has blinded himself by "the habit of universal raillery". He is "moved in spite of himself by that note of passion and sorrow unknown on the more refined stage of European politics". His scepticism fights his interest in Antonia. He alternately calls it an "infatuation" and a "passionate devotion", later demotes it to "the supreme illusion of a lover" and towards the end to something "into which he had worked himself up out of the depths of his scepticism". Finally, on the cargo lighter in the night – with the dark waters and the pitch-black sky suggesting death and the emptiness of life to him, as the lake and the Alps do to Gerald Crich – it has "lost all appearance of reality".

Some have seen his suicide as simply the failure of a pose, but this is unfair because he targets his own pretences: "analysed fearlessly all motives and passions, including his own." Some kind of reductionism seems to be invited by Conrad's commentary, whose severity may be due to his effort of dissociation from a character so close to him mentally.[64] The final summation, for instance – he dies "from solitude and want of faith in himself and others" – refines away some of the complications we have noted. Nevertheless, in the sleepless stress of his last eleven days on the desert island our sympathy is acutely alive as we experience the withering away of his undernourished feelings: "the solitude appeared like a great void, and the silence of the gulf like a tense, thin cord to which he hung suspended by both hands, without fear, without surprise, without any sort of emotion whatever." What fails him is not simply the ability to believe but the strength to make and hold the living contacts with others that normally go with belief.

---

64. There are many Decoud-like comments in Conrad's letters, especially those written in the few years before the composition of *Nostromo* to his friend Cunninghame Graham. For instance: "Half the words we use have no meaning whatever and of the other half each man understands each word after the fashion of his own folly and conceit. Faith is a myth and beliefs shift like mists on the shore." Then he added, saved from an excess of cynicism by his sense of humour, "only the string of my platitudes seems to have no end" (to Cunninghame Graham, 14 January 1898 in *Letters,* II, 17). Conrad's sense of humour saved him from cynicism as often as Dickens's saved him from sentimentality.

In this novel it is attachment to the real not the ideal that sustains, whether for good or ill.

The pre-requisites of that kind of attachment (or "solidarity" to use Conrad's favourite term) are the third major theme of *Nostromo*. They exist pre-eminently in two characters whose actions are creative, or at least curative, because they are attuned to the well-being of others by instinctive sympathy.

Emilia Gould's social ideals – sharing her husband's dream – are essentially an extension of her personal idealization of him: "He was perfect – perfect." But they are always, unlike his, informed by her "genius of sympathetic intuition". Even while officiating as the hostess of the Casa Gould it is her "alert perception of values" that is noticed. Her work alongside Charles at the mine focuses on the welfare of the mineworkers and their families. The three men she helps choose to govern the mountainside community – she calls them "pastors" – are genuinely humane and responsible, as well as devoted to her. Nearly all the characters in the novel from whose standpoint the criminals and failures are finally to be judged are gathered around her: she is its moral centre. As she loses faith in Charles's aims she falls back on a "wisdom of the heart" which has "no concern with the erection or demolition of theories any more than with the defence of prejudices".

Although there is no close psychological examination of her and we see her almost always from the standpoint of an observer, the observation is keenly alert, especially to her distress. At the very end we see "the profound, blind, suffering expression of a painful dream settled on her face with its closed eyes". By then even her personal love of Charles is little more than a cherished memory: "love was only a short moment of forgetfulness, a short intoxication, whose delight one remembered with a sense of sadness, as if it had been a deep grief lived through." Her barren life – "Was it for this that her life had been robbed of all the intimate felicities of daily affection which her tenderness needed as the human body needs air to breathe?" – is a casualty of conditions encouraged for the survival of abstract rather than human causes.

At this point her sole intimate is Doctor Monygham, who offers another twist in the analysis. Long before the start of the novel's events, we are told, he held to a "rule of conduct" which is defined (like Jim's) as "an ideal view". Then, as with Jim, came the shame of treachery to those ideals, when he betrayed his friends under torture. He enters the action of the novel burdened with disillusion and shame.

He hobbles around with his "twisted shoulders, drooping head, sardonic mouth and side-long bitter glance" giving the impression that he has had every moral principle beaten out of him: "the outward aspect of an outcast." His disillusion is more extreme than Jim's, however: "I put no spiritual value into my desires, or my opinions, or my actions." That registers a crucial distinction between the two. The phrase used to define his earlier idealism, "the imaginative exaggeration of a correct feeling" recalls the definition of Emilia's: "the true expression of an emotion." Though it refers to the self it also registers the kind of attachment to the care of others shown originally in his choice of profession. In the end it is his "capacity for passion" and "the sensitiveness of his temperament" that comes to the fore, drawn to Emilia. At a certain crisis of the revolution his devotion to her becomes as dangerous as any other fanatical obsession in the novel, since he is willing, like Charles with his mine, to sacrifice everything for it: "implacable in the expansion of his tenderness." But it is focused on one person and generally monitored by a keen sympathy for others.

As Keith Carabine said, in this novel "the reader is obliged to *criticize* all the characters' viewpoints".[65] It is as much a dialogue of clashing worlds as a novel by Dostoevsky. It is an experience that involves (in Conrad's words) "the courageous recognition of all the irreconcilable antagonisms that make our life so enigmatic, so burdensome, so fascinating, so dangerous – so full of hope".[66] The upbeat of that last phrase is registered in the novel itself in its tribute to Sulaco's newfound prosperity: "It was like a second youth, like a new life, full of promise." Of course, that is not the last note struck, for it is immediately qualified by "of unrest, of toil" and followed by the final gloomy conversation between Emilia and Monygham. But in the novel as a whole the weight of pessimism is laid in the scales against egoism, whether or not allied to idealism, and not against participation as such.

The novel is a great achievement and places Conrad squarely on our map of major thematic novelists, but it is not quite his finest. For that we have to look to the one Lawrence read when it first came out in 1912.

---

65. *Nostromo*, ed. Carabine, xii.
66. Conrad was writing to the *New York Times*, 2 August 1901 on "the only legitimate basis of creative work". See *Letters*, II, 348-9.

In *Under Western Eyes* the social environment is as packed as it is in the previous two novels with powerful, sinister forces and malignant egos.[67] The action is detonated by a revolutionary idealist. These themes are developed with the sharp vividness we have noted in *Nostromo*. The new further exploration here lies in the third theme, in which a nature potentially richer and more responsive than any other in Conrad's novels is destroyed. Focused like *Lord Jim* on a single person, the problem of objectivity was more acute because the character himself is more *sympathique*.

Conrad solved the problem as before, with an independent narrator, but interspersed his account with extracts from the main character's diary which take us directly to the heart of the matter. The discipline involved was the most challenging of his career (it resulted in one of his most severe breakdowns). He said: "It is in order to keep always before myself the effect of a 'performance' that I invented the old teacher of languages."[68] The presence of the teacher provides additional tension between attitude and reality – another factor emphasizing the isolation of the tragic central figure. An ageing English bachelor in a foreign country, he looks on at the episodes in Switzerland from the standpoint of someone no longer under crises who has reached a sardonic adjustment to life, in which the struggle to relate fully is either over or by-passed. His presence produces the same effect as having the denouement take place in Switzerland. They separate the central action from the Russian social context and concentrate all attention on it, emphasizing the universals and highlighting the actuality of Razumov's suffering. All the thematic tendencies in the novel are pointed like arrows at him.

The total effect is to bring the experience closer than any other of our chosen thematic novels to the kind of tragic identification that is generally regarded as one of the glories of the psychological novel (such as *Anna Karenin*). Our demonstration of this achievement will risk making it sound like one, which it very obviously is not. It contains all the general factors that were brought to bear on Jim, but

---

67. Conrad's pages are crammed as full as Dickens's or Dostoevsky's with the vitally maimed. *The Secret Agent*, for instance, is like *Bleak House* and *The Possessed,* filled with the destructively insulated: Yundt, Ossipon and the Professor are like Loerke, Carker and Smerdyakov, the reducers down. The irony directed at these ghoulish predators lets the outrage speak for itself in all its spontaneous vitality while the author's own moral passion (as in the satire of Jonathan Swift) speaks as vividly alongside.

68. Conrad to Macdonald Hastings, 24 December 1916, in *Letters*, V, 696.

here they are focused throughout with sharp sympathy and crystal clarity.

Like Jim, he commits a crime that exiles him forever. As a result of this fact, some readers take a severe view of him. Terry Eagleton, for example, saw in him the "violence, selfish cynicism and autocratic sneering" of a "cruel, arrogant, malicious egoist".[69] Tony Tanner, however, has testified to the success of Conrad's intentions in the matter (as stated in his preface). For Tanner, Razumov is "an intelligent man to whom perception, analysis, deduction and imagination are habits .... His imaginings are more justifiable than those of any other Conrad character."[70]

At the start of the novel Razumov is presented as a young student who has not been challenged enough to force himself to an intellectual appraisal of what his main needs and motives are, or to make necessary a conscious identification with any patterns of thought, political or otherwise. When he is introduced casually to the man he thinks must be his father (a Prince who supports him without acknowledging him) we glimpse a powerfully passionate nature beneath the calm surface of his conformist existence and realize what lies behind his sense of association with autocratic Russia: "This immense parentage suffered from the throes of internal dissensions, and he shrank mentally from the fray as a good-natured man may shrink from taking definite sides in a violent family quarrel."

Into this orphaned, uncertain, insecure yet receptive mental world bursts a neurotic of an altogether different stamp. Haldin, a fellow-student, has just thrown a bomb at a state official and needs a hiding place, choosing Razumov's protection through a misreading of his nature. The hypocrisy and violence of the political obsessive is less explored in Haldin than it had been in Conrad's previous novels, for here the important contrast is between the suffering and doubt of the thinking man forced into political action and the dull complacent sense of martyrdom and virtue to be found in Haldin's more thought-free activity.

The impact of Haldin crystallizes Razumov's basic needs and views, and it is not surprising that his social ideas rely upon the notion of a powerful, benign and uniting autocrat. His aligning himself with

---

69. Eagleton, *Exiles and Émigrés*, 26.

70. Tanner, "Nightmare and Complacency – Razumov and the Western Eye", in *Joseph Conrad,* ed. Carabine, III, 143-46.

the prevailing system is, for a man with the sharp, independent and self-reliant mind shown later, a passional act he is not fully aware of. His situation, pride, independence and sense of his own competence have so far controlled his emotional aspiration, so that it appears only in his desire to claim recognition by merit, not the accident of his birth, and to earn respect and a sense of belonging. When this is threatened by Haldin the anger, outrage and feeling of being trapped takes expression in violence, as when, leaving Haldin in his room, he turns out into the darkness and snow and finds himself beating up a drunken cabbie. (The incident may in externals recall Ivan Karamazov's attack on the drunken peasant, but the emotional realities are quite different.)

Razumov recoils from what the anti-revolutionary General T. represents just as much as he does from Haldin, and this is quite apart from any physical or personal threat to him. Razumov (like Gerald Crich at the crisis of his story) "has a distinct sensation of his very existence being undermined in some mysterious manner, of his moral supports falling from him one by one". Panic prompts betrayal, as it does in Jim's case, but not out of idealism, and not from malice – rather from the sudden eruption of hidden pressures clearing an obstacle out of its way.

The authorities decide to use him. Accepted yet suspected by both sides in the political conflict, and sent by the government as a spy among the émigré revolutionaries in Geneva, he is a victim of both parties, filled with disgust at them and at himself. The trap has become permanent, inescapable. From now on there seems no way out of from the isolation of constant hypocrisy and the fear of self-betrayal.

The accidents of birth and fate have coincided in this personal disaster, but most moving is the way those forces collaborate with his nature, which has been concealed by his situation, by his having been without family and close associative contacts. As it develops (in a way Decoud's does not) we see the change from the soft intellect of the protected academic to the hard intellect using its muscle on observation of reality in itself and others: the awakening of a powerful mind exposed to the total inexperience of a passionate soul. His tragic private integrity sets him apart. He needs to live by what, relying on his own resources, he understands to be constructive and not to be drawn into dubious revolutionary or state activities. He is unable to accept the falsity of his moral position with either group or to accept the extremes with which commitment would have to be associated. In this moral no-man's-land the image of snow returns to his mind:

Rest, work, solitude, and the frankness of intercourse with his kind were alike forbidden to him. Everything was gone. His existence was a great cold blank, something like the enormous plains of Russia levelled with snow and fading gradually on all sides into shadows and mists.[71]

His life has to run a course of isolated and personal damnation or salvation. It is this isolation that makes every step he takes an act of assessment and haunting re-assessment, with no sentimentality or idealism to rely upon. His acts of destruction continue in a fully conscious way – against the generous-hearted Kostia, for instance – in the spirit of violence against self and others that is caused by the impossibility of his position. He has a cruel and vengeful urge to marry Natalia Haldin, the revolutionist's trustful sister, without letting her know he is her brother's betrayer. But in her a different fate awaits him.

Natalia functions partly as a representative of the finer face of political idealism. She endorses social ideals divorced from their fanatical implementation:

"There is too much hate and revenge in that work .... Let the tyrants and the slayers be forgotten together, and only the reconstructors be remembered."[72]

Conrad's revision of the novel, as Keith Carabine showed, brought about the elimination in Natalia of what he himself called her "possibilities" which included some analytical scepticism about the revolutionists. There were sound psychological grounds for the revision: both she and her mother, in their devotion to the memory of Haldin as a person cannot seriously question the principles upon which he acted without reflecting adversely on that loved memory – although the paralysed misery of the mother suggests the magnitude of the suppression of doubts and unposed, unanswered questions. The revision reduced Natalia at times, as Carabine explained, to something like a "Victorian stereotype".[73] Nevertheless, she remains effective in her main role – focused as ever in this novel on Razumov – which is to be, as Conrad pointed out, "a pivot for the action to turn on".[74]

---

71. *Under Western Eyes*, Collected edition, 303.

72. *Ibid.*, 331.

73. Carabine, *Life and the Art*, 168. For further discussion of Natalia's role in the novel see Lissa Schneider, *Conrad's Narratives of Difference*, 2003.

74. Conrad to Olivia Rayne Garnett, 20 October 1911, in *Letters*, IV, 489.

His capitulation to the force of love and admiration, which has from the beginning lain behind the course he has taken towards her, prevents his revenge and eventually destroys him: "You were appointed to undo the evil by making me betray myself back into truth and peace." In the end he delivers himself up to the revolutionaries, but not in the spirit of confession, which implies revealing a sin to representatives of the life or society sinned against. It is done to be rid of the falseness of his position – the sin against himself and those life-values that would make life worth living for him: "It was myself, after all, whom I have betrayed most basely." It is a protest against the suffering caused by his inability to keep his integrity in natural, direct love and hate relationships. The destruction he anticipates is the desired retribution for the sin he feels he has committed against life. The novel presents no urge in Razumov to come to terms: "I am independent – and therefore perdition is my lot." It is his exposure and his fight that are important.

Lawrence read the novel in 1912 and remained curiously resistant – "bored me" – or hostile: "I can't forgive Conrad for being so sad and for giving in."[75] It was a tragic form of affirmation he would not recognize (although he would later create something like it in Gerald's tragedy). At that time he was preoccupied with fighting his own way through the tragic tendencies in Paul Morel at the end of *Sons and Lover,* towards a glimmer of a constructive future for him – attempting there to affirm the kind of positives that are crushed in Conrad's novel. He had long put behind him the tragic melancholia of *The Trespasser.* He had already (probably) turned against Tolstoy's handling of Anna Karenin's tragedy (Frieda was reported reading it that autumn).

A few months later he was recoiling from Thomas Mann's *Death in Venice.* The thematic structure of that tale, depicting a moral collapse that, like that of Conrad's Kurtz in *Heart of Darkness*, spans the whole course of a breakdown from idealism to depravity, might well have interested Lawrence, but he reacted against its subject-matter. In it Gustav Aschenbach is a writer in his fifties, much admired for his sustained posture of nobility and self-sacrifice. His concept of his art requires not merely the suppression of his instincts but their exploitation and sublimation on its behalf. It preys on the passional life, courts it, betrays it and perverts it. The story tells how

---

75. Lawrence to Arthur McLeod, 17 September 1912, in *Letters*, I, 456; and to Edward Garnett, 30 October 1912, in *Letters*, I, 465.

his thus corrupted sensuality takes its revenge. Lawrence in his review, while responding vividly to the symbolism of the city – whose "huddled heart" with its "evil exhalations" mirrors Aschenbach's own – and granting that the picture is "too well done" to be called morbid, still rejected it, classing Mann with Flaubert as one for whom "physical life is a disordered corruption".[76]

Mann, Wells, Bennett and Conrad – these were "the Writers among the Ruins".[77] "Tragedy ought to be a great kick at misery", he declared.[78] His attitude registered more than anything else his own keenness to plunge into life to find something more creative. He was shouldering away these incitements to gloom in order to forge ahead with the construction of his own world of positives, both in life and literature. He was asserting his right to disregard his peers and go his own way.

Lawrence's stated responses to Conrad were no more rejective, however, than those of several other major contemporary novelists. Woolf admired him, but without much discernible influence. Joyce almost totally ignored him, while Forster omitted him from his lectures on *Aspects of the Novel*. Not until the next generation, with novelists such as Greene, Hartley and Lowry, did his influence grow stronger.

---

76. Lawrence, *Phoenix*, ed. Edward McDonald, 312. He referred in his review to *Buddenbrooks*, Mann's earlier novel, comparable in scope with *The Rainbow*, but showed little sign of having read much of it. With Mann's later work he never became familiar.
77. Lawrence to Edward Garnett, 30 October 1912, in *Letters*, I, 465.
78. Lawrence to Arthur McLeod, 4 October 1912, in *Letters*, I, 459.

9

CONTEMPORARIES

Ford, Forster, Joyce and Woolf

The four novelists chosen in this chapter to illustrate other thematic options among Lawrence's contemporaries were all born within ten years of Lawrence and of each other. Therefore they were moulded by similar cultural influences, yet moved towards an interesting diversity of outcomes. They were all drawn at some time in their careers towards solving their artistic problems by adopting a thematic structure for their novels: both Ford and Forster working mainly in the narrative conventions of psychological realism but for a while breaking out of them; Joyce on a path parallel to Lawrence's, out of the developmental structure of *Stephen Hero* into his thematic first novel; and Woolf inspired by Joyce's example to move into her mature thematic style.

Ford Madox Ford, born into a highly cultured family, was closely acquainted with major literary figures, including James, Conrad, Wells and Pound, and, having founded *The English Review*, which in terms of the creative work published (while he was editor) holds the best record of the century was the first to publish Lawrence. At first more famous perhaps for his impact on the literary scene (through journalism and criticism) than for his own fiction, he was a celebrity, behind whose "mask" was a man deeply preoccupied with his own isolation and egoism. As one of his biographers put it: "The pain of living with his own divided nature was unendurable to Ford, and he spent much of his life and his imaginative energy inventing an alternative and more flattering image of himself."[1] His work was as varied and uneven as his life. There are quantities of essays, poems,

---

1. Arthur Mizener, *The Saddest Story*, xv.

memoirs and journalism, besides fiction (he wrote eighty-one books, thirty-two of them novels.).

Undoubtedly the best fiction was written during and just after the First World War. The earlier trilogy about the Tudors he dubbed (along with all historical fiction) "nothing but a *tour de force*, a fake more or less genuine in workmanship but nonetheless a fake".[2] His dissatisfaction with it drove him to write *The Good Soldier* (1915). It is the finest fruit of his literary discipleship of Flaubert and James, and registers, with its narrator and its time switches, the impact of his long association with Conrad. It reads at times like a thriller, with essential information kept back, or like a psychological study of four characters; but the plot is rigged, like Hardy's, to prove an ideological point, while the psychology is a playground for the two themes of idealism and egoism. No regenerative light shines here – that side of Ford's nature, though present in his other novels, is excluded from this one. In that respect it like a fixed card game, the potentialities for winning hidden or disabled. The most impressive aspect of the treatment is the dexterity with which the interplay of the two themes within the characters is handled, and our analysis focuses on that.

Edward Ashburnham – the "good soldier" himself – is a normal, decent man, or seems so (like Conrad's Jim). His friend the narrator insists on it, making all too clear from the beginning his limitations. His eyes

> were as blue as the sides of a certain type of box of matches. When you looked at them carefully you saw that they were perfectly honest, perfectly straightforward, perfectly, perfectly stupid.[3]

The sentence following this indicates the potential threat to others as well as to the self of this kind of stupidity: "But the brick pink of his complexion running perfectly level to the brick pink of his inner eyelids, gave them a curious sinister expression – like a mosaic of blue porcelain set in pink china." The next sentences specify, in the ironic, half grimly jocular tones that, with the admixture of pity, characterize the narrator's approach throughout the book, the area within which the threat operates:

> And that chap, coming into a room, snapped up the gaze of every woman in it, as dexterously as a conjuror pockets billiard balls. It was most amazing. You know the man on the stage who throws up sixteen

---

2. Ford, quoted by Mizener, *The Saddest Story*, 470.
3. *The Good Soldier*, Bodley Head edition, 35. Subsequent page references are to this edition.

balls at once and they drop into pockets all over his person, on his shoulders, on his heels, on the inner side of his sleeves; and he stands perfectly still and does nothing. Well, it was like that.

Married to a woman he finds he cannot love but whose coolness and practicality are as honourably intentioned as his own generosity and sentimentality, he finds consolation elsewhere, in series of infidelities which are inspired by a "mad passion" that is sentimental rather than sensual – "to find an ultimately satisfying woman" – while helplessly tied to notions of feminine purity (afraid for instance to tell his wife for fear of sullying her mind). Unable to disentangle himself from this web of idealism and egoism, towards the end of the novel he falls hopelessly in love with his young niece, Nancy.[4] Rather than sully her he sends her away, and after receiving a calculatedly indifferent telegram from her he commits suicide.

John Dowell, the narrator of the story, shares Edward's idealizing propensities, which in his case protect his inertia and lack of vitality. He idealizes his materialistic wife, and for twelve years, in total ignorance of his wife's infidelities (even with his best friend) and believing her lies about her weak heart, he plays the male nurse in an unconsummated marriage.

The two women are more straightforwardly egoistic, though they share with the men the insulating unreality of their conventional ideals. According to Dowell (in retrospect) Florence his wife is "a cold sensualist with imbecile fears" – her heart morally not physically diseased. "Always play-acting" she "represented a real human being with a heart, with feelings, with sympathies and with emotions only as a banknote represents a certain quantity of gold". After her long-standing affair with Edward she commits suicide partly out of shocked vanity, when she hears of his defection in favour of Nancy, and partly out of fear of her husband's discovering her lies.

Edward's wife Leonora is equally relentless in the pursuit not of pleasure but of security. She devotes her considerable managerial talents to the family property which has been wasted by Edward's generosity and extravagance, and to her marriage – to the extent of persuading herself (with the help of her Catholic religion) that she can overlook and even arrange his infidelities with a view to finally reclaiming him:

---

4. There have been suggestions that Nancy is Edward's illegitimate daughter. See John Sutherland, *Can Jane Eyre be Happy?*

> She saw life as a perpetual sex-battle between husbands who desire to
> be unfaithful to their wives, and wives who desire to recapture their
> husbands in the end. That was her sad and modest view of
> matrimony. (163)

Dowell, after years of living in a dreamworld of deceptions and
self-deceptions, tells his story to get the record straight. He realizes the
harm caused both by the passional self overriding the conscious self's
conception of right conduct – as when Leonora acts "along the lines of
her instinctive desires" in betraying Edward's past infidelities to
Nancy and driving her to offer her body to save his life – and also by
moral concepts inhibiting genuine response, as with Edward's conduct
towards Nancy which is "perfectly ... monstrously ... cruelly correct".

There is irony and even some sardonic fun; there is a sustained
sense of the sinister and some keen observation of personal cruelty,
including the painful silent reading of signs that can be misread:

> No, Edward had no remorse [about Florence's suicide]. He was
> able to say that he had treated Florence with gallant attentiveness of
> the kind that she desired until two hours before her death. Leonora
> gathered that from the look in his eyes, and from the way he
> straightened his shoulders over her as she lay in her coffin – from that
> and a thousand other little things. (119)

But towards the end, as the story moves (even with all its digressions
and flashbacks) "faster and faster and with more intensity"[5] the
accumulation of climaxes – confrontations, surprises, deaths – leads to
what Dowell admits is "melodrama; but I can't help it". These are
"broken, tumultuous, agonized and unromantic lives, periods
punctuated by screams, by imbecilities, by deaths, by agonies". We
see "the black and merciless things that lie behind the façade" of
polite intercourse, "that long, tranquil life, which was just stepping a
minuet":

> No, by God it is false! It wasn't a minuet that we stepped; it was a
> prison – a prison full of screaming hysterics, tied down so that they
> might not outsound the rolling of our carriage wheels as we went
> along the shaded avenues of the Taunus Wald. (18)

The novel operates sometimes on the crudest levels, keeping up the
audience-holding qualities of French farce and Jacobean tragedy, even
black comedy, as in the account of Leonora's finding Maisie Maiden's
body after she has died of heart failure:

---

5. One of Ford's literary recipes: *"progression d'effet."*

> Maisie had died in the effort to strap up a great port-manteau. She had died so grotesquely that her little body had fallen forward into the trunk, and it had closed upon her, like the jaws of a gigantic alligator. (73)

Dowell's mentality is ostensibly responsible for the hysteria and melodrama in the book and also for the ironic corrective, which works sometimes through what he sees himself and sometimes through the irony of the story itself as seen by the reader in spite of him. His passivity in upholding the same "gentlemanly" social codes, contrasted with Ashburnham's bewildered, tortured activity, brings out the menace lying behind such directives uncritically held. The author makes clear the mental limitations of all victims of the code. Both Ashburnham and Leonora, to the degree that they are directed by the best of conventional social, religious or feudal motives, are seen by Dowell as

> two noble natures, drifting down life, like fire-ships afloat on a lagoon and causing miseries, heartaches, agony of the mind, and death .... And why? For what purpose? To point what lesson? It is all a darkness. (146)

This is characteristic both of the narrator's confusion and the general purpose of the plot to keep the dynamics, the melodrama, on the top and the assessments confused and underneath.

Critics over the past 50 years have emphasized widely differing views of Dowell. For Mark Schorer in 1951 he represented chiefly "the madness of moral inertia".[6] Ten years later Samuel Hynes was pointing out his "positive qualities" including moral impartiality and affection, an emphasis the biographer Arthur Mizener later subscribed to by identifying him with his author. More recently, critics have seen the variables and uncertainties as part of the paradoxical dual vision of the novel.[7] In the end Dowell is revealed as even more stupid, uncritical and unself-aware than anyone else. Whether he knows or not what is going on he flounders just as desperately. He starts as a dupe who knows nothing about himself and others, accepts everything at face value and is used as a male nurse and provider by the woman he wants without ever possessing her sexually, and by the end of his story, when the whole seething pit and his own blindness and failure have been revealed to him, he is in the same boat with Nancy, who has

---

6. Schorer, *The World We Imagine*, 102.
7. For a summary of the critics' views, see Martin Stannard's Introduction to the Norton edition of *The Good Soldier*.

been driven insane by the strain of Edward's love and the news of his suicide.

Cynicism and melodrama are the qualities that flourish most energetically in this soil. The dominant tone is inevitably the one that comes from the warped narrator:

> Society must go on, I suppose, and society can only exist if the normal, if the virtuous, and the slightly deceitful flourish, and if the passionate, the headstrong, and the too-truthful are condemned to suicide and madness. (217)

The horror of the "inside" is liberated by a narrator whose lack of vitality dictates an inner preference for remaining on the "outside" as far as possible. The final picture remains one of a "sweltering hell" carrying with it the cliché view that society is both right and wrong and in any case inevitable. For all its technical brilliance the book is flawed by its dependence (however ironically qualified) on Dowell's limited mentality.

After serving as an officer in the war, Ford set about writing his tetralogy centred round his experiences of it. Here the private agony of his characters' lives (some of which recalls the themes of *The Good Soldier*) corresponds to the social agony going on around them. The best of the four volumes – *Some Do Not* and *No More Parades* – concentrate on the agony, while in the later ones we see Ford struggling to find a formula for balance and survival. It is the story (in all four volumes) of one who is full of the feelings that do credit to a gentleman. Christopher Tietjens, built like a "meal-sack" lumbers through a multitude of wartime and peacetime scenes, governed by "right intuitions" and intent on his duties, menaced by the "sexual hatred" of his wife Sylvia – "surely" wrote Graham Greene, "the most possessed evil character in the modern novel" – saved by his long-suffering and sturdy independent integrity and rewarded with the love of a good woman, Valentine Wannop. The style is leisurely, fluid and has been called "impressionistic" It is sometimes mannered and sometimes melodramatic. The war episodes are best: as Bernard Bergonzi pointed out, they show some breadth and richness of scene and character.[8]

E.M. Forster was one of the few literary figures of the time who had little contact with Ford, but he was a friend of Lawrence's. To read him after Lawrence is to see a fascinating array of parallels and

---

8. See Bernard Bergonzi, *Heroes' Twilight*, 166-73.

discrepancies. Parallels for every theme in Lawrence's novels exist in Forster's, although so differently moulded by his personality and experience that they hardly look the same. There is the same condemnation of a preoccupation with self or class or property, from the Herritons in *Where Angels Fear to Tread* to Ronny and his friends in *A Passage to India*. There is a similar preoccupation with the value of male friendship, from the second novel, where Stephen offers a saving comradeship to his half-brother Rickie Elliott, to the last, where the tricky possibilities between Fielding and Aziz are tentatively explored. Throughout there is a steady emphasis on the value of individuality, passion and instinct. In novel after novel female characters like Mrs Elliott, Mrs Wilcox and Mrs Moore stand for "instinctive wisdom". Margaret Schlegel in *Howards End* wants to rebuild human integrity with a "rainbow bridge". In *The Longest Journey* Mrs Elliott, repelled by her barrister husband, has a affair with a young farmer and bears him a child, while in *Maurice* Forster offered his own phallic fable of love with a gamekeeper. There is no need to spell out how different all this is from Lawrence and little question of formative influence, at least of Forster on Lawrence.

One reason for the discrepancy – setting aside the most important one, their individual natures – was Forster's continuing allegiance (which we have seen Lawrence drop after *Sons and Lovers*) to the narrative traditions associated in our study with George Eliot, and in which he was as well educated as Lawrence himself (his *Aspects of the Novel* show that his judgment of the nineteenth century roughly agreed with Lawrence's, except that he liked Jane Austen). Until his last novel, the general themes he so clearly pursued were governed by his psychological interests, and there was an uneasy relationship between the two.

In the first novel, for example, *Where Angels Fear to Tread,* the thematic generalities, the contrast between passionate spontaneity and straitjacketed egoism, run alongside the psychological investigation. The egoism is most effectively presented in the "undeveloped hearts" of the Herriton family, dominated by a mother whose "continued repression of vigour" has turned her into a "well-ordered, active, useless machine". Her daughter Harriet has a relentless, narrow-minded moral fervour which is partially responsible for the tragedy in the novel, the death of the baby she has stolen from its father. The son Philip, in spite of a certain open-mindedness and the educative effect of the novel's events on him, is essentially protected by his priggishness and aestheticism. As Caroline Abbott (to whom he proposes) exclaims, "You appreciate all of us. And all the time you are dead – dead – dead". He admits, "You are quite right; life to me is just a spectacle".

Italian passion is represented with rather less conviction in Gino Carella, the young "cad" who has married Lilia Herriton and after her death is obsessed with their child. He is comparable in function with Ciccio in Lawrence's *The Lost Girl*. The disorder Caroline sees in his home is "the mess that comes of life, not of desolation". When Gino kisses her he appears to her "majestic; he was part of Nature". That phrase may suggest a certain unreality in her responses, but there is no irony here: the unreality lies in the presentation. Caroline, who started by merely offering passive resistance to the Herritons' respectability and the morality of "petty unselfishness" is now in love with Gino, but her "passion" carries little conviction. The generality is superimposed on a realistic psychological context that does not support it. More convincing are her inhibitions, which dictate her return to her English environment.

Criticism of the Herriton style of English middle-class mentality is pursued through the other early novels. In *The Longest Journey* the barrister Mr Elliott is a man who

> passed for a cultured man because he knew how to select, and he passed for an unconventional man because he did not select quite like other people. In reality he never did or said or thought one single thing that had the slightest beauty or value.[9]

The intellectual Cecil Vyse in *A Room with a View* is of "the sort who are all right so long as they keep to things – books, pictures – but kill when they come to people". The Wilcoxes in *Howards End* represent, like Galsworthy's Forsytes, money-mindedness. Margaret Schlegel explains: "love means marriage settlements, death death duties." They have within themselves "nothing to fall back on". Even Henry Wilcox, who, in as much as he admires and wants Margaret, tacitly recognizes some deficiency in himself, merits her accusation – "Stupid, hypocritical, cruel – oh, contemptible!" – although the condemnation is softened by her cherishing pity and by the conviction that the Wilcox mentality and activity is necessary to the maintenance of society.[10]

---

9. *The Longest Journey*, Abinger edition, 24.
10. That attitude made Lawrence reprove Forster for "glorifying those *business* people" (Lawrence to Forster, 20 September 1922, in *Letters,* IV, 301).

In *A Passage to India* (begun 1913-14, restarted 1922, completed 1924) the critique of this mentality is more thoroughgoing. The ten-year interval registered a dissatisfaction with his earlier achievements, as well as his own life (in which he was searching for more complete and balanced social and sexual relationships). Forster now adopted a moral diagram similar to that in his first novel, with the Indians figuring in place of the Italians. Here there is not only greater maturity and precision in the registering of the contrasts but a deeper acknowledgment of what is recognized in Caroline Abbott's development: defeat and insulation in spite of a certain degree of self-knowledge. The uncertainty about positive convictions noticeable in the earlier novel is here turned to advantage as it helps to define more of the factors involved in the formation of responses and relationships and, as part of this, the obstacles to them. The other great advantage this novel has is a firmer coalition between the characterisation and the themes. The universal features of the latter are now more fully explored: they break out with some violence from the context of personal relations, but remain correlated with them.

These fill the picture first. We are introduced to the English ruling class and the complicated reactions produced in the educated Indians by their offensive and insulting behaviour, primarily through the two visiting women, Adela Quested and Mrs Moore, who arrive eager to see and know India and entirely without consciousness of the roles assumed by or forced on to either side. The portrayal of the English is not wholly dismissive. There is a gentle impartiality in the carefully observed diagram of insulation between the two races. An example is the scene where Ronny, the Magistrate of Chandrapore, turns up at the house of Fielding, an English teacher and friend of Aziz, impatient to take his mother (Mrs Moore) and his intended fiancée Adela to a polo game. He barges in on an absorbing conversation between Adela, Aziz and the Hindu Professor Godbole. But he addresses his remarks to Adela, ignoring Aziz and Godbole:

> He did not mean to be rude to the two men, but the only link he could be conscious of with an Indian was the official, and neither happened to be his subordinate. As private individuals he forgot them
>
> Unfortunately Aziz was in no mood to be forgotten. He would not give up the secure and intimate note of the last hour. He had not risen with Godbole, and now, offensively friendly, called from his seat, "Come along up and join us, Mr Heaslop; sit down till your mother turns up."

Ronny replied by ordering one of Fielding's servants to fetch his master at once.

"He may not understand that. Allow me –" Aziz repeated the order idiomatically.

Ronny was tempted to retort; he knew the type; he knew all the types, and this was the spoiled westernised. But he was the servant of the Government, it was his job to avoid "incidents," so he said nothing, and ignored the provocation that Aziz continued to offer. Aziz was provocative. Everything he said had an impertinent flavour or jarred. His wings were failing, but he refused to fall without a struggle. He did not mean to be impertinent to Mr Heaslop, who had never done him harm, but here was an Anglo-Indian who must become a man before comfort could be regained. He did not mean to be greasily confidential to Miss Quested, only to enlist her support; nor to be loud and jolly towards Professor Godbole. A strange quartet – he fluttering to the ground, she puzzled by the sudden ugliness, Ronny fuming, the Brahman observing all three, but with downcast eyes and hands folded, as if nothing was noticeable. A scene from a play, thought Fielding, who now saw them from the distance across the garden, grouped among the blue pillars of his beautiful hall.[11]

The unreality of the social/racial "difference" is brought out by Fielding's reaction.

The narrative gives us an appraisal, which is backed up and qualified by the two women's, of what has gone to make the ruling caste what they are. It adds substantially (at least as much as Kipling's tales do) to the obvious knowledge of their being an insecure minority enduring temperatures of 112 degrees Fahrenheit in an alien country, attempting to impose their Western order upon a disorder they neither understand the nature of nor the reason for. This aspect of the book drew Lawrence's praise, though he saw it in sharper satirical terms: "the repudiation of our white bunk is genuine, sincere and pretty thorough."[12]

In this first part of the book, the reader's sympathies are centred on Mrs Moore, with her ready and unprejudiced affectionate curiosity, and her new-found friend, Aziz, the most engaging and likeable character in the book, who "could discover no rule for this or for anything else in life" and is thus close to the informing intelligence of a novel which continually questions assumptions and judgments.

---

11. *A Passage to India*, Abinger edition, 69-70. The subsequent page references are to this edition.
12. Lawrence to John Middleton Murry, 3 October 1924 in *Letters*, V, 143.

Scenes with him and other Indians are generally without the satirical bias of the scenes with the English, and show a balanced sensitivity which leans towards a lightly indulged exquisiteness of response:

> Of the company, only Hamidullah had any comprehension of poetry. The minds of the others were inferior and rough. Yet they listened with pleasure, because literature had not been divorced from their civilization. The police inspector, for instance, did not feel that Aziz had degraded himself by reciting, nor break into the cheery guffaw with which an Englishman averts the infection of beauty. He just sat with his mind empty, and when his thoughts, which were mainly ignoble, flowed back into it they had a pleasant freshness. The poem had done no "good" to anyone, but it was a passing reminder, a breath from the divine lips of beauty, a nightingale between two worlds of dust. (97)

Terms like "inferior" and "ignoble" together with the whimsy of the last sentence underline a sentimental preference for a set of concepts that the directness and intelligence of the rest of the context denies. These concepts are of course subject like everything else in the book to ironic reservation, which is at its strongest in the Marabar Caves, where a beautiful pattern, "inlaid with lovely colours … delicate stars of pink and grey" makes a fleeting appearance on the walls when a match is struck, is regarded with this kind of appreciativeness, only to be immediately overwhelmed in the minds of the two English women by the dominant ugliness. Traces of preciosity are swept away by the action in Part 2, but return in a different form during the presentation of the Hindu ceremony in Part 3.

The introduction of the impersonal into the carefully observed personal context occurs during the trip to the Marabar Caves. It is carefully prepared for. At first the caves seem to have nothing to recommend them except extreme antiquity. They are being visited as a result of a bungling, well-intentioned desire on the part of Aziz to be a host to the English women and on the part of the two women to see what there is to see and to make their protest against conventional English behaviour by enjoying his company and his India.

But the approach to the caves which will have such a catalytic impact on all the people in the novel reveals inversions of the known and accepted:

> Miss Quested and Aziz and a guide continued the slightly tedious expedition. They did not talk much, for the sun was getting high. The air felt like a warm bath into which hotter water is trickling constantly, the temperature rose and rose, the boulders said, "I am

alive," the small stones answered, "I am almost alive." Between the chinks lay the ashes of little plants. (142)

The boulders come alive and the organic life is in ashes. The timelessness, aridity and heat also suffer the super-imposition of the painted elephant and the ridiculously extravagant picnic provided by Aziz. The details of the picnic in its richness, diversity and colour emphasize the "here and now" as it is imposed in India upon the unimpressionable and incomprehensible. The scene throws a new light on both Aziz's nature and the quality he shares with the other Indians, the rich, crude concentration on the actual, the tactile and visual, those things that are immediately appreciable to the senses, which we see again in the Hindu religious ceremony at the end of the book.

In Adela and Mrs Moore the Marabar caves bring forth images of ugly universals underlying the conflicts and dissatisfactions of their lives. The effect on Adela we get to know only after her collapse. It brings on a hysterical panic that makes her feel she has been sexually assaulted by Aziz. The reader never finds out whether she has been attacked by anyone (guide or tribesman) or whether the whole thing is hysteria-engendered, the subtle shock of the place taking expression in the form most suited to her particular suppressions and insecurities.[13] It reveals at the psychological level how close she has been to a breakdown. At the same time it establishes an impersonal basis for the antagonisms around her:

> the echo flourished, raging up and down like a nerve in the faculty of her hearing, and the noise in the cave, so unimportant intellectually, was prolonged over the surface of her life .... Evil was loose ... she could even hear it entering the lives of others. (185)

For the purposes of the plot her reaction is the means by which the rift between the English and Indian communities can be expressed in action. The English and Indians close ranks:

> All over Chandrapore that day the Europeans were putting aside their normal personalities and sinking themselves in their community. Pity, wrath, heroism filled them, but the power of putting two and two together was annihilated. (156)

The trial of Aziz proceeds until Adela confesses her mistake. Ronny's kind of mentality is seen at its worst, and so is its opposing equivalent

---

13. Forster deleted from an earlier draft a detailed account of an attempted rape, seen from Adela's viewpoint. See Forster, *The Manuscripts of "A Passage to India"*, ed. Oliver Stallybrass, 242-43.

among the Indians. The ensuing crisis vividly highlights the egoism of
the participants, and the way their conception of rules and principles
props up their destructive political antagonism.

Mrs Moore's response to the caves is more profound, revealing and
life-threatening. She has first a semi-hysterical reaction to he crowd,
"crammed with villagers and servants" and then to the echo in there,
which is

> entirely devoid of distinction. Whatever is said, the same monotonous
> noise replies and quivers up and down the walls until it is absorbed
> into the roof. "Boum" is the sound as far as the human alphabet can
> express it .... the echo began in some indescribable way to undermine
> her hold on life. Coming at a moment when she chanced to be
> fatigued, it had managed to murmur, "Pathos, piety, courage – they
> exist, but are identical, and so is filth. Everything exists, nothing has
> value" .... Devils are of the North, and poems can be written about
> them, but no one could romanticize the Marabar, because it robbed
> infinity and eternity of their vastness, the only quality that
> accommodates them to mankind. (138-41)

The "otherness" of India is revealed in its most abstract or
quintessential form, at its most dangerous to European sensitivity.
Insisting on the non-relevance of ordinary assurances, the caves
confound preconceptions about life, death, beauty and value,
suggesting imbalance, madness and the isolation of the individual in a
meaningless universe.

> She had come to that state where the horror of the universe and its
> smallness are both visible at the same time .... in the twilight of the
> double vision, a spiritual muddledom is set up for which no high-
> sounding words can be found; we can neither act nor refrain from
> action, we can neither ignore nor respect Infinity. (197-98)

She loses her grip on life and decides to go home:

> "Say, say, say," said the old lady bitterly. "As if anything can be said!
> I have spent my life in saying or listening to sayings; I have listened
> too much. It is time I was left in peace. Not to die .... I'll retire the
> into a cave of my own." She smiled, to bring down her remark to
> ordinary life and thus add to its bitterness. "Somewhere where no
> young people will come asking questions and expecting answers.
> Some shelf." (190-91)

In Part 3 of the book the personal developments are not neglected,
but they are now more nominal. Fielding gets married and the
friendship struck up in the first part of the novel between him and
Aziz and broken during the trial is partially mended. But any

affirmation is fractured by the problematic. That is true also in the sphere of universals, but they are more prominent, as the thematic propensities liberated by the caves episode expand and the novel tentatively explores some sort of answer to the destructive factors released in Part 2.

When Mrs Moore sails for England an imaginary chorus laughs at her: "So you thought that an echo was India; you took the Marabar Caves as final?" But her influence has already become part of a wider pattern. The almost necromantic effect of the chanting of her name inside and outside the court room (when the defence hopes she will be called to support Aziz's case) has already inspired Adela to make her confession. She is about to become a minor and local legend and religious figure and be absorbed into the complex, adaptable and inclusive Hindu lore, which is shown operating in the Hindu ceremony.

This provides the congregation with a temporary sense of loving unity, of belonging and of acceptance. Although afterwards, "Looking back at the great blur of the last twenty-four hours, no man could say where was the emotional centre of it, any more than he could locate the heart of a cloud" yet "when the villagers broke cordon for a glimpse of the silver image, a most beautiful and radiant expression came into their faces, a beauty in which there was nothing personal, for it caused them all to resemble one another during the moment of its indwelling, and only when it was withdrawn did they revert to individual clods".

The meaningless disparateness of existence that has so horrified Mrs Moore finds a home here. Godbole and his singers

> loved all men, the whole universe, and scraps of their past, tiny splinters of detail, emerged for a moment to melt into the universal warmth. Thus Godbole, though she was not important to him, remembered an old woman he had met in Chandrapore days. Chance brought her into his mind while it was in this heated state, he did not select her, she happened to occur among the throng of soliciting images, a tiny splinter, and he impelled her by his spiritual force to that place where completeness can be found. (276-77)

Godbole's Hinduism, offering a temporary escape from individual isolation is, however, discomposed by the prevalent scepticism. It is "another of mankind's working arrangements".

The thematic handling of material which shows itself in the second half of *A Passage to India* continued in the work Forster wrote (or revised) afterwards, which was published posthumously because of its homosexual content. This, he said, was the only subject he cared to write about after 1923. Some of the tales were written, in part at least, as he admitted, "not to express myself but to excite myself".[14] The best of them, however, develop themes similar to the ones we have looked at in his novels.

For example, in "The Life to Come" (written 1922) the insulated Christian idealism of the missionary Pinmay brings about the defeat in himself, and in the savage chief he has converted, of what his own initial response to the native has seemed to promise, a passionate relationship. "Christ is love" says the savage – that is, for him, homosexual love. Pinmay withers into a superficially conventional clergyman. The converted chief degenerates (with his people) into slavery, both commercial and mental. He despairs of his unrequited passion – "It is my life, whatever else I seem to do" – grows consumptive and dies. The sequence of the stages of the tale, moving from night backward to morning, signifies the reversal of the natural, but the savage's dying action (he knifes Pinmay) reasserts it. The story attempts the fable-like impersonality of a Hawthorne tale: the opening scenes echo Hawthorne's style, and Pinmay's mentality, sin-obsessed and prevaricating, his remorse more sinful than his "sin" recalls Dimmesdale's in *The Scarlet Letter*.

The novel, *Maurice*, written 1913-14 and revised after 1930, is more obviously a thematic fable, though it seems to begin as a study in psychological development. Maurice is "slow" but "sensitive" graduating from schoolboy crushes to a passionate, semi-Platonic affair with the more intellectual Clive, who quite suddenly, a few years later, finds his "body" or life spirit telling him, "You who loved men will henceforward love women". Every development in the novel has this kind of dreamlike simplicity. It becomes for Maurice an unconscious quest for the realisation of his recurring dream, in which a lovely male face appears, together with the words, "That is your friend". From a potentially suicidal loneliness and self-disgust (in which he tries to get his so-called "congenital homosexuality" cured by hypnosis) he is rescued by Clive's gamekeeper, Alex ("blessed are the uneducated") who, hearing the hapless Maurice calling out desperately from his bedroom window the word "Come!" climbs up a ladder:

> But as he returned to his bed a little noise sounded, a noise so intimate that it might have arisen inside his own body. He seemed to

---

14. Forster, *The Life to Come*, xv.

crackle and burn and saw the ladder's top quivering against the moonlit air. The head and the shoulders of a man rose up, paused, a gun was leant against the window sill very carefully, and someone he scarcely knew moved towards him and knelt beside him and whispered, "Sir, was you calling out for me?... Sir, I know .... I know," and touched him.[15]

After some misunderstandings, each repudiates his entire upbringing and they live together: "'All right. To Hell with it' and they passed on together in the rain." No scepticism here.

In spite of its slightness the novel suggests comparisons with *Lady Chatterley's Lover*. Influences have been discussed, both ways. Dixie King argued that Lawrence saw *Maurice* in manuscript because he met Forster just after it was first written, when he was passing it round among his friends.[16] But if he had, he would almost certainly have mentioned it in one of his letters. There is more likelihood in Frederick P. Macdowell's argument that the revisions of *Maurice* after 1930 reveal the influence of Lawrence's novel.[17]

James Joyce was only three years older than Lawrence. His literary background had the same scope (with the addition of medieval Latin and Italian) although his knowledge of nineteenth-century novels was probably slighter. More precocious intellectually, he embarked at an earlier age on his autobiographical novel, which was written in a conventional narrative style, following the hero through his relationships with family and friends. Some of the scenes in the surviving manuscript of that book, now called *Stephen Hero*, correspond to scenes in Part 5 of the final novel. In them Stephen Dedalus's family and friends are more clearly seen as individuals than in the final version, and some of the conversations between him and his mother, his girlfriend and others are vivid and dramatic. Joyce deliberately gave up those virtues in order to construct a novel which is entirely shaped by its themes.

A Portrait of the Artist as a Young Man as finally accomplished after ten years of revision makes Lawrence's *Sons and Lovers* (where the themes are superimposed on a psychological narrative) look

15. *Maurice*, 178.
16. See King, "The Influence of *Maurice* on *Lady Chatterley Lover*", in *E.M. Forster: Critical Assessments,* ed. J.H. Stape, IV.
17. See Macdowell, "Moments of Emergence", in *D.H. Lawrence's "Lady"*, eds Michael Squires and Dennis Jackson.

unfinished. Stephen Dedalus is the threshing ground of the themes. They are woven inseparably into his psychological development and still remain in control of its portrayal. Risking the authorial submergence whose temptations were so dangerous to Flaubert and Conrad, Joyce boldly takes the reader inside Stephen Dedalus's mind, as the writing adopts successive styles that correspond to his changing modes of consciousness. Detachment is achieved by the stylisation, which partially takes on the nature of parody.

Joyce's chosen field is the consciousness of a person whose lack of close personal relationships becomes part of the thematic analysis. He explores the relationship between external pressures and internal needs, some of which are fed by cultural influences, others thwarted by them, and yet others strengthened in rebellion. Stephen's attachment to successive ideologies is seen as an aspect of his permanent disengagement from life and also as necessary to his development. Joyce gives us an analysis of the dissociative mentality and at the same time a study of growth. Our discussion will focus on that duality, uncovering the interplay of the themes.

The basic structure of the novel is wave-like: each successive crest of enthusiasm for an ideal or cultural purpose is followed by a trough of disillusion or else overtaken by a stronger one. The first illusion to suffer in this way is his small boy's idea of family unity, overwhelmed at Christmas dinner by more powerful ones. His father's friend Casey, whose three cramped fingers were got "making a birthday present for Queen Victoria" is shouting:

– We have had too much God in Ireland! Away with God!

and sobbing in pain about Parnell, "My dead king!" with Stephen's father in tears beside him. The religious zealot Mrs Riordan, "starting to her feet and almost spitting in his face" cries:

– Devil out of hell! We won! We crushed him to death! Fiend!

while Stephen's mother, sympathetic to her religious piety, tries to calm her. The main issues of the novel are headlined, though everything in the scene is registered with the naive factual directness of a boy's vision.

He is watching a drama in which the words and representative emotions move him – "Stephen felt the glow rise to his own cheek as the spoken words thrilled him" – but even as early as this it is indicated that his development is likely to take place more in withdrawal from than in participation and conflict with others. The scene is acted out as something totally outside him. There is no specifically personal or affectionate identification with any one speaker nor with each in turn. The voices and emotions reverberate in him like an oil drum and it leads to terror. The bewilderment of failing to understand and of frustrated tentative identification are there, as in the concluding sentence of the scene – "Stephen, raising his terror-stricken face, saw that his father's eyes were full of tears" – but the confusion is reduced to "terror-stricken". The desperation and distress that would be the result of a vigorous need to associate one's feelings with those of the people who are causing the confusion is conspicuously absent, even though it is the cause of the terror. The reaching out towards people is limited, the intensity of the reverberations the outside world makes on his inner one is unlimited, and so his experience seems to validate withdrawal and self-protective dissociation.

During adolescence he moves steadily away from the "hollow-sounding voices" that urge the ideals of honour, school, nation, church and family, but he is held prisoner by the idealizing process – so that for instance when his suppressed sexuality breaks from him on a visit to the red light quarter it has to come under the enchantment of religious experience in order to escape into action:

> He had wandered into a maze of narrow and dirty streets. From the foul laneways he heard bursts of hoarse riot and wrangling and the drawling of drunken singers. He walked onward, undismayed, wondering whether he had strayed into the quarter of the jews. Women and girls dressed in long vivid gowns traversed the street from house to house. They were leisurely and perfumed. A trembling seized him and his eyes grew dim. The yellow gas flames arose before his troubled vision against the vapoury sky, burning as if before an altar. Before the doors and in the lighted halls groups were gathered arrayed as for some rite. He was in another world: he had awakened from a slumber of centuries.[18]

That his "surrender" to sexuality is a religious act and at the same time a desecration – that his extremism has dictated the form of the experience and now colours his response to it – keeps in the forefront of the reader's attention Stephen's greed for the ideologies he is damaged by, as well as revealing how the conflict with them is forcing his development. The instinctual factors, unpredictable and potentially chaotic, are the sources of growth.

---

18. *The Essential James Joyce*, ed. Harry Levin, 249. Subsequent page references to *A Portrait of the Artist as a Young Man* are to this edition.

During and after Father Arnall's sermon on the terrors of hell we see how the religious rejection of these factors co-operates with Stephen's own experience. His horror of the rift his actions have caused in himself abets the indoctrination:

> The sentence of saint James which says that he who offends against one commandment becomes guilty of all had seemed to him first a swollen phrase until he had begun to grope in the darkness of his own state. From the evil seed of lust all other deadly sins had sprung forth: pride in himself and contempt of others, covetousness in using money for the purchase of unlawful pleasures, envy of others whose vices he could not reach to and calumnious murmuring against the pious, gluttonous enjoyment of food, the dull glowering anger amid which he brooded upon his longing, the swamp of spiritual and bodily sloth in which his whole being had sunk. (253)

The ideas of restraint for the purposes of order and apparent harmony, and of giving the self to others at one remove, giving by a mental act and by an abasement of the demon-ego, appeal to him, as does the idea of "the Judgment" with its detailed and elaborate terrors designed to strengthen one's egoistic concern and preoccupation with the state of one's own soul. The pattern put forward by his religion, of the solitary battle of the individual soul and its reacceptance into the general enhances his feeling of the isolation of the individual psyche, its importance and the need to protect it. Even his horror of himself implies a kind of vanity – a sense of the largeness of his capacity – though this is also part of a more valuable recognition of his difference from others. The terrors and confusions that follow his disgust-filled dream –

> A field of stiff weeds and thistles and tufted nettlebunches. Thick among the tufts of rank stiff growth lay battered canisters and clots and coils of solid excrement.[19]

– and the self-pitying vision of lost innocence – "His eyes were dimmed with tears and, looking humbly up to heaven, he wept for the innocence he had lost" – are the results of the hysteria of a soul locked in itself and sustaining the state by the very earnestness and noble intentions of its egotism. On the other hand his overwhelming need for confession, both during and after the "retreat" expresses the longing to

---

19. *The Essential James Joyce*, 277. Stephen's excremental vision, including the final exclamation of "Help!" was derived from an "epiphany" written about 1904, which is quoted in *The Workshop of Daedalus*, eds Robert Scholes and Richard M. Kain, 16.

be at one with life, to be accepted by others and part of them, and this longing has lain behind the sin itself. He wants his prayer to be as acceptable as that of the lowest, most humble, and is forced into his agony of shame and submission by the vanity of his assumption that it is not. He hankers after a sin worse than sensuality, a crime of denial rather than acceptance, an assertion of the ego rather than a mere animal indulgence.

Through the whole of this third chapter runs a child-like impressionability and a sensitive wish to excel along the approved lines of moral development laid out for him. The balanced ironic appraisal shows in general terms in the scene where the priest confesses him. The words of the priest reflect his simply held beliefs but they indirectly sustain Stephen's vanity while condemning it, condemn life at the same time as working on behalf of it, and reflect the same failure to make a whole of life as Stephen feels. The scene ends on an affirmation that is all the more touching for its ironic undertones:

> He knelt to say his penance, praying in a dark corner of the dark nave: and his prayers ascended to heaven from his purified heart like perfume streaming upwards from a heart of white rose .... It would be beautiful to die if God so willed. It was beautiful to live in grace a life of peace and virtue and forbearance with others. (283)

That feeling of self-dedication takes him in the next chapter to the verge of the priesthood, with its strong appeal both to his ego and his doctrinaire fanaticism. Then, in the first rapture of release and regeneration when he abandons the religious ideal for the artistic we see the same factors at work as before. The style highlights them, mimicking a relevant literary fashion, the repetitions enforcing the irony:

> He was alone. He was unheeded, happy and near to the wild heart of life. He was alone and young and wilful and wildhearted, alone amid a waste of wild air and brackish waters and the seaharvest of shells and tangle and veiled grey sunlight and gayclad lightclad figures of children and girls and voices childish and girlish in the air .... Her image [of a girl on the beach] had passed into his soul for ever and no word had broken the holy silence of his ecstasy. Her eyes had called him and his soul had leapt at the call. To live, to err, to fall, to triumph, to recreate life out of life! A wild angel had appeared to him, the angel of mortal youth and beauty, an envoy from the fair courts of life, to throw open before him in an instant of ecstasy all the ways of error and glory. On and on and on and on! (303-304)

The closer the affirmation comes to the author's current standpoint the more emphatic the irony, relentlessly underlining that habit of idealistic withdrawal which is seen as a failure, however unavoidable and however much it is associated with the beginnings of his artistic creativity. At the same time there is no minimizing of the positive that is interwoven with it: Stephen is being driven, at least in imagination, towards a more inclusive experience, in which sexuality and aspiration may be unified.

The details of sordid poverty at the start of the final chapter stress again the degree to which the idealist's elation has been an evasion of the piecemeal nature of disorganized everyday experience. They show a wretchedness and self-and-world disgust suffered so sharply that the recoil from it provides the impetus for the next pendulum swing. The writing, as sure and subtle as before[20] first underlines the refuge aspects of Stephen's new aspirational world and the consequent likelihood of further disenchantment. He gravitates to those aspects of his new medium of expression and experience that will indirectly maintain his dissociation, vanity and self-preoccupation (as he did with religion) and the novel makes clear that this is also part of the conventional approach. Literature screens his experience, as we see on his walk to college where he responds to everything through the veils of his favourite authors, Hauptman, Newman, Pater and Ibsen. The irony is directed three ways, at the influences themselves, at the immaturity of Stephen's understanding of them and at the way they are offered to him, limited and formalized. The cliché-ridden villanelle he composes to a "beloved" he hardly knows mocks both Stephen and the literary tradition it belongs to. It is a fashion of feeling and of writing that Joyce, identifying Yeats at the centre of the cult, rejected.[21]

Stephen's religious training dictates his peculiar version of the current cult of art, which he pursues with a priestly dedication and a more than priestly pride – not just God's vicar but God himself in the only world that counts:

> – The aesthetic image in the dramatic form is life purified in and
> reprojected from the human imagination. The mystery of aesthetic

---

20. Some of the older critics, notably Hugh Kenner (*Dublin's Joyce*) and Wayne C. Booth (*The Rhetoric of Fiction*) found "uncertainty" or "moral ambiguity" in the last chapter of *A Portrait of the Artist*.

21. Joyce specified Yeats in Stephen's diary. David Seed in his *James Joyce's Portrait of the Artist* meticulously summarized the villanelle's relationship to current literary fashions.

like that of material creation is accomplished. The artist, like the God of the creation, remains within or behind or above his handiwork, invisible, refined out of existence, paring his fingernails. (337)

Those last few phrases underline the parody of Flaubert's ideal, but that is only the surface level of irony. We see again in the presentation of this artistic credo an equal weight of irony falling on the ideas themselves, derived as they are both from late-nineteenth-century aestheticism and from church scholasticism, and on Stephen himself and his motives for adopting them.[22] Even the most promising formulations are little more than studied platitudes:

> – Pity is the feeling which arrests the mind in the presence of whatsoever is grave and constant in human sufferings and unites it with the human sufferer. Terror is the feeling which arrests the mind in the presence of whatsoever is grave and constant in human sufferings and unites it with the secret cause. (328)

Moreover, the notions quickly reveal a moral bias that discredits them. What emerges as their aim is the creation of a state of mind "above desire and loathing" whose "luminous, silent stasis" makes it unassailably superior to any other. Stephen is obsessed with working out a substitute for the absolutes that have been offered him all his life, with rediscovering the protective inflexibility of codes of thought that will absolve him from the variables of direct involvement in life.

The egomaniac side of Stephen's nature prevails in this part of the novel and the vulnerable is suppressed, but not entirely. He watches the migrant swallows flying about his home: "The inhuman clamour soothed his ears in which his mother's sobs and reproaches murmured insistently and the dark frail quivering bodies wheeling and fluttering and swerving round an airy temple of the tenuous sky soothed his eyes which still saw the image of his mother's face." He doubts his choice: "was it for this folly that he was about to leave the house of prayer and prudence into which he had been born and the order out of which he had come?"

In the end it is the call of undifferentiated life, as before, that drives Stephen through shame and doubt and through pretensions and ideologies, on towards creative participation, even when this aim

---

22. Stephen's aesthetic dogmas were derived almost verbatim from the notes Joyce made in Paris in 1902. See Scholes and Kain, eds, *The Workshop of Daedalus*, 52. S.L. Goldberg in his *The Classical Temper* demonstrated how carefully Joyce filtered his early thoughts on art into Stephen for the purposes of satire.

looks to be turned awry by the urge to achieve balance by withdrawal. His final stance is an acknowledgment that he needs "a new terminology" in order to "encounter for the millionth time the reality of experience and forge in the smithy of my soul the uncreated conscience of my race".[23] The proclamation carries the same seeds as before, indicated by the same ironies, for the processes of thought and response are not conquered but experienced and challenged endlessly.

The trough after that crest of enthusiasm comes at the start of the next novel, *Ulysses*, where we find Stephen returned home to his mother's deathbed (these episodes of *Ulysses* were originally placed at the end of *A Portrait*). He is wracked with guilt at his own refusal to pray for her soul, yet his cynicism is all the more radical, ingrained, bitter and pervasive. His supercilious arrogance is matched only by his self-contempt. He lives in weary futility, his mind tricked out with studied literary and academic musings and infected with a death-obsession that gives rise to the most memorable passages in these "Telemachus" episodes, where everything is sharply observed and highly charged with the mixture of emotions and aspirations we are familiar with from the *Portrait*, but now in a more splintered state:

> The grainy sand had gone from under his feet. His boots trod again a damp crackling mast, razorshells, squeaking pebbles, that on the unnumbered pebbles beats, wood sieved by the shipworm, lost Armada. Unwholesome sandflats waited to suck his treading soles, breathing upward sewage breath. He coasted them, walking warily.[24]

He walks as if over broken glass towards the kind of balance between acceptance and rejection, dissociation and integration he longed for in *A Portrait*. He continues self-protectively analysing his experience along lines that return him to a position where contemplation is the only action – to a false "stasis" – until in his meeting with Bloom, and the touching and separating of the two natures, is suggested the active understanding that a greater maturity must involve. Joyce's attitude towards both characters is one of balanced, compassionate, exuberant irony. The pendulum swing he showed operating in Stephen and that

---

23. Stephen echoes his author: "I am one of the writers of this generation who are perhaps creating at last a conscience in the soul of this wretched race" (Joyce to Nora Joyce, 22 August 1912 in *Letters,* II, 311).

24. *Ulysses*, Everyman edition, 57. The complicated disunity of episode 3 of *Ulysses*, where Stephen is alone on the beach, reads like a prose equivalent of parts of T.S. Eliot's *The Waste Land*. As it appeared in *The Egoist* in 1918, while Eliot was editor and Pound closely involved, it may well have influenced the composition of that poem.

he mentioned in one of his letters as characteristic of himself – "one moment high as the stars, the next lower than the lowest wretches"[25] – is arrested in the tension that the irony maintains. The artistic maturity of *Ulysses* (based as it had to be on a personal one) is a fuller realization of Stephen's dream at the end of *A Portrait* than any he can at that time envisage. His ideal is made manifest in a mutation that both affirms and criticizes it.

In rejecting (or putting behind him) the self-conscious, isolated intellectual Stephen, Joyce rejected (or no longer needed) the technique of high definition and selection used to portray him. As *Ulysses* progressed, his style grew more expansive, not selecting but adding, and the range of coverage grew as wide (though in a different direction) as the "loose, baggy monsters" of the previous century. "The thought is always simple", as he once remarked to a friend,[26] but complexity is achieved by impacting items – impressions, emotions, ideas – on top of each other, so presenting the vitality, the growing potential of his subjects at the same time as the disappointment, dissatisfaction and disillusion prompted by the extremes of his and their demands on life. Joyce's personal difficulty in distilling down the fragments, the apparently unorganizable and unrelated extremes of his knowledge and responses, into a fuel to power rather than destroy is helped by the comedy involved in the process. The complexity of the raw material, the fragments, is there all the time, not forgotten and not assimilated except by these technical means. Joyce meant not to miss an ounce of the complexity both of man's nature and the forces at work on it, nor of that nature's resultant bungling, uneven, indistinct movement. For the same purpose, on the chaotic and diffuse mass of the basic experience he superimposes endless references, parallels, parodies and symbols. The intention is not simply to show up a squalid everyday Dublin life by putting it into an epic framework and mocking it with a variety of literary and academic approaches, but to send up a wide variety of visions of reality and question the validity of seeing life in terms that separate and develop elements of it for the purpose of constructing a conveniently portable frame of reference. In *Ulysses* as in *A Portrait* he wanted to reveal the confusion behind motivation, behind action, and at the same time portray the processes of challenge and assimilation, assertion and submission that have to

---

25. Joyce to Nora Joyce, 2 September 1909 in *Letters*, II, 243.
26. Frank Budgen, *James Joyce and the Making of Ulysses,* 291.

become inextricably united, almost forming one process, in order to achieve a living competency.

Finnegans Wake gives us the same procedure on an even more ambitious scale. The multi-layered, seething mass of happenings is organized in a pattern of repetition, wheeling through successive cycles of nature, history and individual lives. It was "the heroic attempt" according to Samuel Beckett, "to make literature accomplish what belongs to music".[27] Like music it can combine different, even antithetical tendencies simultaneously, its exuberant affirmativeness riddled with subversive ironies.

The range of Virginia Woolf's writing was more diverse than that of any of her major contemporaries except Lawrence. There is a mass of journalism, letters and diaries, often with a sharp exactitude of observation about people and places not to be found (or found with a different focus) in the most characteristic and highly valued of her novels. There are memoirs of her early life, published as *Moments of Being*; biographies that are fanciful like *Orlando* or actual like *Roger Fry*; and what might be called feminist books, *A Room of One's Own* and *Three Guineas*. "She was full of interests", said E.M. Forster, "and the number increased as she grew older, she was curious about life, and she was tough, sensitive but tough".[28]

The directions and sources of her cultural development were strongly influenced by her father, the distinguished Victorian intellectual, Leslie Stephen. She read English literature, she said, "in conjunction with English history".[29] Without formal university training she took in almost as much of the nineteenth-century novel as that other auto-didact, Lawrence. Her respect and admiration went most to George Eliot and Jane Austen, and this is reflected in the style of her earliest novels. This line of literary interest sponsored her preference, among her contemporaries, for James and Proust. But she also responded vividly to Conrad, whom she once called "a much better writer than all of us put together",[30] and Lawrence, a reading of whose *Women in Love* prompted the remark to their mutual friend Koteliansky, "He is 100 times better than most of us".[31] She might

---

27. Beckett, 1937, quoted in James Knowlson, *Damned to Fame: The Life of Samuel Beckett*, 258.

28. Forster, *Two Cheers for Democracy*, 251.

29. *Virginia Woolf's Reading Notebooks*, ed. Brenda R. Silver, 6.

30. Woolf to Pernel Strachey, 3 August 1923 in *Letters*, III, 62.

31. Woolf, 25 June 1921 in *Letters*, II, 476.

well have found an impetus in these towards the thematic organization of her materials, and if so, it was reinforced (as we will see) by her admiration of her friend Forster's *A Passage to India*. However, in the development of her style, Joyce was the decisive influence, for the way he exploited the technique of the "stream of consciousness".[32]

His example encouraged her in her reaction against Arnold Bennett and the trends he represented (although their style was rooted in traditions she respected). She repudiated the way such "materialists … spend immense skill and industry making the trivial and transitory appear the true and the enduring", and she mocked the "air of probability embalming the whole so impeccable that if all his [Bennett's] figures were to come to life they would find themselves dressed down to the last button of their coats in the fashion of the hour".[33] For her life consisted of states of mind: "Let us record the atoms as they fall upon the mind in the order in which they fall, let us trace the pattern, however disconnected and incoherent in appearance, which each sight or incident scores upon that consciousness."[34] Although she was to make of it something quite unlike Joyce's, "*la monologue intérieure*" showed her a way into the inner world she needed to explore.

Her own style came to maturity in *Mrs Dalloway* which focuses on the manic alienation of the suicidal depressive, Septimus. Our discussion will focus on the next novel, *To the Lighthouse,* because of the way in which that theme is combined there with others. The most interesting aspect of the book from our point of view (as with Joyce's *Portrait*) is the way the conflict of the themes shapes and governs the exploration of the characters. The three main characters all have their ideals, they are all egoists, all seek regenerative ends. Whereas in Joyce's novel the positives narrowly prevail, here it is the reverse.

Lily Briscoe (the same age, 44, at the end of the novel as Woolf was when she wrote it) is a loner, uneasy in the fluctuating world of daily sensation and social happenings. She wants in her paintings both to find something more permanent and communicate it to others. But she is a self-confessed failure as a person, and to that degree also as an

---

32. The term "stream of consciousness" was first applied to Dorothy Richardson (see John Rosenberg, *Dorothy Richardson*, 90) although its French equivalent had appeared some years earlier. Richardson's experiments in that direction must be accounted an influence on Woolf, although she often reacted against what she saw as self-indulgence in her work.
33. Woolf, "Modern Fiction" (1925) in *Essays*, IV, 159-60.
34. *Ibid.*, IV, 161.

artist. She contrasts her own "poverty of spirit" with Mrs Ramsay's "abundance" of feeling. Seeing young Minta and Paul in love – "entering into illusion glittering eyed" – she backs away:

> She need not undergo that degradation. She was saved from that dilution. She would move the tree rather more to the middle.[35]

The last sentence refers to her painting, which offers refuge and compensation: "in the midst of chaos there was shape." Whenever she sets out on the "exciting ecstasy" of artistic creation, she feels like a "soul bereft of body" preparing to exchange "the fluidity of life for the concentration of painting". In the early manuscript version of the novel, this feeling was taken further, Lily imagining herself in the act of creation enjoying "that intensity and freedom of life which, for a few seconds after the death of the body, one imagines the souls of the dead to enjoy". It is an experience to be preferred to "the gratification of bodily human love" because it is more final: "an awful marriage; forever".[36] In the final version of the novel, meaning appears for her out of the meaningless like "matches struck unexpectedly in the dark". The image connects her with Forster's scene in the Marabar caves in *A Passage to India,* while another aspect of her mentality may remind one of Beckett: "to follow her thought was like following a voice which speaks too quickly to be taken down by one's pencil, and the voice was her own voice saying without prompting undeniable, everlasting, contradictory things." At the end of the novel there is a stronger sense of her achievement, both as a woman who has freed herself from the influence of Mrs Ramsay's kind of sex role (while coming to terms with the grief of her loss) and as an artist: "I have had my vision" are the last words of the book. However, these like all the other positives in the novel are subject to question.

In the portrait of Mr Ramsay there is a kindred criss-crossing of qualifications. Lily's final vision of him is of a "very distinguished" man of letters, and at the same time "a figure of infinite pathos". Partly because of this duality he is the most dynamic character in the novel, vividly struggling to live fully as well as to achieve much in his

---

35. Woolf, *To the Lighthouse*, ed. Susan Dick, 87. Subsequent page references are this Shakespeare Head edition.

36. Woolf, *To the Lighthouse: the Original Holograph Draft,* ed. Susan Dick, 280. Clarissa in the previous novel, *Mrs Dalloway*, afflicted by a sense of isolation and by "incapacity" of feeling (the nun-like or virginal "cold spirit" which she blames for a certain degree of failure in her marriage) also feels a penchant for death, seen in her sentimental salute to Septimus's suicide, as a "defiance" of conventional complacency and an "embrace" of an absolute.

work. But he is isolated, even in his own family, by his own nature – difficult, exacting, egotistical and lacking in sympathy for the feelings and needs of others – and by his obsession with his writings. His philosophical perplexities and his anxieties about the value of his work reflect Woolf's own.[37] The metaphor of the Ramsays' marriage that appears (rather implausibly) in their young son James's imagination – the mother as a fountain, "a rain of energy" and a "delicious fecundity" into which "the fatal sterility of the male plunged itself, like a beak of brass, barren and bare" – stresses irreconcilable opposition. The meagre dialogue between them softens yet corroborates this impression. The scene at the end of the first part of the novel, where they are both reading, is a dumb show of estrangement, with conversation limited to practicalities. They are locked in themselves, taking each other and their love for granted, he condescending towards her "simplicity" and she indulging in delusions about some sort of "triumph" – "Nothing on earth can equal this happiness" – achieved in spite of her mysterious unwillingness to say "I love you".

Mrs Ramsay is explicitly offered as an integrating force, a force for good, and in spite of her lack of robustness she seems to achieve it by sympathy and sensitivity. Her friend Lily comments sentimentally: "It was her instinct to go, an instinct like the swallows for the south, the artichokes for the sun, turning her infallibly to the human race, making her nest in its heart." She herself is sustained in her best moments by the sense of "a coherence in things, a stability":

> something, she meant, is immune from change, and shines out (she glanced at the window with its ripple of reflected lights) in the face of the flowing, the fleeting, the spectral, like a ruby. (89)

In her portrait the creative factors in the novel are most explicitly developed, but the negatives are correspondingly stronger. They show up to some extent in her character itself: her self-admitted "wishing to dominate, wishing to interfere, making people do what she wished" and her habitual reaction to masculinity: "she felt, without hostility, the sterility of men." But these are less significant for the reader than the way the scope of her character is limited and confined to the itemized thoughts and responses of a single day, and a day in which in spite of her sympathy and patience she feels isolated and up against

---

37. The most sophisticated examination of the book's philosophical ramifications, especially with regard to Mr Ramsay, is Gillian Beer's essay, "Hume, Stephen and Elegy in *To the Lighthouse*", in her *Virginia Woolf: The Common Ground*.

life: "And again she felt alone in the presence of her old antagonist, life." She comments on her husband:

> He said the most melancholy things, but she noticed that directly he had said them he always seemed more cheerful than usual. All this phrase-making was a game, she thought, for if she had said half what he said, she would have blown her brains out by now. (60)

Herta Newman noticed in her "a pessimism more profound than Mr Ramsay's philosophic gloom". The "maternal model" she upholds is "exposed as a deception".[38]

In her the main trend of the novel emerges. The fact that she is a woman of weak resilience who makes few demands and generally offers passive participation, but is warm-hearted and beautiful finally serves to increase the seductive persuasiveness of enervation:

> she began all this business [of being the kind hostess] as a sailor not without weariness sees the wind fill his sail and yet hardly wants to be off again and thinks how, had the ship sunk, he would have whirled round and round and found rest on the floor of the sea. (72)

Her sympathy begins to seem spurious; it is the experience of isolation that dominates:

> the things you know us by, our apparitions, are simply childish. Beneath it is all dark, it is spreading, it is unfathomably deep; but now and again we rise to the surface and that is what you see us by. (55)

Gillian Beer praised the "extraordinary serenity of the book" which

> even while it includes desolation and harassment, depends upon its acceptance of attenuation. Loss, completion, ending, absence, are acknowledged. Evanescence is of the nature of experience.[39]

An apter term than serenity for the whole experience might be acquiescence. At the core of her acceptance there is a weariness of life:

> Not as oneself did one ever find rest, in her experience (she accomplished here something dexterous with her needles) but as a wedge of darkness. Losing personality, one lost the fret, the hurry, the stir; and there rose to her lips always some exclamation of triumph over life when things came together in this peace, this rest, this eternity; and pausing there she looked out to meet that stroke of the Lighthouse, the long steady stroke, the last of the three, which was her stroke .... (55)

38. Newman, *Virginia Woolf and Mrs Brown*, 90.
39. Beer, *Virginia Woolf: The Common Ground*, 45-46

The character in its position of central relevance to the book, sharing its vision, provides a triumph of the imprisoned self and a glorification of the burdened and deathward:

> She praised herself in praising the light, without vanity, for she was stern, she was searching, she was beautiful like that light. It was odd, she thought, how if one was alone, one leant to things, inanimate things; (55-56)

There is a family resemblance to Mrs Moore in Forster's *A Passage to India,* which Woolf had read two years before. She too stands for sympathy and family values, and suffers the deconstructive vision of a meaningless universe. But (as we have seen) her vision is later half-mocked and her positive influence enlarged. Here there is little to offset the pervasive quality of enervation which is subtly established as Mrs Ramsay offers the reader gratuitous and uncertain familiarities with life, little epiphanies of vision. Her thoughts and fantasies, not necessarily related at every point to her motivation or immediate circumstance but developed often for their own sake demonstrate the random contingency of moment-by-moment existence and reveal a helplessness and purposelessness that can be regarded (in the lingering light of idealism) as painful or ugly or (when appreciated with a childlike naivety) beautiful.

The static quality does not come merely from her view. The source lies in the whole concept of the book with its material consciously shaped, selected and contained, even its major symbols riddled with ambiguities. It is structured so that the overall effect is static. It avoids normal action or limits it to symbolic relevance only (as in the last section). The scenes are of actions rather than action and are representative – snapshot symbolism. Conversation, an active ingredient, is smoothed in in bits and pieces and deactivated by its inconsequentiality so that it blends unresisting into the blandness. The minor details of mood and experience that Woolf concentrates on, and the symbols that attempt to extend their influence make the novel top-heavy, in spite of the subtlety and naturalness with which they arise in the context.

As a result of this naturalness one might be forgiven for feeling that the part of the book that holds together as an unbroken vision with the maximum potential for expressing this theme is the middle one where there are no characters at all and no need for them and where the representatives of people (the cleaners) wander on and off stage with their mime of the human lot. It expands the underlying sense of emptiness and unreality worked elsewhere into the characters' responses. Here it is conveyed entirely by the visual symbols on which the author has so firm a grip, and here, where these are unadulterated by character or action of any kind other than the mimetic, the reader's appreciation of the desperation behind such a grip is at its strongest. What gives rise to dissatisfaction in the complex generalizing of the other parts of the book is the intrusion of any action or any purpose.

The overall effect is to turn the reader into a connoisseur of subtly preserved responses, for there are few places in prose where it is done so well. Woolf's grip on the relation between mood and what appears to be visual reality is keen and constant, apart from lapses into preciosity, as in this passage where the author is following the progress of "certain airs, detached from the body of the wind":

> Almost one might imagine them, as they entered the drawing room, questioning and wandering, toying with the flap of hanging wallpaper, asking, would it hang much longer, when would it fall? Then smoothly brushing the walls, they passed on musingly as if asking the red and yellow roses on the wall-paper whether they would fade, and questioning (gently, for there was time at their disposal) the torn letters in the wastepaper basket, the flowers, the books, all of which were now open to them and asking, Were they allies? Were they enemies? How long would they endure? (108)

At its best the technique offers a tasteful recording of some of the processes of response, a record of minor reactions that relate at a tangent to active participation, haphazardly shaping, reshaping, destroying, distracting or insulating.

The mind wavers while the senses hold on to an illusory pattern and beauty, which adds to what is the pleasanter aspect of the book's passivity a drugged stillness, as if it had been written under narcosis:

> And dismissing all this, as one passes in diving now a weed, now a straw, now a bubble, she felt again, sinking deeper, as she had felt in the hall when the others were talking, There is something I want – something I have come to get, and she fell deeper and deeper without knowing quite what it was, with her eyes closed. (100)

The novel, in so far as it intends more than making patterns with what are after all on their own quite commonplace abstracts about life, is attempting a record of certain features of it, and as a record it is limited in being removed from the kind of dramatic action which brings out complexity and rescues the content from paralysis through the grip of the author. The responses recorded are trivial not because people's daily thoughts and reactions are necessarily trivial and unexplored but because the author does not want to explore but to express a fixity and sameness. The book is weighted unfavourably against Mr Ramsay, however hard it struggles to be just. It is weighted against activity, purpose and assertion as well as mere egotism.

Woolf in her reaction against the "materialism" of Arnold Bennett nevertheless retained his visualizing habit, even though it is that of the impressionist rather than the naturalistic painter; so that in spite of her disclaimer of the trappings and furniture of such novels she replaced their attempt at realism with her own, and the concomitant in each case, the urge to generalize from the very specific or to take certain things for granted, is unsatisfying. Symbols of spiritual conditions become her furniture and reveal aspects of personality and lifestyle hardly more comprehensively than Bennett's rooms, clothes and facial expressions. The two writers offer two halves of a technique that even if put together might still cause life to "refuse to live there" unless the obsessional concentration on the circumstantial, whether physical or spiritual, were relaxed.

At its worst her approach is a materialism of the feelings, and the expression of it occasionally lapses into mixed metaphors and rag-bag symbolism – even on the first page:

> Since he belonged, even at the age of six, to that great clan which cannot keep this feeling separate from that, but must let future prospects, with their joys and sorrows, cloud what is actually at hand, since to such people even in earliest childhood any *turn in the wheel* of sensation has the power to *crystallise and transfix* the moment upon which its *gloom or radiance* rests... [our italics]

Even at its best the finest dramatic complexity is sacrificed. She rejected one set of artistic limitations for another. If Bennett's characters are in danger of spending their time (in her words) "in some softly padded first-class railway carriage, pressing bells and buttons innumerable" her own are in danger of losing the ability to make a journey and the finger with which to press.

Her next novel, *The Waves,* developed the theme and technique of the middle section of *To the Lighthouse.* In it the characters speak not with their own accents but as it were through an interpreter who delivers their essential thought-experience (how the "white wax" of their nature has responded to the impressions of their environment) in a homogeneous style. Those who search for some pattern in the flux of experience – whether in personal love (Neville) or the study of history (Louis) or in art (Bernard) – are disappointed. In Bernard is combined the dual consciousness that was separated in Septimus

Smith and Clarissa Dalloway. One half he calls "the enemy" which admits defeat and self-deception, acknowledges the fundamental chaos of existence and drives towards suicide. The other half affirms the community of individuals, the harmony of life, "the eternal renewal, the incessant rise and fall and rise again". The two are ambiguously fused in his final gesture (the last words of the novel):

> "Against you I will fling myself, unvanquished and unyielding, O Death!"
>
> *The waves broke on the shore.*

The book represents an ultimate destination in her pursuit of the possibilities of thematic structure, before returning in her next, *The Years*, to the tradition of psychological realism, chronicling the fortunes of a family. Finally, in *Between the Acts*, she symbolized the theme of creative effort in a historical pageant with its vision of community and harmony (which its deviser calls "a failure, another damned failure") and placed alongside it the psychological examination of characters who are all caught in unsuccessful relationships.

10

THE NEXT GENERATION

Huxley, Orwell and Beckett

Here we shall be looking at just three authors (and focusing chiefly on one thematic narrative from each) in order to examine some of the processes that forge new links in the chain of tradition. Themes we have explored in Lawrence and others, especially the attack on idealism and the experiences of isolation and despair, are subject to fresh developments, as these writers take in the influence of those we have already examined, reacting both with it and against it and searching further afield in the narrative tradition for the purpose of creating new variants.

We start with Aldous Huxley because of his direct and personal connection with Lawrence, who has been the focal point of this whole investigation. He called Lawrence "the most extraordinary and impressive human being I have ever known".[1] The complicated process of his receiving and challenging that influence extends all the way from his fourth novel, *Point Counter Point*, to his last, *Island.*

Point Counter Point was written in the thirteen months (a relatively long gestation for Huxley) when he was meeting Lawrence fairly regularly. Lawrence himself was in the didactic phase of his own novels. He figures in Huxley's novel directly, as Rampion, whom Huxley described as "just some of Lawrence's notions on legs" and Lawrence called "boring" and "a gas-bag".[2] The initial sketch in the novel of the Lawrences as Huxley saw them is biographically interesting, but the rest of the picture is relatively a fake, and this undermines what is positive in the novel, which in any case is partially sent up as well as endorsed. In spite of the divisiveness that inhabits him as well most of the other characters in the novel, Rampion expounds an ideal of balance that can be found better expressed in

---

1. Huxley to E. F. Saxton, 3 March 1930, in *Letters*, 332.

2. Huxley, quoted by Sybelle Bedford, *Aldous Huxley*, I, 202; and Lawrence to Huxley, 28 October 1928, in *Letters*, VI, 601

Lawrence's *Apropos of Lady Chatterley's Lover*, as well as in Huxley's own essays of that time. Rampion's later rantings sometimes bear a closer resemblance to those of Annable in Lawrence's first novel, *The White Peacock*. But Lawrence's general influence can be seen in many ways throughout *Point Counter Point*, and not just in the pursuit of idealism. Echoes of *Women in Love,* for instance, occur when Spandrell, like Loerke, boasts of seducing young girls, or Lucy, like Gudrun, adopts a deliberate sensuality.

In this novel the only theme worth taking seriously is idealism, analysed along Lawrencian lines, quite subtly in the case of the main author-figure, Philip Quarles, and less so in the others. On Quarles (who is writing a novel much like *Point Counter Point*) his wife Elinor comments:

> All that the intelligence could seize upon he seized. She reported her intercourse with the natives of the realm of emotion and he understood at once, he generalised her experience for her, he related it with other experiences, classified it, found analogies and parallels. From single and individual it became in his hands part of a system. She was astonished to find that she and her friends had been, all along, substantiating a theory, or exemplifying some interesting generalisation.[3]

She concedes that his is a "quick comprehensive ubiquitous intelligence that could understand everything, including the emotions it could not feel and the instincts it took care not to be moved by". That somewhat glamorizing assumption is shared by Philip when he entertains a vision of himself as so receptive and plastic that his mind might be called "amoebic".

But the analysis is taken a step further when Elinor wonders "whether it was that the habit of secrecy had made it impossible for him to give utterance to his inward feelings, or whether the very capacity to feel had been atrophied by consistent silence and repression". And later it is more relentless, when both his wife and his mother agree that in crucial ways he is "impregnable" and even somewhat of a mollusc. Elinor comes to the conclusion that the limitations of his understanding proceed from the limitations of his feelings: "Nobody understands what he does not feel. Philip couldn't understand her because he didn't feel as she felt." She later reflects, "She had begged for love; but what he had given her was a remote

---

3. *Point Counter Point*, Collected edition, 1971, 107. Subsequent page references are to that edition.

impersonal benevolence". Quarles himself towards the end of the book defines the simplifying tendencies of his mentality: "Living's much more difficult than Sanskrit or chemistry or economics. The intellectual life is child's play; which is why intellectuals tend to become children."

The general lines of the analysis are obviously Lawrencian, yet it is finely specific, and genuinely exploratory and self-critical – "in part a portrait of me" as he said.[4] For the purposes of definition and analysis he was developing to an extreme the intellectuality which he regarded in himself as comparatively moderate. Quarles suspects his condition is immutable:

> Shall I ever have the strength of mind to break myself of these indolent habits of intellectualism and devote my energies to the more serious and difficult task of living integrally? And even if I did try to break these habits, shouldn't I find that heredity was at the bottom of them and that I was congenitally incapable of living wholly and harmoniously? (324)

Through Quarles Huxley was making an endlessly fair-minded attack on a tirelessly resilient intellectuality.

The novel elsewhere pursues this theme in terms less demanding and rewarding. Analogies with the musical technique of counterpoint are used to represent, as Peter Firchow put it, "the isolation of his characters within their closed systems of thought".[5] Huxley's articulate facility spins generalizations that smother the specific and leave one's sympathies only faintly involved, and the drama comes only fitfully to life.   However, the basic mechanism whereby the ideas and ideals are sponsored by and also endorse the personal limitations of the characters is clearly outlined. Marjorie Carling's codes of self-repression and self-sacrifice, for instance, are seen as the product of and excuse for a deficient vitality. The scientific intellectuality of Lord Edward helps cause and protect an arrested emotional development. His assistant Illidge's scientific and socialist interests minister to his envy and spite. The pretentious and self-applausive spirituality and devotion to art and thought shown by the editor Burlap conceal a pappy but predatory self-indulgence. And in

---

4. Huxley, quoted by Peter Firchow, *Aldous Huxley*, 112.

5. Peter Firchow, *Aldous Huxley*, 102. The alternative title for the novel, which Huxley had in mind and preferred was "Diverse Laws", which with its reference to the book's epigraph is more descriptive.

Spandrell we witness a disappointed, mother-dominated love of God turning into diabolism.

The next novel, *Brave New World*, takes Lawrence's influence into the area the latter had occupied in the final phase of his work, the didactic fable, but does so in a style adopted from older reaches of the tradition. Here the influence of Swift joined forces with Lawrence's to give Huxley's satirical bent its head.[6] The fiercest satirical light is thrown on the directors and controllers of this world, and their intellectualist craving to create it according to an abstract blueprint. In this scenario the emotional deficiency identified in Quarles now rules the world. As with Galsworthy and his Forsytes, writing this book involved the criticism of one half of the author by the other.

Orwell criticized the novel for its Wellsian liberal rationality, which fails to take account of the fact that "the energy that actually shapes the world springs from emotions – racial pride, leader-worship, religious belief, love of war".[7] He ignored the fact that this kind of rationality, out of touch with the springs of action and sadistically inimical to the spontaneity of individual life was Huxley's chief target. Orwell saw his own fable, *Nineteen Eighty-Four,* as a corrective to Huxley's, but there is more congruence than this suggests. The Ministry of Truth where Winston Smith works recalls Huxley's College of Emotional Engineering. Like Winston, Bernard Marx in *Brave New World* wonders "What would it be like … if I were free – not enslaved by my conditioning?". Mustapha Mond is as much a manic idealist as O'Brien, although the sadism is latent. For him too, "Science is dangerous". In the manuscript of *Brave New World*, Mond even goes so far as to declare, like O'Brien, "The Past, the stupid unnecessary Past, has been abolished".[8]

The complete subjugation of the spontaneous and individual to the regularized collective will is the keynote in this fable. Only function counts, in a rigid five-caste social machine in which each individual

---

6. A more recent influence in the same direction, of course, was H. G. Wells. David Bradshaw has demonstrated in *The Hidden Huxley* how many similarities there were in the mental attitudes of the two. Huxley began his novel as a parody of Wells' recent *Men like Gods*, in order to attack the Wellsian ideal of technological progress. It has some of the playful inventive facility seen in Wells' early scientific romances, with a wide range of contemporary reference, some of it witty, often crudely or facetiously so.

7. Orwell, *Collected Essays*, II, 141.

8. Quoted by Donald Watt, "Manuscript Revisions of *Brave New World*", in *Critical Essays on Aldous Huxley*, ed. Jerome Meckier, 77.

component is determined and conditioned in the bottle from which it is born:

> On Rack 10, rows of next generation's chemical workers were being trained in the toleration of lead, caustic soda, tar, chlorine. The first batch of two hundred and fifty embryonic rocket-plane engineers was passing the eleven hundredth metre mark on Rack 3. A special mechanism kept their containers in constant rotation. "To improve their sense of balance" Mr Foster explained .... "They learn to associate topsy-turvydom with wellbeing; in fact, they're only truly happy when they're standing on their heads."[9]

The Director has just explained to the students that all conditioning aims at "making people like their inescapable destiny". The picture recalls Wells' Selenites in *The First Men on the Moon* but has a sharper edge:

> He waved his hand again, and the Head Nurse pressed a second lever. The screaming of the babies suddenly changed its tone. There was something desperate, almost insane, about the sharp spasmodic yelps to which they now gave utterance. Their little bodies twitched and stiffened; their limbs moved jerkily as if to the tug of unseen wires. (15)

There is a cold inverted passion of power and ego behind the Director's benevolent prescription of subliminal training:

> "Till at last the child's mind *is* these suggestions, and the sum of the suggestions *is* the child's mind. And not the child's mind only. The adult's mind too – all his life long. The mind that judges and desires and decides – made up of these suggestions. But these suggestions are *our* suggestions!" The director almost shouted in his triumph. "Suggestions from the State." (22)

Even among the highest castes, who are not so drastically engineered, human responses are systematically denatured and devalued through conscious indoctrination and the elimination and censorship of the arts and sciences. With them, any residue dissatisfaction is subdued with drugs (which include the official religion and arts). Motherhood is a dirty word and sex reduced to the casual and promiscuous, for reasons the Controller explains:

> "Think of water under pressure in a pipe." They thought of it. "I pierce it once" [he] said. "What a jet!"

---

9. *Brave New World*, Collected edition, 1970, 12-13. Subsequent page references are to this edition.

> He pierced it twenty times. There were twenty piddling little
> fountains ....
> "Fortunate boys!" said the Controller. "No pains have been spared
> to make your lives emotionally easy – to preserve you, so far as that is
> possible, from having emotions at all." (32-35)

The outrage is called in question by two Alpha-plus intellectuals
whose difference from the norm – Bernard Marx is physically
diminutive for his type, while Helmholtz Watson has "too much
ability" – has made them aware of their individuality. Marx complains
like Quarles in *Point Counter Point* of their being "adults
intellectually" but "infants where feeling and desire are concerned".
He is demoted and Watson is sent into exile, but not before a
discussion with the Controller-in-Chief, Mustapha Mond, whose
rationalism has the plausibility of a maniac. "We believe in happiness
and stability" he says, and everything in his argument follows with
specious logic from that. At this point the logic of *Brave New World*
connects with that of *Nineteen Eighty-Four*. In both we see ideologies
becoming dangerous when, as Hannah Arendt put it: "taken literally
they become the nuclei of logical systems in which, as in the systems
of paranoiacs, everything follows comprehensibly and even
compulsorily once the first premise is accepted. The insanity of such
systems lies not only in their first premise but in the very logicality
with which they are constructed."[10]

The outrage is challenged most strongly by the introduction of
John the Savage, through whom Lawrence casts his light over this
book. Brought up on a reservation for primitives, his responses to
people are normal in our sense of the word and his understanding has
been brought to consciousness by reading a copy of Shakespeare's
works that happened to be lying around. Brought into the New World,
he cannot come to terms with it. Some of his responses are facilely
generalized, but through him the premises of the New World are
thoroughly denied.

Not quite categorically, however, for in the picture of the Old
World, the Reservation where John has lived, a note of distaste makes
itself felt. Huxley revealed his ambivalence towards the primitives'
life – dirty, vulnerable, burdened and precarious – in his later
Foreword when he called it "hardly less queer and abnormal" than the
Brave New World. In the novel he capitalizes on his own distaste,

---

10. Arendt, *The Origins of Totalitarianism*, 457-58.

both in the picture of the Reservation itself and in the reactions of Lenina, the standard Alpha woman, to John's mother:

> And suddenly the creature burst out in a torrent of speech, rushed at her with outstretched hands and – Ford! Ford! It was too revolting, in a moment she'd be sick – pressed her against the bulge, the bosom, and began to kiss her. (97-98)

Huxley was beginning to repudiate the Lawrencian influence.

Brave New World is of course in one sense a vacation from the graver problems of relating ideals to their psychological necessity within the individual. In his next novel, *Eyeless in Gaza* we see Huxley, like Wells in *Tono-Bungay,* attempting to come to grips with those realities. The main character, Anthony Beavis, is called by his doctor "an admirable manipulator of ideas, linked with a person who, as far as self-knowledge and feeling are concerned, is just a moron". He lives in what he himself calls "a prison of knowledge" and self-escapism: "there is nothing, to make oneself forget a particular and personal feeling, so effective as a good generalisation." This is the kind of mentality outlined in Quarles in *Point Counter Point*. For Anthony, "The thirty-five years of his conscious life made themselves immediately clear to him as a chaos – a pack of snapshots in the hands of a lunatic". The structure of the novel reflects this: it is like a disarranged pack of cards, each chapter dated but out of sequence.

The book is not, however, a repeat of the earlier one, for it launches a psychological study in depth of Anthony's predicament. Some of the scenes in which his emotional retardation is traced back to his childhood are sensitively drawn. After his mother's death we see a conflict between his childish vulnerability and intellectuality, and there are painfully embarrassing encounters with his father, who is described by a friend as one of those who are "cripples in spirit". The friend, Mrs Foxe, offers an explanation of Anthony's psychological mechanism when she observes that he is sensitive to hurt and grief but "wears a kind of armour" to protect himself against it.

His development reveals a perspective quite different from that supplied by Rampion, and we realize that Huxley is reconsidering Lawrence's influence. What Lawrence stood for had demanded from Huxley an emotional development which he pictured, in the emotionally atrophied Quarles, as out of the question. What had been seen in Quarles as a failure to rise to a challenge is now in Anthony represented as a considered rejection. When he reads a passage from Lawrence's tale, "The Man who Died" vividly expressive of the undifferentiated call to life, he comments: "But life, life as such, he protested inwardly – it was not enough .... And, oh, the horror of that display of sub-mental passion, of violent and impersonal egotism!" He needs something more rarefied. As Pierre Vitoux put it: "Huxley, through Anthony, has now moved on to a hierarchical vision, with Life subordinate and Reason in control."[11]   Several years earlier Huxley had complained that Lawrence's books were "oppressively *visceral* .... one longs for the open air of intellectual abstraction and pure spirituality".[12]

The last part of Anthony's development sees him accepting from the anthropologist Miller a mystical philosophy of self-transcendence. Few readers have found it convincing. The crucial mystical illumination of "wholeness" conveyed largely in abstract terms, gives little assurance that he has done more than exchange one Plato's cavern for another. These broad didactic ideas are superimposed upon a context that cannot support them. The novel shows, like Wells' *Tono-Bungay*, an imagination defeated by the complexities of the problems it poses and falling back on generalities.

In Huxley's later novels there is a similar uneasy attempted amalgamation (or alternation) of psychological analysis and a didactic or satirical overview. The kind of idealism which had been the focus of such sharp criticism in the ten years before *Eyeless in Gaza* had now gained an immunity from scepticism because it was needed to prop up the beliefs that were meant to save the author from scepticism. In each novel characters appear – Propter in *After Many a Summer*, Rontini in *Time Must Have a Stop* – who hold up that didactic flag.

There were two further excursions into the form that had proved so rewarding in *Brave New World*. The first, *Ape and Essence,* came in 1948, given impetus by observation of the horrors of the Second World War. Written before Huxley had read Orwell's *Nineteen Eighty-Four,* it bears some resemblance to it, for it is set in a repressive, fear-ridden society of the future, in which debased instincts rule. A combination of worldwide devastation and "gamma-rays" has reduced people almost to the level of apes. Their degeneracy and their worship of "Belial" are intended as a sardonic comment on humanity.

> Surely it's obvious.
> Doesn't every schoolboy know it?
> Ends are ape-chosen; only the means are man's.

---

11. Vitoux, "Aldous Huxley on Lawrence's Philosophy of Life", in *Now More than Ever: A Symposium*, ed. Bernfried Nugel, 315.
12. Huxley to G. Wilson Knight, 15 September 1931, in *Letters*, 353.

The satiric method is cruder than in *Brave New World*. Huxley's scepticism, made caustic through pain and revulsion, had slipped into cynicism.[13]

Finally in *Island* (1962) Huxley produced what he called "a kind of reverse *Brave New World*".[14] Like its predecessor it adopts the structure and style of a fable, harking back to the didactic narratives of the eighteenth century – though this time to Voltaire rather than Swift. It continued the attack on the forms of idealism that bugged him throughout his life – there are flashbacks to marital fixations in the hero and a Calvinist upbringing – but the main effort is to put forward, in a breakaway community whose ideologies are culled eclectically from various Eastern and Western schools of thought, the way of regeneration that will lead the individual and the community to "Good Being". It is Wellsian in its subscription to the world-transforming potentialities of liberal enlightenment, and Huxleyan in its mistrust of what is challenging and unpredictable in normal human relationships, and a desire to defuse them. That had been characteristic of the idealism attacked in *Point Counter Point* and *Brave New World*. Now it is endorsed (as, for example, in the voluntary eugenics programme for the choosing and mating of human eggs) as an integral part of a rational system imposed on life. Huxley was no longer fighting his intellectualism but going to sleep in its coils.

George Orwell inherited from Lawrence's generation, if not so directly as Huxley from Lawrence himself, the theme of idealism, ingrained in him by his upbringing and then by his struggle to escape it, for he used antithetical ideas in order to do so and then had to release himself from them in turn. He learned the necessity and the treachery of them all. He fought a battle longer and bitterer than Huxley's, but eventually more victorious, against the class- and ideal-ridden mentality behind an upbringing that was in some ways similar.[15]

---

13. During this phase of his career scepticism was sometimes made genial by sympathy and sentiment. One of the best examples of this is the tale, "The Genius and the Goddess", written partly as a tribute to the memory of Frieda Lawrence. Here the contradictions and "booby-traps" of life are enjoyed and celebrated in a spirit of fun, endorsing "the creative otherness of love and sleep" which restores to Katy (the goddess) her life-giving strength.
14. Huxley, quoted by Firchow, *Aldous Huxley*, 178.
15. He was sent to the same school, Eton (and actually taught by Aldous for a short while) after a childhood that was as intellectually hard-pressed and probably more

The first novel, *Burmese Days*, shows Flory, the main character, up against the imperialist set-up as Orwell experienced it in his early twenties. Each of the three subsequent novels of the 1930s pits an individual against some aspect of the system in contemporary England. Orwell's choice of narrative style at this time was governed by a characteristic desire to be direct and intelligible to ordinary people, which went with an admiration (much qualified with reservations) for writers like Dickens, Kipling and Wells – accompanied by some distaste for the current anti-realist fashions of Woolf and Waugh.

However, after six years filled with war-work and journalism, he looked for inspiration to the oldest forms of the thematic tradition. *Animal Farm* was the first book, he said, in which he tried "to fuse political purpose and artistic purpose into one whole".[16] The result, for all its apparent artlessness, reverberates with the kind of significance we have been studying in more obviously sophisticated constructions. He wrote in the Preface to the Ukrainian edition: "On my return from Spain I thought of exposing the Soviet myth in a story that could be easily understood by almost anyone."[17] But the satire applies to any revolutionary "ism" and any form of subsequent dictatorship. The classic formula itself guarantees the presence of universals of behaviour and experience beyond the topical. The whole fabric is based upon an assessment of the relation between ideology and human nature. Jeffrey Meyers once suggested a comparison with Conrad's *Nostromo* which might seem far-fetched were it not for the shared interest in the mechanism of idealism and barbarism in the revolutionary setting.[18] The scenes with General Montero in Conrad's novel, for instance – the success of his barbaric energy and childish egotism when posed against an egoist-idealist of a different sort in Gould – are recalled by the picture of the pig Napoleon in his skirmishes with Snowball, who can be read in general terms (not just as a reference to Trotsky) as an idealist and dangerous as such but posing a threat of a different order.

From the start the purist is sent up and understood to be a potential danger. The old boar Major pronounces:

---

emotionally deprived. His classic essay on his schooling, "Such, such were the Joys" records the struggle of an isolated individual against a tyrannous code, which is the central motif of his work.

16. Orwell, "Why I write," in *Collected Essays*, I, 7.

17. Orwell, *Collected Essays*, III, 405.

18. See Meyers, *A Reader's Guide to George Orwell*, 143.

"And above all, no animal must ever tyrannize over his own kind. Weak or strong, clever or simple, we are all brothers. No animal must ever kill any other animal. All animals are equal."[19]

The absurdity of these dictates delivered to a motley audience containing cats, dogs and rats establishes from the start the inevitability of failure for the ideal, and already suggests a hidden motive behind it. Quite apart from its reference to Karl Marx's appearance, it is not for nothing that this original idealist is described as a pig with a "wise and benevolent appearance in spite of the fact that his tushes had never been cut". Then again, his idealism does involve a genuine desire for a better life for the animals.[20]

The fable is kept balanced in many ways, all of which underline its validity as an analysis of causes and effects. It emphasizes, for instance, the ease with which an oppressor uses in ju-jitsu fashion the strength of his victims against themselves as well as their weakness. The pigs use Boxer's earnestness, loyalty and hard work, which are more of an inspiration to the animals than the pigs' processions, slogans and intellectual sleights of hand. The deception is made possible, as Boxer says, by "something in ourselves" which is seen for example in the stupidity of the sheep, the comfort-seeking non-involvement of the cat who is found to have voted on both sides, the tendency to expect pie tomorrow which is reflected in the Raven's stories, and a general bewildered apathy:

> As for the others, their life, so far as they knew, was as it had always been. They were generally hungry, they slept on straw, they drank from the pool, they laboured in the fields; in winter they were troubled by the cold, and in the summer by the flies. Sometimes the older ones among them racked their dim memories and tried to determine whether in the early days of the Rebellion, when Jones's expulsion was still recent, things had been better or worse than now. They could not remember. There was nothing with which they could compare their present lives: they had nothing to go on but Squealer's lists of figures, which invariably demonstrated that everything was getting better and better. The animals found the problem insoluble; in any case, they had little time for speculating on such things now. Only old Benjamin professed to remember every detail of his long life and to know that things had never been, nor ever could be, much

---

19. *Animal Farm*, ed. Peter Davison, 6. Subsequent page references are to this edition.
20. Florence and William Boos pointed out a resemblance between the Major and William Morris in their "Orwell's Morris and Old Major's Dream", in *English Studies*, LXXI.

> better or much worse – hunger, hardship, and disappointment being,
> so he said, the unalterable law of life
>   And yet the animals never gave up hope (87)

That last note typifies the buoyancy of the story, a buoyancy achieved paradoxically, like Swift's, in the very completeness of its scepticism. It is one of the qualities that sets it apart from *Brave New World*. The pigs' greedy and vicious duplicity is balanced by the long-suffering nobility and fellow-feeling of some of the other animals (notably the horses) and by the sense of achievement these animals have in work – and in the fact that finally they are indomitable. The satisfaction they find in building the windmill in the face of all natural and man-made opposition is so great that in one of their battles with men they dash out from their fearful hiding, and in self-forgetful anger at the blowing up of the mill rout their attackers. This is an event that their dictator could not have counted on but is quick to take advantage of in his usual way.

In *Nineteen Eighty-Four* the analysis is more intimately personal and at the same time more wide-rangingly abstract. Here Orwell, reacting partly in sympathy with and partly against the work of Wells, Zamyatin and Koestler[21] set out once more to attack Socialist idealism and the utopianism that lies behind it, but transferred the focus of attention from the idealism itself to the self-imprisoning isolation it belongs with. The book has been discussed as if it were an already discredited prophecy, or a warning of what might happen at a more distant date, or as if it were a neurotic nightmare which shows how ill Orwell was when he wrote it. Alok Rai is one of the most recent of those who have called *Nineteen Eighty-Four* "the rationalisation of a specific state of paranoid anxiety" and the expression of "a metaphysic of impotence".[22] He quoted Isaac Deutscher, who six years after the publication of the novel called it "a cry from the abyss of despair".[23] But the consideration of Orwell's despair is strictly marginal to an appreciation of a novel in which Winston's despair is critically placed in a setting that is thematically focused. The book is of course both topically political and intimately personal, and the two strands are inextricable, but they are woven into a work of art whose significance is universal and impersonal.

---

21. See Orwell, "Arthur Koestler" (1944), in *Collected Essays*, III, 234-44; and his Review of Zamyatin's *We*, 1946, in *Collected Essays*, IV.
22. Rai, *Orwell and the Politics of Despair*, 136.
23. Deutscher, *Heretics and Renegades*, 44.

Orwell was clear both about his intentions – "a show-up of the perversions to which a centralized economy is liable and which have already been partly realized in Communism and Fascism"[24] – and about the technical difficulties of writing what was, he said, "in a sense a fantasy, but in the form of a naturalistic novel".[25] The triumph of the book consists in the compounding of these elements, without the contradictions we found (for instance) in *Lady Chatterley's Lover*. In Orwell's own mental context and idiom it explores some of the conflicts broached in Lawrence's last novel between the destructive tendencies of modern social life and the possibilities of personal salvation.

The naturalism (or observation of people and circumstances) is especially evident in the early chapters, with their picture of a dreariness – uniformity of clothing, shortages and political jargon – that many of the first British readers must have associated with the post-war austerity of the 1940s. Instantly recognizable are the hypocritical power-politics of a divided world, and political and social behaviour which is crystallized into expressions like "Big Brother", "doublethink" and "thoughtcrime" that were to become part of the common language. The details of the regime are built up with a remorseless thoroughness, with at its centre Winston's "locked loneliness". From the beginning the writing is highly charged with fear and loathing. It is also compassionate, and even at times buoyant with quick observation and sardonic humour.

From the start the realism is infused with the thematic concerns, but the latter show their controlling dominance in Part 2, where Winston and Julia are both in love with each other and in battle against the system. They discover in themselves what the system is opposed to, what is missing in their lives. Casual sex, even what Winston calls "corruption" is revolution: "the animal instinct, the simple, undifferentiated desire: that was the force that would tear the Party to pieces":

> Their embrace had been a battle, the climax a victory. It was a blow struck against the Party. It was a political act.[26]

Out of willed rebellion comes sex, and then, unexpectedly, out of sex comes love: "a deep tenderness, such as he had not felt for her before,

---

24. Orwell to Francis A. Henson, 16 June 1949, in *Collected Essays*, IV, 502.
25. Orwell to F. J. Warburg, 31 May 1947 in *Collected Essays*, IV, 329-30.
26. *Nineteen Eighty-four*, Everyman edition, 133. Subsequent page references are to this edition.

took hold of him." Nevertheless, that most personal experience
becomes an expression of the theme: no sooner do they discover it
than they throw it away, betraying its primacy (the need to protect it)
by going to O'Brien to offer themselves to kill and die in the anti-
Party cause. Julia's sole stipulation, that they shall not be parted, is
meaningless in the context of their other vows. They are as much
fanatics as those they oppose.

As Winston reads Goldstein's book on the system, he and we are
penetrating further into a world of unreality, where everything makes
intellectual sense and at the same time is humanly senseless – a world
of "doublethink" indeed – a kind of maniacal lucidity (the sort one
associates with Marx and Lenin) that calls forth a Swiftian disgust. In
order to preserve "oligarchy" according to Goldstein (i.e. O'Brien)
"the prevailing mental condition must be controlled insanity".

The last, most wholly "fantastic" part of the story holds us fixed in
feelings of horror which are reinforced by the remnants of
"naturalism" that persist: the grim and funny details, for example, of
the downfall of Ampleforth (who couldn't find a rhyme for "rod"
other than "God") and Parsons with his farcical servility (wanting to
say Thank you to the Thought Police for saving him from himself).
But chiefly we are imprisoned in Winston's terrified mentality. As
Laura Tanner showed, the reader at first has to "rely on Winston's
severely limited perspective" and then, as O'Brien penetrates
Winston's mind, "that perspective is stolen away from the narrator by
O'Brien" with the effect of "frightening immediacy".[27]

The social regimentation, while not as complete as in *Brave New
World* is more compelling. It is carried out not by the elimination of
emotion but by its canalisation, in the service of the Party. Submission
and infliction are built into a system offering a dream of ultimate
security. O'Brien expounds:

> "Alone – free – the human being is always defeated. It must be so,
> because every human being is doomed to die, which is the greatest of
> all failures. But if he can make complete, utter submission, if he can
> escape from his identity, if he can merge himself in the Party so that
> he *is* the Party, then he is all-powerful and immortal." (277)

This "collective solipsism" as O'Brien calls it, is more humanly
inhuman than what prevails in *Brave New World*. It needs enormous
reserves of dammed-up emotion to achieve the distortion of the
natural it requires to make it work. It gets this by repressions inducing

---

27. Laura E. Tanner, *Intimate Violence*, 43-47.

the more manageable commodities of hysteria or fanaticism. The degradation and perversion of sexual and family ties for instance is systematically pursued by the Party "not merely to prevent men and women from forming loyalties which it might not be able to control" but "to remove all pleasure from the sexual act" – the natural made unnatural. O'Brien triumphantly proclaims, "We shall abolish the orgasm" to be replaced by "the intoxication of power". The denial of instinctive responses accumulates the hate and fear that is discharged by the rank and file against the "enemy" and by the rulers against the rank and file. The Party is the triumph of organization over the unorganizable, of the ego (located in the intellect, in the need for predictable and therefore controllable patterns) over anything that is not it.

O'Brien appeals to sadism as a motive, but that gratification of a physical craving is yoked to an ego-enhancing idea of power, and that idea itself is an abstract: "The object of power is power." Winston sees in O'Brien's face "an exaltation, a lunatic intensity" derived from the notion that "reality exists in the human mind and nowhere else .... we make the laws of nature .... we create human nature". The Party denies "not merely the validity of experience but the very existence of external reality." Puritanical perfectionism goes hand in hand with the sadism: "We make the brain perfect before we blow it out." Winston will be "washed clean".

Some have criticized the set-up for its unlikelihood. Carl Freedman, for instance, saw it as an example of "the most orthodox kind of irrationalism" on Orwell's part.[28] He adopted Isaac Deutscher's phrase, "the mysticism of cruelty" to sum up Orwell's perversity in this respect.[29] A more recent complaint has come from Richard Posner: "It is unrealistic to suppose the 'Inner Party' of a totalitarian state dominated by lunatics or even sadists" – although he realized that the novel has a more important satirical dimension.[30] But Orwell was making a passionate outcry similar to Lawrence's in *Women in Love* against regarding the intellect as the main point of reference in determining behaviour and general good, and also against developing too explicit principles of general good. The whole system, beyond the obvious target of the political satire, represents the fixity and therefore deadliness of the products of the intellect as opposed to

---

28. Freedman, *George Orwell*, 162.
29. Deutscher, *Heretics and Renegades*, 48.
30. Posner, "Orwell versus Huxley", in *Philosophy and Literature*, XXIV, 25.

the forces of life. Winston's struggle in the prison of idealism relates not only to Lawrence but to Conrad, and to Joyce's battle with Catholicism. And to Dostoevsky: Winston, struggling to understand the Party line, offers a lame summary of the Grand Inquisitor's argument in *The Brothers Karamazov* – "You are ruling over us for our own good" – which O'Brien brushes aside. Alan Sandison put the general situation between Winston and O'Brien into its widest context: "O'Brien appears as the Inquisitor joined with the heretic in combat with the Devil .... In other words the Devil they are fighting is individualism."[31]

Those forces of life that go on and are not self-destructive are chiefly represented by the "proles". They are left "outside" and not taken into account by the Party. It is there, Winston feels, that "hope lies":

> They were not loyal to a party or a country or an idea, they were loyal to one another .... The proles had stayed human. (172)

By setting up Party and Proles Orwell divides the death-dealing and life-giving sources and leaves himself free to concentrate his passionate anxiety on the former. Alongside the detailed analysis of the negatives of mental oppression, the values of "privacy, friendship, love" remain, like Conrad's positives, undetailed but definite.

Winston's love affair with Julia puts him in touch with these positives. He comes to recognize in her, in the thrush that sings in their hideout and in the Proles the same beauty and regenerative power:

> It had never occurred to him that the body of a woman of fifty, blown up to monstrous dimensions by child-bearing, then hardened, roughened by work till it was coarse in the grain like an over-ripe turnip, could be beautiful. But it was so, and after all, he thought, why not? The solid, contourless body, like a block of granite, and the rasping red skin, bore the same relation to the body of a girl as the rosehip to the rose. Why should the fruit be held inferior to the flower?
>
> "She's beautiful", he murmured. (228)

Some have deplored what they see as the thematic simplification of the set-up. Raymond Williams, for instance, called the picture of the proles and the hope they represent "stale revolutionary romanticism".[32] But it is Winston's feelings we are given, not the

---

31. Sandison, *The Last Man in Europe*, 186.
32. Williams, *George Orwell*, 78.

author's, and Winston is a spiritual cripple. It is with a sense of patronage and awe, not of belonging, that he describes his yearning, the yearning of an idealist:

> Sooner or later it would happen, strength would change into consciousness. The proles were immortal, you could not doubt it when you looked at that valiant figure in the yard. In the end their awakening would come. And until that happened, although it might be a thousand years, they would stay alive against all the odds, like birds, passing on from body to body the vitality which the Party did not share and could not kill. (229)

Winston is trying to rehabilitate himself to his own nature and escape the conditioning in which reality has lost its meaning. He sees where regeneration lies but views it from the angle of an indoctrinated party member unable to achieve it and inevitably falling back on the sophistry he started with: "Until they become conscious they will never rebel, and until after they have rebelled they cannot become conscious." His dream of their potential remains "a mystical truth and a palpable unreality".

Winston's defeat comes from within himself. He is the victim of the Party because he is one of them. So much of him wants the simplified solution in which aspiration is booby-trapped by egotism and fear of life. Sado-masochistic as his training has made him, he loves as well as hates and fears his tormentor O'Brien – they are "intimates". He longs to give himself and the complexities of response up to an absolute, while the rest of his nature fights it. The inevitability of the tragedy is there from the start – as Winston says: "thoughtcrime equals death." He has been under surveillance for seven years. "We are the dead", he and Julia say just before their arrest, during which Winston's precious glass paperweight with a piece of coral at its centre is smashed. Purchased from Charrington (who is a member of the Thought Police) it provides a double vision, of escape and entrapment: it is "the room he was in, and the coral was Julia's life and his own, fixed in a sort of eternity at the heart of the crystal".

In *Nineteen Eighty-Four*, as in *Women in Love*, the theme of idealism is yoked to that of self-imprisonment and the struggle to escape it.

That was Beckett's major theme also.[33] He exhaustively explored all the elements of that compound experience: isolation, cynicism, and the suicidal tendency, the backlash of violence, the sense of chaos and a total insecurity rooted in self- and life-loathing. Moreover, this complex experience, related to the ideologies that reinforce it, is placed in an evaluative perspective created by the piecemeal reference (from within the condition) to positive themes of release and renewal, in the presence of a subversiveness that ranges in mode from anarchic Rabelaisian to categorical Swiftian.

His achievement came about not only in a reaction, encouraged by Joyce's example, against the conventions of nineteenth-century but also against that example itself: "I realized that I couldn't go down that same road", he said.[34] Getting free involved a search for inspiration in earlier literature, especially Bunyan, Swift and Sterne; and in Rabelais he encountered and was later to employ aspects of the "carnival" tradition explored by Mikhail Bakhtin.[35] Contemplating the expansive movement of Joyce's work, he decided that his own way would be "in subtracting rather than adding".[36] He restricted the scope of his art so severely that he was able to refer aptly to the figures in it as a "gallery of moribunds".

In Beckett's one pre-war novel, Murphy himself is the theme, though it is also glimpsed from the outside in most of the minor characters, as well as showing up in images of prisons and cages. Beckett had already learned from Joyce how to take the reader right into the hero's mentality; with Murphy, that is an imprisonment in itself. But the main theme is offset, and detachment achieved, by a ceaseless, funful exuberance, an implicit manifestation of the theme of release, which is separately symbolized in the rapture and pathos of the final kite-flying scene. The surface realism of the narrative (including some precise topographical features taken from fact) is ridiculed by outbreaks of the fantastic and non-sequitur: order and rationality mocked by chaos and incoherence.

The full flowering of Beckett's potential, like Orwell's, had to wait until after the war, when he adopted the monologue as his basic narrative technique and began to explore more fully the negatives of

---

33. A feeling of self-imprisonment was something he was born into. He even claimed to have pre-birth memories of being trapped and unable to escape, imprisoned and in pain (see Knowlson, *Damned to Fame*, 2).
34. Beckett, 1989, quoted by Knowlson, 105
35. See Bakhtin, *Rabelais and his World*.
36. Knowlson, 352.

his nature and experience: "I can now accept this dark side as the commanding side of my personality. In accepting it, I will make it work for me."[37]

Generally, in most novels, isolation, impotence and insulation are put in a context where they can be "placed" by normal experience. In Beckett's Trilogy the normal experience, for the purpose of discovery, is placed by them. The narrative views the whole complex experience of self-imprisonment through the eyes of the paralytic, who is presented, not satirically, from the security of a superior set of values, but from within his predicament – not indulging in it either but with insatiable curiosity and ceaseless, meticulous questioning: a relentlessly unsentimental but compassionate attention to outrage, pain and confusion that rouses in the reader the same feelings. The novels view complexity from its uniform side, positives from their negative side and potency from its impotent side, in order to offer a vision that gains dramatic impact from the inversion of the normal process of exploration: working in the dark instead of the light. On occasions the same reading attitude has to be adopted as for Swift sometimes, that of standing back from the act of demolition to wait for the dust to settle, so as to see what else can be seen or envisaged when the edifice is no longer there. The customary idea of order and proportion having been challenged and some of the parts more closely examined, the apparently destructive act can be seen as a positive one, as all intensive efforts of exploration are, in its impact on the reader, who is stimulated to put together afresh in his own mind the dislocated items of his experience.

The life-paralysis of Molly in the first narrative is central. For that reason it is chosen here for detailed examination. But the others are further developments of it. *Malone Dies* views the same experience from a different angle by incorporating the comfort and security of the final paralysis. The tone is more relaxed from within this security. The aim is to play with the ideas given him when young, merely to relieve the tedium while waiting for death. But the duality, the removal of the self and the hopeless involvement, continues. In *The Unnameable*

---

37. Beckett, quoted by Deirdre Bair, *Samuel Beckett*, 299. Maturity also involved the change from writing in English to writing in French. This freed Beckett from affectation "parce qu'en Français" he explained, "c'est plus facile d'écrire sans style". It was an escape from what he called "Anglo-Irish exuberance and automatisms" and another way of loosening the ties with Joyce. Self-translation into English poses some problems for the critic (see the discussion of these in Leslie Hill's *Beckett's Fiction*) which are marginal to our concerns here.

there are no characters: "the unnameable" is that which has underlain all "the appearances elsewhere ... put in by other parties" and the centre round which all its "delegates" such as Molloy have wheeled "like a planet round its sun". This central unsocial core gives a sustained cry of dismay and hatred at what has been foisted on it in the way of roles, ideas, and words. Not having been "properly born" it cannot live with them or without them. The suffering and disgust is kept at a pitch near hysteria. The condition is summed up in "their" terms – "Through the splendours of nature they dragged a paralytic" – and in his: "in my life, since we must it call so, there were three things, the inability to speak, the inability to be silent, and solitude, that's what I've had to make the best of."

Molloy is written in a dry, undemonstrative prose that makes disconcerting shifts and can rise from flatness to hysteria in a moment. There is little narrative continuity and the only development is Molloy's increasing incapacity (he ends up paralysed in a ditch). Time is circular not progressive, even though there is, as Leslie Hill pointed out, "a genealogical fable" buried in the text.[38] The natural features of the region Molloy inhabits correspond to facets of Beckett's subject. There is a constant movement between a number of closely allied situations, mainly productive of pain and isolation, and between the causative responses, disgust, fear and confusion. The situation is for Molloy inescapable, insupportable – "a veritable calvary, with no limit to its stations, and no hope of crucifixion". But the fragmentary nature of Molloy's experiences is a factor in the cleansing of the narrative. He flits from one to the next, and the final effect is not of a lingering cry or moan so much as a balanced presentation that puts forward a long-drawn-out agony at the same time as an ability to respond spontaneously to the fun or pain or aggression or irony available in the context of the experience. The humour, sometimes crude and sometimes painful, in the way Swift's irony is both crude and painful, is one of the chief narrative means of keeping the tone on this side of hysteria, sentimentality and self-indulgence, and sometimes only just achieves it.

The freshness and alertness of the writing lies in its multiplicity of statement. The themes are as inextricably intertwined in every sentence as they are in *Finnegans Wake*. However, what holds the whole structure together and gives it a readable unity is the pattern of thinking that can be traced through the multiplicity, in spite of the

---

38. Hill, *Beckett's Fiction*, 81.

seemingly endless doubling back, the cancellations and restatements of thoughts as soon as they are made. The analysis that follows seeks to draw attention to both the "disparates" and the kind of pattern of thematic analysis with which we have become familiar throughout this study and which holds the disparate elements together. It is important to appreciate this in order to pierce through the apparent negativity of the work.

The attack on idealism and rationality is as relentless and far-reaching as Joyce's or Lawrence's. To ideas, analysis, the tabulation or "naming" of things Molloy has been over-exposed. He sees the complexity and difficulty of his experience, the inadequacy if not destructiveness of the words that express it and the insufficiency of the ideas which direct and in turn are directed by that expression. These are at variance with each other, but he acknowledges that life cannot be managed without words and ideas – "Saying is inventing. Wrong, very rightly wrong":

> Yes, even then, when already all was fading, waves and particles, there could be no things but nameless things, no names but thingless names. I say that now, but after all what do I know about then, now when the icy words hail down upon me, the icy meanings, and the world dies too, foully named. All I know is what the words know, and the dead things, and all that makes a handsome little sum, with a beginning, a middle and an end, as in the well-built phrase and the long sonata of the dead.[39]

He has been made over-aware. Exposure to too much light has made definition or naming impossible. In the absence of protecting beliefs and motivating positives the insecurity of total exposure makes him retire. The more he retires the more exposed he becomes to the confusions of thoughts and words when they have to be used. For him the exigencies of experience have not helped him build barriers in the form of abstracts. Once the abstracts are isolated and formed in words they are ready to condition, limit and mislead thought. They are the life-line, the means of seeking a balance – hence this story and the rest of the trilogy – and at the same time they are the death-trap.

Any attempt to think a way out is ridiculed. The speciousness and self-serving qualities of ratiocination, for instance, are brought out in its employment to solve his anxiety about the number of times he farts: "Damn it, I hardly fart at all, I should never have mentioned it.

---

39. *"Molloy"... A Trilogy*, Paris, 1959, 31-32. Subsequent page references are to this edition.

Extraordinary how mathematics help you to know yourself." Both the
need for and the absurdity of formally trained thinking, the energy
expended in it and the limited pointless objectives to which it is
directed, are exposed in a six-page discussion of the problem of the
stones in his pockets, a send-up of the processes of scientific or
academic investigation, its objectives and ideals, which grows funnier
by its persistence and over-loading. Carrying the joke to inordinate
lengths, like Swift or Rabelais, bullies the reader beyond the bounds
of boredom and into submission to the motives. At the same time the
length enables Molloy to incorporate all his usual daily anxieties and
insecurities, weaving them in so that their presence sheds light on the
general conditions under which such so-called scientific and
mathematical investigations take place, emphasizing the side of them
that is life-wasting, evasive or a manifestation of a mere mental
restlessness or anxiety which is out of the same stable and serves as
much purpose as the enquiry into the farts. Not only does each would-
be solution to the problem produce new ones, the inherent flaws in
the whole procedure, in so far as it aims to impose reason, order and
harmony, are revealed together with the need for it. It is a futile
attempt at "setting the whole system of nature at naught" – as in the
little parable of the woman who takes her old dog for a walk on a lead
on a pavement, only to have it run over and killed by that
ungovernable chaos, Molloy.

He lives out the same kind of feelings of defeat and pointlessness
that in Chapter 9 we have seen overcome Mrs Moore in *A Passage to
India* and are reflected in Woolf's Mrs Ramsay. Mrs Moore expresses
the same conviction that "everything exists, nothing has value" and
the same dissatisfaction with words and communication, the urge to
retire, the obstinacy of a desire to hold on. Even some of the terms
used to describe the experience overlap: Forster refers to "something
snub-nosed ... the undying worm" while Worm is one of the figures in
The Unnameable. Mrs Moore is haunted by an echo which is "entirely
devoid of distinction. Whatever is said the same monotonous noise
replies." Molloy too hears a sound "not like the other sounds, that you
listen to, when you choose, and can sometimes silence, by going away
or stopping your ears, no, but it is a sound which begins to rustle in
your head, without your knowing how, or why":

> I listen and the voice is of a world collapsing endlessly, a frozen
> world, under a faint untroubled sky, enough to see by, yes, and frozen
> too. And I hear it murmur that all wilts and yields, as if loaded down,
> but there are no loads, and the ground too, unfit for loads, and the

light too, down towards an end it seems can never come. For what possible end to these wastes where true light never was, nor any upright thing, nor any true foundation, but only these leaning things, forever lapsing and crumbling away, beneath a sky without memory of morning or hope of night. (40)

Beckett pushes this experience to its limits, and used as a means of studying old issues from an unexpected angle it becomes extremely comprehensive. The narrative circles round and round the issues, stating and unstating. Every condition contains its opposite, every proposition provokes its contradiction (as we have seen with Dostoevsky and Lawrence). "Two incompatible bodily needs at loggerheads", for example, is a rich seam for exploration along Beckett's lines. Intense futile activity (mental or otherwise) is set against giant lethargy: "For in me there have always been two fools, among others, one asking nothing better than to stay where he is and the other imagining that life might be slightly less horrible a little further on."

But nothing is what it seems: the inactive or submissive element is at the same time a form of adaptability in which even the hopelessly confined experience of being bedridden can expand to include exploration and interest and can of course accommodate obsession. There is endless, mercilessly vital adaptability and activity within impossible restriction, as there is robustness within collapse. Even his much-sought dissociation is itself contradicted by the movement towards "solving this business with my mother" (who represents his umbilical attachment to life) and is shown to be as rich in illusion as any other:

> In your box, in your caves, there too there is a price to pay. And which you pay willingly, for a time, but which you cannot go on paying forever. For you cannot go on buying the same thing forever, with your little pittance. And unfortunately there are other needs than that of rotting in peace, it's not the word, I mean of course my mother whose image, blunted for some time past, was beginning now to harrow me again. (75)

Molloy is given a sufficiently hampered, suppressed normality of vital response to ensure the reader's commitment to his progress or lack of it. He craves contact with others, though he is powerless to achieve it and disgusted by the thought of it. For example, he passes a man with a dog on a walk, watches him disappear, wills his disappearance – "From things about to disappear I turn away in time" – and imagines hailing him back:

> He hears my cries, turns, waits for me, I am up against him, up against the dog, gasping between my crutches. He is a little frightened of me, a little sorry for me, I disgust him not a little. I am not a pretty sight, I don't smell good. (13)

The mixture of fear – "I am full of fear, I have gone in fear all my life" – and of needs, with an angry dismissal of the whole complex inter-relationship, underpins every event, together with his powerlessness to cope with it all and his bewilderment as to why it exists. The humour sometimes produces an effect of lively animality or childishness that adds its own gloss of pathos, as in the passages about his bicycle, where the symbolic role of the bicycle (associated with the theme of release) is joined to its role as provider of fun and promoter (in the reader) of compassion.

A reader's identification with these aspects of Molloy's predicament is tested by other features of the life-impotence: for instance, the anger and aggression shown in his reaction to the man who demands friendship (he retaliates by kicking him with his paralysed legs) or the disgusted preoccupation with the pathetic and ugly, or the mechanically physical and the gratefully, gratuitously tender in sexual love. But the aggression is seen as genetically inescapable – "Ah the old bitch, a nice dose she gave me, she and her lousy unconquerable genes" – and the sexual act does give rise, however selfishly, to a momentarily compassionate outgoing towards someone else. Beckett made sure the reader joins to some extent in Molloy's personal bitterness on the subject: in one of his favourite expressions, "making a balls of it" the commonness of the association (attraction and rejection in one, the symbols of life epitomizing chaos) is brought home.

In any case the balance is held between Molloy as something to be identified in the reader and Molloy as an objective creation with its own separate identity – a confined area for analysis. The maniacal limitation is given an independent innocence of existence that at times recalls Caliban: "And if ever I'm reduced to looking for a meaning to my life, you can never tell, it's in that old mess I'll stick my nose to begin with, the mess of that poor old uniparous whore and myself the last of my foul brood, neither man nor beast." The innocence comes in its very incapacity to be anything else: locked in itself, away from the rest of the world, vividly feeling and suffering. The sense of his painful exposure to the benign and the non-benign, his movements towards and away from each, the failure to relate his experience of each to the other, makes his impotence moving:

.... while on my face and great big Adam's apple the air of summer
weighed and the splendid summer sky. And suddenly I remembered
my name, Molloy. My name is Molloy. I cried, all of a sudden, now I
remember. Nothing compelled me to give this information, but I gave
it, hoping to please, I suppose. (23)

Layered references are employed throughout to increase the scope of
the fable, sometimes by ironic contrast, sometimes by direct
association with other myths. Thomas Cousineau pointed to the
evocation of classical figures – Oedipus, Odysseus – alongside others
from the Old Testament.[40] Here the "great big Adam's apple" is not
only a touching physical expression of his exposure but also a recall
of Adam's apple of knowledge or self-consciousness and the idea
pervading the book that life is one long expiation of the original sin of
being born.

Moran (in the second half of the book) is not so insulated as
Molloy in some respects and in others not so open and exposed, more
normal in some ways and more inhuman in others. Greater contact
with normal life is made available to him through a greater degree of
insentience. The kind of stupidity required for this kind of adaptability
– his receptivity to the overlay of training that gives him his wider
contacts – has also given him scope to be a greater menace, to his son
and his housekeeper, for example. He starts off seeing himself in all
the normal roles, but aggressively ill-at-ease with them, as
householder, father and a conventionally religious man. His ill-
satisfying experience sets going the process of self-inquiry and
discovery that eventually reduces him to the unstable and uncertain
isolated core that is Molloy. Sent on a quest (to track down Molloy)
that has no solution and no purpose except to de-activate, he finds the
experience cleansing: "And to tell the truth I not only knew who I
was, but I had a sharper and clearer sense of my identity than ever
before." The Molloy process is set in motion: bewilderment, the
unending battle with the untrue in desires, sensations, and the
presentation of the self to the self and to others (and vice versa) along
with the admission of the inescapability of it and the need of it for the
purposes of continuation. At the end we are back at the beginning of
the book. If his narrative were set down further it would be Molloy's.

Molloy then has all the features to be found in the earlier novels of
the thematic tradition, but in a strikingly new and original form. It
may have suggested to its early readers that the next great thematic

40. See Cousineau, *After the Final No: Beckett's Trilogy*, 83-84.

novel would be just the same, just as different. And so it was. *How it is*, Beckett's final novel, is even more relentless in its portrayal of a cruel alternation of victim and tormentor endlessly repeated, and still more uncompromisingly purist in its style than the Trilogy, for it distils and refines the disparates of experience further, attempting effects normally associated with poetry.

The same applies post-Beckett. Challenge and continuity: the thematic novel alive, mutating.

BIBLIOGRAPHY

THE WORKS OF D.H. LAWRENCE

The following Cambridge editions, published by Cambridge University Press, are cited:

Aaron's Rod, ed. Mara Kalnins, 1988.
The First and Second Lady Chatterley Novels, eds Dieter Mehl and Christa Jansohn, 1999.
The First "Women in Love", eds John Worthen and Lindeth Vasey, 1998.
Kangaroo, ed. Bruce Steele, 1994.
Lady Chatterley's Lover, ed. Michael Squires, 1993.
The Letters of D H, Lawrence, eds J. T. Boulton and others, 8 vols, 1979 – 2000.
The Lost Girl, ed. John Worthen, 1981.
Mr Noon, ed. Lindeth Vasey, 1984.
Paul Morel, ed. Helen Baron, 2003.
The Plays, eds Hans-Wilhelm Schwarze and John Worthen, 1999.
The Plumed Serpent (Quetzacoatl), ed. L. D. Clark, 1987.
The Rainbow, ed. Mark Kinkead-Weekes, 1989.
Reflections on the Death of a Porcupine and Other Essays, ed. Michael Herbert, 1988.
Sons and Lovers, eds Carl Baron and Helen Baron, 1992.
Studies in Classic American Literature, eds Ezra Greenspan, Lindeth Vasey and John Worthen, 2003.
A Study of Thomas Hardy and other Essays, ed. Bruce Steele, 1985.
The Trespasser, ed. Elizabeth Mansfield, 1981.
The White Peacock, ed. Andrew Robertson, 1983.
Women in Love, eds David Farmer, Lindeth Vasey and John Worthen, 1987.

Phoenix: the Postumous Papers of D.H. Lawrence, ed. Edward McDonald, London, 1936.
Phoenix II, eds Warren Roberts and Harry T. Moore, London, 1968.

OTHER WORKS CITED

Arendt, Hannah, *The Origins of Totalitarianism*, enlarged edition, London,1958.

Arvin, Newton, *Hawthorne*, London, 1930.

Baines, Jocelyn, *Joseph Conrad:A Critical Biography*, revised edition, London, 1967.

Bair, Deirdre, *Samuel Beckett: A Biography*, London, 1978.

Bakhtin, Mikhail, *Problems of Dostoevsky's Poetics*, trans. and ed. Caryl Emerson, Minneapolis, 1984.

Bakhtin, Mikhail, *Rabelais and his World*, trans. Helene Iswolsky, Bloomington (Indiana), 1984.

Balbert, Peter, *D.H. Lawrence and the Phallic Imagination*, London, 1989.

Balzac, Honore de, *Eugénie Grandet*, trans. Ellen Marriage, Everyman edition, 1992.

Barker, Dudley Raymond, *The Man of Principle: A View of John Galsworthy*, London, 1963.

Beckett, Samuel, *"Molloy", "Malone Dies" and "The Unnameable": A Trilogy*, trans. Patrick Bowles and the author, Paris, 1959.

Bedford, Sybelle, *Aldous Huxley:A Biography*, 2 vols, London, 1973.

Beer, Gillian, *Virginia Woolf: The Common Ground*, Edinburgh, 1996.

Bennett, Joan, *George Eliot: Her Mind and her Art*, Cambridge, 1948.

Bergonzi, Bernard, ed., *H. G. Wells: A Collection of Critical Essays*, London, 1976.

Bergonzi, Bernard, *Heroes' Twilight: A Study of the Literature of the Great War*, 3rd edition, London, 1996.

Boos, Florence and William, "Orwell's Morris and Old Major's Dream", in *English Studies*, LXXI (1990).

Booth, Wayne C., *The Rhetoric of Fiction*, London, 1983.

Boumelha, Penny, *Charlotte Brontë,* London, 1990.

Boyle, Ted, *Symbol and Meaning in the Fiction of Joseph Conrad*, London, 1965.

Bradley, A.C., *Shakespearean Tragedy*, London, 1905

Brontë, Charlotte, *Jane Eyre*, eds Jane Jack and Margaret Smith, London, 1969.

Brontë, Charlotte, *Letters*, ed. Margaret Smith, 2 vols, London, 1995 and 2000.

Brontë, Charlotte, *Shirley*, eds Herbert Rosengarten and Margaret Smith, London, 1979.

Brontë, Emily, *Wuthering Heights*, eds Hilda Marsden and Ian Jack, London, 1976.

Budgen, Frank, *James Joyce and the Making of "Ulysses"*, revised edition, London, 1972.

Burden, Robert, *Radicalizing Lawrence*, Amsterdam, 2000.

Burwell, Rose, "D.H. Lawrence's Reading", in *D.H. Lawrence Review*, III (1970).

Carabine, Keith, "From Razumov to *Under Western Eyes*: The Case of Peter Ivanovitch", in *Conradiana*, XXV (1993).

Carabine, Keith, ed., *Joseph Conrad: Critical Assessments*, 4 vols, Mountfield, 1992.

Carabine, Keith, *The Life and the Art: A Study of Conrad's "Under Western Eyes"*, Amsterdam, 1996.

Chambers, Jessie, *D.H. Lawrence:A Personal Record*, 2nd edition, London, 1965.

Conrad, Joseph, *Collected Letters 1861-1916*, eds Frederick R. Karl and Laurence Davies, 5 vols, Cambridge, 1983-96.

Conrad, Joseph, *Lord Jim*, Collected edition, London, 1946.

Conrad, Joseph, *Nostromo*, ed. Keith Carabine, London, 1984.

Conrad, Joseph, *Under Western Eyes*, Collected edition, London, 1947.

Cousineau, Thomas J., *After the Final No: Beckett's Trilogy*, London 1999.

Daleski, H. M., *Thomas Hardy and the Paradoxes of Love*, London, 1997.

D'Annunzio, Gabriele, *The Triumph of Death*, trans. Georgina Harding, London, 1898.

Davidson, Arnold E., *Conrad's Endings*, London, 1984.

Deutscher, Isaac, *Heretics and Renegades*, London, 1955.

Dickens, Charles, *Dombey and Son*, ed. Alan Horsman, London, 1974.

Dostoevsky, Fyodor, *The Brothers Karamazov*, trans. Constance Garnett, London, 1951

Dryden, Linda, *Joseph Conrad and the Imperial Romance*, London, 2000.

Dunbar, Janet, *J.M. Barrie: The Man Behind the Image*, London, 1970.

Eagleton, Terry, *Exiles and Emigrés*, London, 1970.
Edel, Leon and Gordon Ray, eds, *Henry James and H. G. Wells: A Record of Their Friendship*, London, 1958.
Eliot, George, *Adam Bede*, ed. Carol A. Martin, Oxford, 2001.
Eliot, George, *The George Eliot Letters*, ed. Gordon S. Haight, 9 vols, London, 1955.
Eliot, George, *The Mill on the Floss*, ed. Gordon S. Haight, Oxford, 1996.
Ellis, David and Ornella De Zordo, eds, *D.H. Lawrence: Critical Assessments*, 4 vols, Mountfield, 1992.
Ellmann, Richard, *James Joyce*, revised edition, London, 1983.
Engelhardt, Dorthe G.A., *L.N. Tolstoy and D.H. Lawrence*, Frankfurt, 1996.

Firchow, Peter, *Aldous Huxley: Satirist and Novelist*, Minneapolis, 1972.
Flaubert, Gustave, *Correspondance*, ed. Jean Bruneau, 4 vols, Paris, 1973-98.
Flaubert, Gustave, *Letters*, trans. and ed. Francis Steegmuller, 2 vols, London, 1981-82.
Flaubert, Gustave, *Madame Bovary*, trans. Eleanor Marx-Aveling, London, 1886.
Ford, Ford Madox, *The Good Soldier*, ed. Martin Stannard, London, 1995.
Ford, Ford Madox, *The Good Soldier*, Bodley Head edition, London, 1962.
Forster, E.M., *A Passage to India*, ed. Oliver Stallybrass, London, 1979.
Forster, E.M., *Aspects of the Novel*, London, 1927.
Forster, E.M., *The Life to Come and Other Stories*, London, 1972.
Forster, E.M., *The Longest Journey*, ed. Elizabeth Heine, London, 1984
Forster, E.M., *The Manuscripts of "A Passage to India"*, ed. Oliver Stallybrass, London, 1989.
Forster, E.M., *Maurice*, London, 1971.
Forster, E.M., *Two Cheers for Democracy*, London, 1951.
Freedman, Carl, *George Orwell: A Study in Ideology and Literary Form*, London, 1988.

Gibson, Andrew and Robert Hampson, eds, *Conrad and Theory*, Amsterdam, 1998.

Glen, Heather, *Charlotte Brontë: The Imagination in History*, London, 2002.

Goldberg, S.L., *The Classical Temper,* London, 1961.

Guerard, Albert J., *Conrad the Novelist*, Cambridge (Mass.), 1958.

Guerard, Albert J., *The Triumph of the Novel*, London, 1976.

Hardy, Barbara, *The Appropriate Form*, London, 1964.

Hardy, Thomas, *Far from the Madding Crowd*, New Wessex edition, London, 1974.

Hardy, Thomas, *Tess of the d'Urbervilles*, New Wessex edition, London, 1974.

Hart Davis, Rupert, *Hugh Walpole*, London, 1985.

Hawthorne, Nathaniel, *The Blithedale Romance and Fanshawe*, Centenary edition, Columbus (Ohio), 1964.

Hawthorne, Nathaniel, *The House of the Seven Gables*, Centenary edition, Columbus (Ohio), 1965.

Hawthorne, Nathaniel, *The Scarlet Letter*, Centenary edition, Columbus (Ohio), 1962.

Hervouet, Yves, *The French Face of Joseph Conrad*, Cambridge, 1990.

Hill, Leslie, *Beckett's Fiction*, Cambridge, 1990.

Hoddinott, Alison, "Charlotte Brontë and D.H. Lawrence", in *Brontë Studies*, XXVII (2002).

Holderness, Graham, *D.H. Lawrence: History, Ideology and Fiction*, London, 1982.

Huxley, Aldous, *Brave New World*, Collected edition, London, 1970.

Huxley, Aldous, *The Hidden Huxley*, ed. David Bradshaw, London, 1994.

Huxley, Aldous, *Letters of Aldous Huxley*, ed. Grover Smith, London, 1969.

Huxley, Aldous, *Point Counter Point*, Collected edition, London, 1971.

Hyde, Virginia, *The Risen Adam: D.H. Lawrence's Revisionist Typology*, Pennsylvania, 1992.

James, Henry, *Letters*, ed. Percy Lubbock, 2 vols, London, 1920.

James, Henry, *Selected Literary Criticism*, ed. Morris Shapira, London, 1963.

John, Juliet, *Dickens's Villains: Melodrama, Character, Popular Culture*, London, 2001.

Joyce, James, *The Essential James Joyce*, ed. Harry Levin, London, 1948.

Joyce, James, *Letters*, eds Stuart Gilbert and Richard Ellman, 3 vols, London, 1957.

Joyce, James, *Ulysses*, Everyman edition, London, 1994.

Kaye, Peter, *Dostoevsky and English Modernism*, London, 1999.

Kenner, Hugh, *Dublin's Joyce*, New York, 1987.

Kinkead-Weekes, Mark, *D.H. Lawrence: Triumph to Exile 1912-1922*, Cambridge, 1996.

Knowlson, James, *Damned to Fame: the Life of Samuel Beckett*, London, 1996.

Lary, N.M., *Dostoevsky and Dickens*, London, 1973.

Leavis, F.R., *D.H. Lawrence: Novelist*, London, 1955.

Leavis, F.R., *The Great Tradition*, London, 1950.

Levenson, Michael, *Modernism and the Fate of Individuality*, London, 1991.

Lodge, David, *After Bakhtin: Essays on Fiction and Criticism*, London, 1990.

Lodge, David, *The Language of Fiction*, London, 1966.

Mack, Maynard and Ian Gregor, eds, *Imagined Worlds*, London, 1968

Mackenzie, Norman and Jeanne, *The Life of H.G.Wells: The Time Traveller*, revised edition, London, 1987.

MacPike, Loralee, *Dostoevsky's Dickens: a Study of Literary Influence*, London, 1981.

Matlaw, R.E. "Recurrent Images in Dostoevsky", in *Harvard Slavic Studies*, III (1957).

Meckier, Jerome ed., *Critical Essays on Aldous Huxley*, London, 1996.

Melville, Herman, *Moby Dick*, Evanston (Illinois), 1988.

Menon, Patricia, *Austen, Eliot, Charlotte Brontë and the Mentor Lover*, London, 2003.

Meyers, Jeffrey, *A Reader's Guide to George Orwell*, London, 1975.

Mizener, Arthur, *The Saddest Story: A Biography of Ford Madox Ford*, London, 1972.

Moore, George, *George Moore on Parnassus: Letters*, ed. Helmut E. Gerber, London, 1988.

Najder, Zdzislaw, *Joseph Conrad: A Chronicle,* London, 1983.

Nehls, Edward, ed., *D.H. Lawrence:A Composite Biography*, 3 vols, Madison (Wisconsin), 1957-59.

Newman, Herta, *Virginia Woolf and Mrs Brown*, London, 1996.

Newton, K. M., *George Eliot: Romantic Humanist*, London, 1981.

Nixon, Cornelia, *Lawrence's Leadership Politics and the Turn against Women*, London, 1986.

Nugel, Bernfried, ed., *Now More than Ever: Proceedings of the Aldous Huxley Centenary Symposium,* Frankfurt, 1995.

Orwell, George, *Animal Farm*, ed. Peter Davison, London, 1998.

Orwell, George, *Collected Essays, Journalism and Letters*, eds Sonia Orwell and Ian Angus, 4 vols, London, 1968.

Orwell, George, *Nineteen Eighty-Four*, Everyman edition, London, 1992.

Panichas, George, *Adventure in Consciousness,* The Hague, 1964.

Parrinder, Patrick, "Wells's Cancelled Endings for 'The Country of the Blind'", in *Science Fiction Studies*, XVII (1990).

Perlina, Nina, *Varieties of Poetic Utterance: Quotation in "The Brothers Karamazov"*, London, 1985.

Posner, Richard A., "Orwell versus Huxley", in *Philosophy and Literature*, XXIV (2000).

Preston, Peter and Peter Hoare, eds, *D.H. Lawrence in the Modern World*, London, 1989.

Pritchett, V.S., *The Living Novel*, London, 1946.

Pykett, Lyn, *Charles Dickens*, London, 2002.

Ragussis, Michael, *The Subterfuge of Art*, London, 1978.

Rai, Alok, *Orwell and the Politics of Despair*, London, 1988.

Rosenberg, John, *Dorothy Richardson, the Genius they Forgot*, London, 1973.

Sandison, Alan, *The Last Man in Europe: An Essay on George Orwell*, London, 1974.

Schapiro, Barbara Ann, *D.H. Lawrence and the Paradoxes of Psychic Life,* London, 1999

Schneider, Lissa, *Conrad's Narratives of Difference*, London, 2003.

Scholes, Robert and Richard M. Kain, eds, *The Workshop of Daedalus,* Evanston (Illinois), 1965.

Schorer, Mark, *The World We Imagine*, London, 1969.

Seed, David, *James Joyce's "Portrait of the Artist as a Young Man"*, London, 1992.

Squires, Michael and Dennis Jackson, eds, *D.H. Lawrence's "Lady"*, Athens (Georgia), 1985.

Stape, J.H., ed., *E.M. Forster: Critical Assessments*, 4 vols, Mountfield, 1998.

Stendhal, *Correspondance,* eds Henri Martineau and V. del Litto, 3 vols, Paris, 1968.

Stendhal, *Romans et Nouvelles*, ed. Henri Martineau, 2 vols, Paris, 1952.

Stendhal, *Scarlet and Black*, trans. C.K. Scott Moncrieff, London, 1927.

Stendhal, *To the Happy Few: Selected Letters*, trans. and ed. Norman Cameron, London, 1952.

Stewart, Jack, "Linguistic Incantation and Parody in *Women in Love*", in *Style*, XXX (1996).

Stewart, Jack, *The Vital Art of D. H. Lawrence*, London, 1999.

Stock, Irvin, *William Hale White*, London, 1956.

Sutherland, John, *Can Jane Eyre be Happy?* London, 1996.

Swigg, Richard, *Lawrence, Hardy and American Literature*, London, 1972.

Tanner, Laura E, *Intimate Violence*, Bloomington (Indiana), 1994.

Tillett, Margaret, *Stendhal: The Background to the Novels*, London, 1971.

Tolstoy, Leo, *Anna Karenin*, trans. Constance Garnett, London, 1901.

Tolstoy, Leo, *Resurrection*, trans. Louise Maude, London, 1912.

Tolstoy, Leo, *War and Peace*, trans. Constance Garnett, 2 vols, London, 1904.

Turgenev, Ivan, *Fathers and Sons*, trans. Constance Garnett, Traveller's Library, London, 1928.

Vitoux, Pierre, "The Text of *Women in Love*", in *Texas Studies in Language and Literature*, XVII (1976).

Watt, Ian, *Conrad in the Nineteenth Century*, London, 1980.

Watts, Cedric, "Bakhtin's Monologism and the Endings of *Crime and Punishment* and *Under Western Eyes*", in *The Conradian*, XX (2000).

Wells, H.G., *Ann Veronica,* Everyman edition, London, 1993.

Wells, H.G., *The Complete Short Stories,* ed. John Hammond, London, 1998.

Wells, H.G., *The First Men in the Moon,* Everyman edition, London, 1993.

Wells, H.G., *Tono-Bungay*, Everyman edition, London, 1994.

Wharton, Edith, *A Backward Glance*, London, 1934.

Williams, Raymond, *George Orwell*, London, 1971.

Williams, Raymond, *Modern Tragedy*, London, 1966.

Woolf, Virginia, *Diary*, eds Anne Olivier Bell and Andrew McNeillie, 5 vols, London, 1977-84.

Woolf, Virginia, *Essays*, ed. Andrew Mc Neillie, 4 vols, London, 1986-94.

Woolf, Virginia, *Letters*, eds Nigel Nicholson and Joanne Trautman, 6 vols, London, 1975-80.

Woolf, Virginia, *To the Lighthouse*, ed. Susan Dick, London, 1992.

Woolf, Virginia, *To the Lighthouse: The Original Holograph Draft*, ed. Susan Dick, London, 1983.

Woolf, Virginia, *Virginia Woolf's Reading Notebooks*, ed. Brenda R. Silver, London, 1983.

Worthen, John, *D. H. Lawrence: The Early Years 1885-1912*, London, 1991.

Worthen, John, "The First *Women in Love*", in *The D.H. Lawrence Review*, XXVIII (1999).

Zola, Emile, *Germinal*, ed. Ernest Alfred Vizetelly, London, 1901.

INDEX